MW00716757

Revised Edition

ACTIVE TOTAL RETURN MANAGEMENT OF FIXED-INCOME PORTFOLIOS

RAVI E. DATTATREYA
FRANK J. FABOZZI

IRWIN
Professional Publishing®

1333 Burr Ridge Parkway
Burr Ridge, IL 60521
(800) 634-3966

This publication is designed to provide accurate and authoritative information in regard to the subject matter covered. It is sold with the understanding that the author and the publisher are not engaged in rendering legal, accounting, or other professional service.

ISBN 1-55738-565-3

Printed in the United States of America

BS

1 2 3 4 5 6 7 8 9 0

PG

Dedication

To Goda, SriRanga, Lakshmi, and Srivatsa
Ravi E. Dattatreya

To Francesco Fabozzi
Frank J. Fabozzi

Contents

Preface

The last ten years have seen a revolution in fixed-income portfolio management. At one time, the primary focus of a fixed-income portfolio manager's attention was yield numbers such as yield to maturity, yield to call, and yield spreads and indicators of credit quality. While concern for credit quality has not changed, money managers now focus on other measures in evaluating fixed-income securities and constructing portfolios. There are two reasons the tools available to money managers had to be expanded.

First, the era of the "plain vanilla" bond was dead. Complex securities in which the issuer and/or the bondholder had an option to do "something" were introduced and continue to be brought to market. Traditional tools for evaluating these securities failed to recognize the value of the embedded option. Even the callable bond which has been around for decades could no longer be evaluated using the traditional measure of yield to call. Second, as a result of volatile interest rates beginning in the 1970s, the traditional "buy-and-hold" strategy was no longer appropriate for most bond market participants. Active traders needed tools to assess the potential outcome of trades. Those who managed the funds of insurance companies, pension funds, commercial banks, and thrifts needed tools to construct portfolios that would satisfy liabilities in a volatile interest rate environment. Traditional yield measures offered little to assist these managers.

The seeds for this revolution in fixed-income portfolio management can be traced back to several important works published in the early 1970s. In 1972, Sidney Homer and Martin Leibowitz's *Inside the Yield Book: New Tools for Bond Market Strategy* was published. This now-classic book clearly demonstrated that traditional yield measures such as yield to maturity and yield to call were of limited value in assessing the potential return of a bond. Instead, they proposed an alternative measure of potential return which they called *realized compound yield*, and is now more popularly referred to as *total return* or *horizon return*. Homer and Leibowitz also demonstrated the characteristics of a bond that will determine its price volatility. Yet, a measure that quantifies price volatility was not presented.

The link between bond price volatility and interest rate changes was the next step in the development of modern fixed-income portfolio management. The link was based on theoretical works developed independently several decades earlier by several economists—Frederick Macaulay in 1938, Paul Samuelson in 1945, and John Hicks in 1946—and in the insurance literature in 1952 by F. M. Redington. In these earlier works, these researchers developed a measure of bond price volatility that is now popularly referred to as *duration*. (Because Macaulay was the first to develop this measure, it is often referred to as Macaulay duration.) Despite the existence of these published works, as late as the mid 1970s duration was still not a measure used by practitioners. However, two articles published in prestigious academic journals in the early 1970s brought greater attention to the potential usefulness of duration. In 1973, the *American Economic Review* published an article by Professors Michael Hopewell and George Kaufman that demonstrated the usefulness of duration in explaining price volatility. In 1971, Professors Lawrence Fisher and Roman Weil in an article appearing in the *Journal of Business*, published by the University of Chicago, showed the importance of duration for portfolio strategies.

Once portfolio managers and traders realized the significance of duration, duration-based portfolio and trading strategies were developed. New measures of duration were proposed. Unfortunately, some strategies were developed without a full understanding of the limitations of duration as a measure of price volatility.

In the early 1980s, Stanley Diller and Ravi Dattatreya worked to extend the application of the analytical tools, as well as to understand and demonstrate their limitations. This work resulted in a 1984 paper published by Goldman Sachs titled *Parametric Analysis of Fixed Income Securities.* The study demonstrated that duration was only one parameter (measure) that summarizes the potential price performance of a fixed-income security. To properly assess the potential price performance of a fixed-income security due to interest rate changes, another parameter is needed. This parameter was called convexity. In addition, the same study was the first to point out that the standard duration measure was of limited value in assessing the performance of bonds with embedded options such as callable bonds and mortgage pass-through securities. The price performance value of these securities can only be assessed by taking into consideration the price performance and value of the embedded options. This was therefore the first work that tied together fixed-income analysis and option theory.

Recent years have seen two further developments essential to modern fixed-income portfolio management. First, theoretical and empirical evidence has brought greater recognition of the need to incorporate the term structure of interest rates into fixed-income analysis in order to eliminate inconsistencies. Sophisticated statistical tools for estimating the term structure are now being used. Second, option pricing theory focusing on fixed-income instruments has demonstrated the limitations of applying models commonly used to price stock options. New option pricing models for fixed-income securities have been developed. The state-of-the-art models incorporate the term structure of interest rates.

In *Active Total Return Management of Fixed-Income Portfolios,* we set forth a framework for modern fixed-income portfolio management that builds on the analytical concepts developed in the research cited above. Therefore, many of the concepts presented are not new. The primary focus of the book is in the logical rather than mathematical development of the concepts, emphasizing their application to the valuation of Treasuries, callable corporate bonds and mortgage-backed securities, and portfolio strategies (indexing, immunization and active strategies).

ACKNOWLEDGMENTS

Parts of this book were written when Ravi Dattatreya was Director of the Financial Strategies Group of Prudential-Bache Capital Funding. He thanks Lisa Pendergast, Joe Reel, and Edward Peterson of Prudential-Bache Capital Funding. The product of his initial research was a Prudential-Bache Capital Funding report with the same title as this book. He also thanks Paul V. Scura of Prudential-Bache Capital Funding for encouragement in the preparation of the report and for granting him permission to use material from that report in this book, so that more market participants can be educated on the latest technologies.

Frank Fabozzi used drafts of portions of the first edition of this book in both his Fixed Income Seminar (15.449) and Investment Banking and Markets course (15.438) at MIT, and portions of the second edition of this book in his Investment Banking Seminar at Yale's School of Management. The comments of many of the students in these courses were helpful.

Finally, we wish to acknowledge that many of the concepts and ideas in this book are influenced by the thoughts, published and unpublished, of Stanley Diller.

Chapter 1

Introduction

Today, detailed analysis of fixed-income securities is a standard practice for the astute investor. However, this has not always been the case. Not too long ago, the relative stability of interest rates and the lower liquidity of the securities encouraged passive investment behavior, which required little analysis. As long as an issue's credit quality and term-to-maturity met the simple objectives of the investor, the issue was usually purchased and held to maturity. Active trading in the security was the exception rather than the rule.

The recent dynamic evolution in the fixed-income markets, as seen by the introduction of complex securities and hedging instruments, and an enormous increase in the volatility of interest rates, have forced a more active approach to investment in this market. The increased liquidity of fixed-income securities has both resulted from and contributed to this more active market. Suddenly, what used to be a safe, passive investment in a fixed-income security has become loaded with risk. Changes in financial reporting requirements for financial institutions that have moved them closer to marked-to-market accounting have also decreased the attractiveness of some passive portfolio management techniques and encouraged more performance-oriented active management.

Choosing an investment now requires a careful comparative evaluation of the various instruments. Such excruciating analyses of alternative investments is not just an intellectual exercise, but a prudent business requirement. It is no longer sufficient to ask how an investment will perform. Investors must now ask how it will perform relative to the risk taken. The investor's primary task now is to find an acceptable balance between risk taken and rewards expected. The methodologies that have evolved for evaluating fixed-income securities in this context are called *frameworks*.

WHAT IS A FRAMEWORK?

There is enormous variety in the universe of fixed-income securities: bonds with short and long maturities; bonds with zero, low, and high coupons; amortizing and bullet bonds; callable and puttable bonds; mortgages and their derivatives such as CMOs and strips;[1] as well as futures and options on these securities.[2] The value of these securities changes in response to changes in environmental variables, such as interest-rate levels, volatilities, etc. The value of a security depends on how it responds to market changes, i.e., on the positive and negative attributes of the security, as well as how these attributes vary as a result of changes in their determinants. Different securities offer different risks and rewards. Portfolio management can be viewed as the procedure by which the trade-off between risk and reward is balanced. However, certain assumptions must be made to define and to determine the returns and the risks obtainable from different securities.

The definitions of *risk* and *reward,* along with the set of assumptions that are used to determine them, make up a framework. Basically, a framework relates risk and reward, which are the two summary attributes of all securities. Therefore, the robustness of a framework depends on how completely and accurately risk and reward are defined and how their relationship is determined.

RISKS ASSOCIATED WITH FIXED-INCOME INVESTMENTS

The return obtained from a fixed-income security from the time it is purchased to the time it is sold can be divided into two conceptual parts: (1) the market value of the security when it is eventually sold,

---

[1] Mortgages and their derivatives are reviewed in Chapter 9.
[2] Options and futures are reviewed in Chapters 7 and 10.

and (2) the cash flows received from the security during the holding period, plus any additional income from reinvestment of the cash flow. Several environmental factors impact one or both of these two parts of return. We can define the risk in any security as a measure of the impact of these market factors on the return characteristics of the security. The different types of risk in fixed-income securities are described below.

Market or Interest-Rate Risk

The price of a bond moves in a direction opposite to that of the change in interest rates: As interest rates rise (fall), the price of a bond will fall (rise).[3] For an investor who plans to hold a bond to maturity, the change in the bond's price prior to maturity is not of concern; however, for an investor who may have to sell the bond prior to the maturity date, an increase in interest rates will mean the realization of a capital loss. This risk is referred to as *market risk* or *interest-rate risk,* which is by far the major risk in the fixed-income market, and a major portion of this book is devoted to exploring this type of risk in detail.

It is customary to represent the market by the yield levels on Treasury securities. Most other yields are compared to the Treasury levels, and are quoted as spreads off appropriate Treasury yields. To the extent that the yields of all fixed-income securities are interrelated, their prices respond to changes in Treasury rates. As discussed in Chapter 2, the actual magnitude of the price response for any security depends on various characteristics of the security such as coupon, maturity, etc.

Reinvestment Risk

The cash flows received from a security are usually (or, are assumed to be) reinvested. The additional income from such reinvestment, sometimes called "interest-on-interest," depends on the prevailing

---

[3] There are fixed-income instruments whose price changes in the same direction as interest rates. Examples are put options (see Chapter 7) and certain stripped mortgage-backed securities (see Chapter 9).

interest-rate levels at the time of reinvestment, as well as on the reinvestment strategy. The variability in the returns from reinvestment from a given strategy due to changes in market rates is called *reinvestment risk*. Reinvestment risk is greater for longer holding periods. It is also greater for securities with large early cash flows, such as high-coupon bonds. This risk is analyzed in more detail in Chapter 4.

Call or Timing Risk

Many bonds contain a provision that allows the issuer to retire or "call" all or part of the issue before the maturity date. The issuer usually retains this right to have the flexibility to refinance the bond in the future if market interest rates decline below the coupon rate.

From the investor's perspective, there are three disadvantages of the call provision. First, the cash-flow pattern of a callable bond is not known with certainty. Second, because the issuer will call the bonds when interest rates have dropped, the investor is exposed to reinvestment risk. That is, the investor will have to reinvest the proceeds received when the bond is called at relatively lower interest rates. Finally, the capital appreciation potential of a bond will be reduced. The price of a callable bond may not rise much above the price at which the issuer will call the bond.

Many long-term Treasury and agency bonds, most corporate bonds, and almost all mortgage-backed securities have embedded in them the option on the part of the borrower to call or terminate the bond. Even though the investor is usually compensated for taking the risk of call by means of a lower price or a higher yield, it is not easy to determine if this compensation is sufficient. In any case, the returns from a bond with call risk can be dramatically different from that obtainable from a noncallable bond. The magnitude of this risk depends on the various parameters of the call as well as on market conditions. Call risk (also called *timing risk)* is so pervasive in fixed-income portfolio management that we consider it next only to market risk in importance. A framework for analyzing callable bonds and one for mortgage-backed securities are presented in Chapters 8 and 9, respectively.

Call risk is also called *convexity* or *option risk*. Convexity, discussed later, refers to the property that the value of a security changes faster (positive convexity) or slower (negative convexity) than linearly in response to a change in a market parameter such as interest rates. The presence of optional features such as the right to call a bond can change the convexity of a security significantly. When using one security for another as a substitute, or when hedging one security with another, the difference in the convexity of the securities results in convexity risk.

Credit Risk or Default Risk

Credit risk (or *default risk*) refers to the risk that the issuer of a fixed-income security may go into default, i.e., will be unable to make timely principal and interest payments on the security. Credit risk is gauged by quality ratings assigned by commercial rating companies such as Moody's Investor Service, Standard & Poor's Corporation, Duff & Phelps Credit Rating Company, and Fitch Investors Service, as well as by dealer firms and institutional investor concerns.

Because of this risk, most bonds are sold at a lower price than, or at a yield spread to, comparable U.S. Treasury securities, which are considered free of credit risk. However, except for the lowest credit securities, known as "junk bonds," the investor is normally concerned more with the changes in the perceived credit risk and/or the cost associated with a given level of credit risk than with the actual event of default. This is because even though the actual default of an issuing corporation may be highly unlikely, the impact of a change in perceived credit risk or the spread demanded by the market for any given level of risk can have an immediate impact on the value of a security.

Yield Curve or Maturity Risk

Sometimes a bond of a given maturity is used as an alternative to another bond of a different maturity. To the extent that rates at different maturities move differently, the alternative bond has *yield curve* or *maturity risk*.

Volatility Risk

The price of a bond with an embedded option depends on the level of interest rates and factors that influence the value of the embedded option.[4] The value of an option rises when interest-rate volatility increases. In the case of a callable bond or mortgage-backed security, since the investor has granted an option to the borrower, the price of the security falls because the investor has given away a more valuable option. The risk that a change in volatility will affect the price of a security is called *volatility risk*.

Marketability or Liquidity Risk

Marketability risk (or *liquidity risk*) involves the ease with which an issue can be sold at or near its value. The primary measure of marketability/liquidity is the size of the spread between the bid price and ask price quoted by a dealer. The greater the dealer spread, the greater the marketability/liquidity risk. For an investor who plans to hold the bond until the maturity date and need not mark the position to market, marketability/liquidity risk is less important.

Inflation Risk or Purchasing Power Risk

Inflation risk or *purchasing power risk* arises because of the variation in the value of cash flows from a security, as measured in terms of purchasing power, due to inflation.

Exchange Rate or Currency Risk

A bond that pays in a foreign currency has unknown cash flows in terms of the domestic currency. The cash flows will depend on the foreign exchange rate at the time they are received. Such a bond exposes the investor to *exchange rate risk* or *currency risk*.

Political or Legal Risk

Sometimes the government can declare withholding or other additional taxes on a bond, or declare a tax-exempt bond taxable. Or a regulatory authority can conclude that a given security is unsuitable

---

[4] See Chapter 6 for a discussion of the factors that influence the value of an option.

for investment entities that it regulates. These actions can adversely impact the value of the security as well as reduce the cash flows from it. Similarly, it is also possible that a legal or regulatory action impacts the value of a security positively. The probability of such actions and their impact on the value of a security is known as *political risk*.

Event Risk

Occasionally the ability of an issuer to make the interest and principal payments is seriously and unexpectedly changed by a natural or industrial accident, or by an acquisition or a leveraged buyout (such as that of RJR Nabisco, for example). Such risk is called *event risk*.

Sector Risk

Bonds in different sectors of the market respond differently to environmental changes due to a combination of some or all of the above risks, as well as others. Examples include discount versus premium coupon bonds, industrial versus utility bonds, corporate versus mortgage-backed bonds. The differential movement of the different sectors of the market is called *sector risk*.

Basis Risk

This list of the various risks in investment in the fixed-income markets is by no means intended to be exhaustive. In the marketplace, it is customary to combine almost all risks other than market risk (interest-rate risk) and refer to it as *basis risk*. In this book, our main concerns are market risk, reinvestment risk, call risk, yield curve risk, and volatility risk.

FIXED-INCOME PORTFOLIO MANAGEMENT STRATEGIES

The nature of an institutional investor's liabilities will dictate the investment strategy it will request its money manager to pursue. By the liabilities of an institutional investor we mean both the *amount* and *timing* of the cash outlays that must be made to satisfy the contractual terms of the obligations issued. Depository institutions seek to generate income by the spread between the return that they earn on their assets and the cost of their funds. Life insurance companies are in the spread business. Pension funds are not in the spread business, in that they themselves do not raise funds in the market. Defined-benefit pension funds seek to cover the cost of pension obligations at a minimum cost, which is borne by the sponsor of the pension plan.

Fixed-income portfolio management strategies can be broadly divided into active and structured portfolio strategies.

Active Management Strategies

Active management strategies usually seek to capitalize on implicit or explicit expectations about (1) the direction of future interest rates, (2) changes in yield spreads between and within market sectors, (3) changes in interest-rate volatility, or (4) changes in credit quality, etc.

Structured Portfolio Management Strategies

A structured portfolio management strategy is one in which a portfolio is designed to match the performance of some predetermined benchmark regardless of how interest rates move. Strategies in this category are not usually driven by expectations. Examples are:

Immunization and Cash-Flow Matching. When the need is to satisfy a single future liability, a strategy known as *immunization* is used.[5] When multiple future liabilities must be satisfied, *multiperiod immunization* or *cash-flow matching* is used.

Indexing. Indexing a portfolio means designing a portfolio so that its performance will match the performance of some bond index. While it is common to refer to indexing as a passive strategy, it is actually a structured portfolio strategy. Indexing an equity portfolio is commonplace. On the bond side, indexing is a relatively recent phenomenon. In 1980, for example, only $40 million of assets was

---

[5] This strategy is discussed in Chapter 4.

managed under bond indexing strategies.[6] Currently, more than $75 billion of funds under fixed-income management is indexed. Since 1980, the number of investment advisors who manage funds on an indexed basis has increased from a few to about 50.[7]

Several factors explain the recent popularity and phenomenal rate of growth of bond indexing.[8] First, the empirical evidence suggests that historically the overall performance of active bond investment advisors has been poor. Second, an advantage of bond indexing is reduced advisory management fees charged for an indexed portfolio compared to active management advisory fees. Advisory fees charged by active managers typically range from 15 to 50 basis points. The range for indexed portfolios, in contrast, is 1 to 20 basis points, with the upper range representing the fees for enhanced and customized benchmark funds.[9] Finally, lower nonadvisory fees, such as custodian and master fees, is the third explanation for the popularity of indexing. While indexing matches the performance of some index, the performance of that index does not necessarily represent optimal performance. Moreover, matching an index does not mean that a money manager will satisfy the return requirement objective of a client.

Surplus Hedging. The *surplus* of a financial institution or a pension fund is the difference between the value of its assets and liabilities. *Surplus hedging* is a strategy to prevent the surplus from decreasing or falling below a specified level. Corporate pension plan sponsors, for example, are encouraged to hedge the fund's surplus by the financial reporting requirements for pension funds (Financial Accounting Standards Board Statement No. 87). The financial report-

---

[6] Sharmin Mossavar-Rahmani, "Understanding and Evaluating Index Fund Management," in Frank J. Fabozzi and T. Dessa Garlicki, eds., *Advances in Bond Analysis and Portfolio Strategies* (Chicago: Probus Publishing, 1987), p. 433.

[7] Sharmin Mossavar-Rahmani, *Bond Index Funds* (Chicago: Probus Publishing, 1991), p. vii.

[8] Ibid., pp. 2–12.

[9] Sharmin Mossavar-Rahmani, "Understanding and Evaluating Index Fund Management," op. cit., p. 434.

ing requirements specify that under certain conditions a corporate pension plan must report a liability if the present value of the pension liabilities exceeds the market value of plan assets. In this case the objective of surplus hedging is to maintain the value of the surplus above zero.

Active Management within a Structured Portfolio Strategy

Within a structured portfolio management strategy, active management strategies can still be utilized. For example, immunized portfolios can be rebalanced to take advantage of expected changes between market sectors. In a cash-flow-matched portfolio, if securities are mispriced it might be possible to replicate the cash flow of a bond in the portfolio with other bonds at a lower cost. This strategy, referred to as *cash-flow swapping*, enables funds to be withdrawn from the portfolio while still satisfying the original objective of meeting the liability stream.

Contingent immunization is a strategy that allows the money manager to actively manage a portfolio unless and until the market value of the portfolio falls below a specified value, at which time the portfolio is fully immunized. The client in this strategy is willing to accept a lower guaranteed return in exchange for the upside potential from active management.

Enhanced indexing uses active strategies to shift the indexed portfolio from the target benchmark portfolio. This can be done by tilting the indexed portfolio toward sectors of the bond market that are expected to outperform others and/or including sectors in the bond market that are not included in the target index.

The framework that we set forth in this book can be used in all of the fixed-income portfolio strategies discussed above, including structured portfolio management.

ACTIVE TRADING ENHANCES RETURNS

There are several reasons why active trading is a prudent investment practice. They can be classified broadly into two categories: availability of relative values in the market and suitability of investment to purpose.

Values Can Still Be Found in the Market

Notwithstanding the fact that the market today is much more efficient than ever before, due mainly to advances in communication and modern evaluation techniques, relative values can still be found. Some of the reasons are:

Taxes.   The impact of taxes varies from one market segment to another. For example, discount bonds used to have two types of tax advantages:[10] (1) a part of the interest income was not taxed when earned (accrued), but only when the bond was sold or at its maturity, and (2) even at this later date, this part of interest was taxed at a lower, capital gains rate. Another example is that some holders of premium bonds do not sell their bonds as they prefer not to realize the gains for tax reasons.

Accounting.   Many holders of discount bonds purchased them at a higher price and are reluctant to realize the loss by selling the bonds for accounting or performance-related reasons. Therefore, the supply of discount bonds for trading is diminished. Premium bonds are less attractive to those who have to amortize the "loss," i.e., the premium paid over par.

Supply.   Several participants tend to "buy and hold" bonds, thus effectively taking the bonds out of circulation. Structured portfolio strategies such as cash-flow-matched portfolios follow such a practice. Tax, accounting, or other advantages might encourage borrowers to favor a particular financing technique, thus increasing supply. Regulatory changes also impact supply.

Liquidity.   Due to the reasons above, and others, trading activity is relatively lower in discount and premium bonds than in current

---

[10] This advantage is not present in original issue discount bonds in the United States.

bonds. Current bonds enjoy a higher level of liquidity. The liquidity needs clearly differ among different investors.

Demand.   The relative demand for different securities changes continually. For example, the total short interest in a security might be excessive, resulting in a short-squeeze and the corresponding higher demand and price for the security. Another example is where a given security suddenly comes into demand because of its use in creating a derivative product such as the Treasury or mortgage strips or CMOs.

Needs.   Different market segments have differing investment needs. These needs, themselves, change continually. For example, the cash-flow needs of the insurance industry might change due to demographic effects, thus impacting the class of securities that are appropriate investments for them.

Frameworks.   Different market participants use different frameworks to evaluate bonds. Also, not all of the valuation methodologies are consistent or correct, and this causes mispricings to occur.

Preference.   For various reasons securities are preferred to different extents by market participants. Some investors, for example, prefer to deal only with simple securities because their values are more easily estimated.

New Products.   When new and innovative products are introduced, their value is not clearly understood by all market participants, leading to possible mispricing. This is most common in the market for CMOs, where market participants have demanded a high risk premium for complex structures when they are introduced. As market participants come to better understand these new structures, the risk premium demanded declines.

Regulatory Constraints.   Certain institutional investors operate under significant regulatory constraints. Any changes in their economic status or any relaxation or tightening of the restrictions will impact the market. Two examples are savings and loan associations and mutual funds. Restrictions on savings and loan associations by some state regulators on investing in certain derivative mortgage-backed securities have impacted values in that sector of the market. Many mutual-fund investment policies were dominated by advertising considerations, encouraging them to invest in securities with high current yield. Changes in reporting requirements for mutual funds shifted the emphasis to total return performance, thereby changing the yield relationships between premium bonds and the other coupon sectors.[11]

Risk Valuation. Each security has embedded in it several different types of risk, which we discussed earlier in this chapter. The perceived level of each of these risks changes continually. In addition, the perceived value of each unit of such risk itself changes over time. To complicate matters further, different market segments value risks differently. For example, pension funds, which are nontaxable, are less concerned about the risk of changes in the tax law.

   For these and many other reasons, values can always be found in the market. It is the goal of a framework to discover these values.

Suitability of Investments

The needs and demands of investment change continually, and a portfolio has to be managed to bring it to a balance. Some of the reasons are listed below.

Change in Market Conditions. The changes in interest-rate levels, for example, change the properties of investments, and the portfolio characteristics may deviate from the original goal. Even just the passage of time can cause such changes. In addition, changes in the credit quality of some issuers may indicate rebalancing.

Liquidity Needs. As demand for cash depletes the liquid part of the portfolio, the relatively longer term investments have to be sold to generate cash. Changes in liquidity needs can also trigger a move to short-term investments.

---

[11] Securities and Exchange Commission, Release Number 33-6753, February 2, 1988.

Market Outlook. The management of a portfolio almost always implies a bullish, bearish, or neutral market outlook. As the outlook changes, the portfolio has to be adjusted by trading.

Changes in Liabilities. As explained earlier, a portfolio is usually constructed in order to meet certain explicit or implicit liabilities. As these liabilities mature or otherwise change, the portfolio has to be correspondingly altered.

New Products. Innovations in product development are constantly being made. When a new product more closely matches an investment need, it is prudent to consider purchasing it.

The twin requirements of portfolio management—capturing values in the market and keeping the portfolio in balance relative to needs and objectives—can be met through active trading. A complete framework is an essential tool in the proper execution of this process.

WHAT DRIVES INVESTMENT RETURNS?

Empirical studies have investigated the factors that have affected the historical returns on Treasury portfolios. A recent study found that three factors explained historical bond returns.[12] The first factor was changes in the level of rates, the second factor was changes in the slope of the yield curve, and the third factor was changes in the curvature of the yield curve.

The study employed regression analysis to determine the relative contribution of these three factors in explaining the returns on zero-coupon Treasury securities of different maturities. Exhibit 1-1 summarizes their results. The second column of the exhibit shows the coefficient of determination, popularly referred to as the "R^2," for each zero-coupon maturity. In general, the R^2 measures the percentage of the variance in the dependent variable explained by the independent variables. The R^2 will have a value between 0 percent and 100 percent. In terms of the experiment conducted by Litterman and Scheinkman, the R^2 measures the percentage of the variance of

---

[12] Robert Litterman and Jose Scheinkman, "Common Factors Affecting Bond Returns," *Journal of Fixed Income* (June 1991), pp. 54–61.

Exhibit 1-1. Factors Explaining Treasury Returns

Factor 1: Changes in the level of interest rates
Factor 2: Changes in the yield curve slope
Factor 3: Curvature of the yield curve

Zero-coupon maturity	Variance of total returns explained	Proportion of Total Explained Variance Accounted for by		
		Factor 1	Factor 2	Factor 3
6 months	99.5%	79.5%	17.2%	3.3%
1 year	99.4	89.7	10.1	0.2
2 years	98.2	93.4	2.4	4.2
5 years	98.8	98.2	1.1	0.7
8 years	98.7	95.4	4.6	0.0
10 years	98.8	92.9	6.9	0.2
14 years	98.4	86.2	11.5	2.2
18 years	95.3	80.5	14.3	5.2
Average	98.4	89.5	8.5	2.0

Source: Robert Litterman and Jose Scheinkman, "Common Factors Affecting Bond Returns," *Journal of Fixed Income* (June 1991), p. 58. This copyrighted material is reprinted with permission from *The Journal of Fixed Income*, 488 Madison Avenue, New York, NY 10022.

historical returns explained by the three factors (i.e., the independent variables). As can be seen in the second column, the R^2 was very high for all maturities, meaning that the three factors had a very strong predictive or explanatory effect.

The last three columns show the relative contribution that each of the three factors had in explaining the return on the zero-coupon maturity bond. For example, let's look at the 18-year zero. The second column indicates that 95.3 percent of the variance of the return in the 18-year zero is explained by these three factors. The first factor—which can be viewed as changes in the level of rates, holding all other factors constant (in particular, yield curve slope)—contributes about 81 percent of the explanatory power. This factor has the greatest explanatory power for all the maturities, averaging about 90 percent. The implication is that a portfolio manager should control for exposure to changes in interest rates by adjusting the market risk or interest-rate risk of the portfolio. For this reason it is important to have a way to measure or quantify this risk.

The second factor, changes in the yield curve slope, is the second largest contributing factor. For the 18-year zero-coupon bond, the relative contribution is about 14.3 percent. The average relative contribution is 8.5 percent. Thus, changes in the yield curve slope are, on average, about one-tenth as significant as changes in the level of rates. While this may not seem very significant, remember that the study examined a portfolio containing a series of Treasury zero-coupon bonds which typically have much less yield curve slope risk than securities such as CMOs. Moreover, while the relative contribution is only 8.5 percent, this can still have a significant impact on the return for a portfolio, and a portfolio manager must control for this risk.

Notice that the third factor, changes in the curvature of the yield curve, contributes relatively little to explaining historical returns. For simplicity we therefore ignore this factor.

This study has been replicated for mortgage-backed securities.[13] Instead of looking at three factors, they consider only two factors: changes in the level of interest rates and changes in the yield curve slope. Exhibit 1-2 reports the regression results for current coupon fixed-rate pass-throughs, one-year CMT adjustable-rate pass-throughs, a principal-only strip, a high coupon interest-only strip, and four CMO bonds (a 7-year PAC, a 10-year VADM, a short-average-life floater, and a long-average-life floater). The dependent variable in the regression is the return on the particular mortgage-backed security. The independent variables are the level of rates and changes in the yield curve slope. The time period studied was December 1983 to December 1992.

The second column shows the R^2. The third and fourth columns report the estimated regression coefficient for the two factors and show in the last two columns the corresponding T-statistics. The results are quite interesting. With the exception of the short-average-

---

[13] Michael P. Schumacher, Daniel C. Dektar, and Frank J. Fabozzi, "Yield Curve Risk of CMO Bonds," in Frank J. Fabozzi, ed., *CMO Portfolio Management* (Summit, NJ: Frank J. Fabozzi Associates, 1993).

Exhibit 1-2. CMO Bond Returns vs. Changes in Level and Slope of the Yield Curve: Regression Results 12/83 through 12/92

Dependent variable	R^2	Coefficients		T-statistics	
		Level	Slope	Level	Slope
Current coupon fixed-rate mort.	79%	–4.01	–1.20	–18.5	–5.7
1-year CMT adjustable-rate mort.	30	–1.30	0.03	–4.9	0.1
Principal-only strip	64	–11.43	–2.66	–10.2	–2.4
High coupon interest-only strip	32	12.47	1.13	5.0	0.5
7-year PAC	86	–6.70	–1.15	–14.0	–2.8
10-year VADM	95	–8.00	–2.31	–9.6	–2.9
Short-average-life floater	11	–0.43	–0.22	–1.9	–1.1
Long-average-life floater	13	–0.64	–0.51	–1.1	–0.9

Source: Michael P. Schumacher, Daniel C. Dektar, and Frank J. Fabozzi, "Yield Curve Risk of CMO Bonds," in Frank J. Fabozzi, ed., *CMO Portfolio Management* (Summit, NJ: Frank J. Fabozzi Associates, 1994).

life floater and the ARM, the R^2s are good. While not reported here, there have been periods where the R^2 for these two floating-rate securities has been much higher. The PAC and VADM had very high explanatory power.

The R^2 gives the explanatory power of the two factors collectively. The T-statistics shown in the last two columns indicate the statistical significance of each factor separately. Generally, a T-statistic with an absolute value greater than 2 is considered statistically significant at the 5 percent level of significance. The T-statistics reported for changes in the level of interest rates are statistically significant for all but the short and long average-life floater. The T-statistics reported for changes in the yield curve slope are statistically significant for the PO strip, the IO strip, the PAC, the VADM, and the current-coupon mortgage. The only instruments for which changes in the yield curve slope were not statistically significant were the floaters and the ARM. These results further support the importance of yield curve risk. Thus, in addition to a measure of market risk or interest-rate risk, a measure to quantify yield curve risk is needed.

THE FOUR M'S OF RISK MANAGEMENT

As we noted earlier, institutional investors assume various types of
financial risk. Even though our focus is on interest-rate risk, the concepts developed apply to many other types of risks as well.

It is important to view interest-rate risk as an integral part of a
comprehensive risk management program.[14] Risk management can
be defined as a systematic approach that attempts to provide the
institution a degree of protection from risk and makes such risk
acceptable. Any complete interest-rate risk management program,
therefore, should provide the necessary framework for the implementation of the four M's of risk management: measurement, monitoring, modification, and management.

> *Measurement* defines exactly what types of risks will be
> managed under the program. For each risk, the appropri-
> ate risk measures and acceptable procedures for measure-
> ment are defined as well.

> *Monitoring* sets forth the mechanics of locating which parts
> of the institution are sources of different forms and quan-
> tities of risk and the frequency with which these risks will
> be measured and reviewed. It puts in place the necessary
> systems and procedures to ensure that the information can
> be and is obtained when desired.

> *Modification* provides the risk manager with the tools nec-
> essary to modify any particular risk to desired levels. For
> example, here is where we determine whether futures or
> swaps are appropriate instruments for the institution and
> the limits on quantities and purposes for which these will
> be used. In actual use, optimization by the risk manager—
> i.e., selection of tools and quantity—is also done here.

> *Management* is the collection of policies and procedures for
> the exercise of the other three M's. Here we define the

---

[14] Risk management is known as asset liability management (ALM) in
many contexts.

upper and lower[15] bounds for each risk category, as well as the conditions under which an action will be required to initiate the modification step. In addition to routine policy, this part of risk management includes some emergency powers for the risk manager and guidelines as to how and when these powers can be used. As an example, the emergency powers could include relaxation of the limits on the tools or amounts that can be employed.

In a way, we can compare risk management to a form of insurance. It can shield the institution from risk where its assumption is necessary. For example, in the absence of automobile insurance, we would probably find the risks of driving a car unacceptable. It is insurance that makes it possible for us to drive. The main function of risk management is similar: it is to enable the institution to be in business, that is, to assume the necessary risks. For example, it facilitates a bank to make long-term loans that are in demand regardless of whether long-term funding for the loan is available, by providing acceptable techniques to hedge the resultant interest-rate risk. In general, the more leveraged an institution, the more critical risk management is to that institution. This is because its net worth then is a small fraction of the size of its assets, and even modest market moves can result in wide swings in the net worth. Risk management is therefore simply the process of preservation of net worth.

---

[15] The goal of risk management is not risk elimination. Lower bounds for risk are required, as risk and reward are interrelated. In most cases, risk cannot be eliminated, only transformed, anyway. This fact was realized best by corporations that issued (or converted via interest-rate swaps to) fixed-rate debt just before the long rally in the bond market in the early 1990s. Even though these corporations had fixed-rate debt, which is considered a no-risk situation in most cases, they soon realized the risk in fixing as the market rates plummeted and they found themselves paying higher-than-market coupons on their debt or on interest-rate swaps. One way to look at this situation is to consider both fixed rate and floating rate as risky: the former when rates fall, and the latter when rates rise. For more discussion of this topic, see Ravi E. Dattatreya, Raj E. Venkatesh, and Vijaya E. Venkatesh in *Interest Rate and Currency Swaps* (Chicago: Probus Publishing, 1994).

The function of risk management is not just protection from risk. The safety achieved through it also opens up opportunities for enhancing the net worth. An effective risk management program can make it possible for an institution to take on positions that would have been considered too large or too risky in the absence of the protection offered by risk management. Such a program can also enable an institution to enter into new business areas as the demands of the marketplace change and grow. In many cases these businesses would have been beyond the reach of the institution without the comfort of the insurance provided by risk management.

Every manager has two fundamental priorities. The first priority is to protect and preserve the existing business or investment and provide damage control.[16] The second priority is to enhance the returns, strengthen the business and enrich the institution. Risk management, as discussed above, can be a vital ally to the manager in fulfilling these two needs.

Of the financial risks discussed earlier, interest-rate risk and option risk fall neatly within the risk management framework, mainly because it is possible to quantify the risks easily and appropriate hedging vehicles are available. Any acceptable risk management policy will also help measure and monitor liquidity risk and provide suitable strategies for its management. Other risks are more complex to manage. Consider credit risk. It is difficult to manage it in the traditional sense. It is best controlled by limiting it before it is assumed.

The focus of our attention in this book will be the quantifiable risks, interest-rate risk in particular. As a consequence, we will be dealing mainly with risks associated with fixed-income assets and liabilities.

OVERVIEW OF THE BOOK

In this book, we develop the progression of thinking that led to two popular frameworks, the simple duration analysis, and its extension, the parametric approach. We illustrate how various securities can be

---

[16] Damage control is where emergency powers are used most often by the risk manager.

rated as rich or cheap using different techniques within these frameworks. We demonstrate some serious shortcomings of these frameworks in their use for decision making in transactions even in the case of very simple straight Treasury bonds. We then introduce a new robust framework based on total returns. The total return is the return of an investment over some horizon. In computing total returns, we still have to make certain assumptions on the future behavior of interest rates. We state some conditions that any acceptable set of such assumptions should satisfy. We extend the discussion to options, callable bonds, and mortgage-backed securities.

Many of the concepts developed in this book are not new. Duration has been known for 50 years, and convexity for decades. The arbitrage arguments in the total return analysis are well established in academic literature, especially in the modeling of options. The major contribution of this book is in the logical rather than mathematical development of the ideas. We present logical equivalents to complex mathematical equations. The intent is to clarify the underlying truths and their implications, and perhaps even make them obvious. Another equally important contribution is in the application of the option modeling technology to valuing all fixed-income securities, thus providing a common, universal framework.

Chapter 2

The First Generation: Duration Analysis

The most important risk to consider is the variation in the market value of a security as the environmental variables change. The major factor affecting a simple fixed-income security (that is, a security without option-like features such as callability) is, of course, the general level of interest rates, which in turn influences the yield on the security. The way a bond responds to changes in yields depends on its maturity, coupon, and the current price (or, effectively, yield). In other words, the price sensitivity of a bond depends on the timing and size of all cash flows from the bond.

As a basis of discussion, we need a measure of price sensitivity.

We define price sensitivity to be the percentage change in price for a small change in yield.

Price sensitivity is expressed as a percentage change in price for a 100-basis-point change in yield.

In this chapter we present a measure of price sensitivity called duration and illustrate how this measure can be used in portfolio management. In the next chapter, we take a closer look at duration and highlight its limitations as a sole measure of price sensitivity.

TERM-TO-MATURITY AS A MEASURE
OF PRICE SENSITIVITY

Many investors use the term-to-maturity of a bond as an indication
of price sensitivity. However, even though maturity does provide a
crude measure, it alone is not enough to determine price sensitivity,
as it provides information only about the timing of the final payment.

To illustrate this, we compare in Exhibit 2-1 two bonds—Bond
A, which is a 15-year, 10 percent coupon bond, and Bond B, which
is a 30-year, 10 percent coupon bond, both priced to yield 10 percent, i.e., the initial price of both bonds is par. If the yield declines
by 100 basis points to 9 percent, the price of the 15-year bond
increases to 108.14, a change of 8.14 percent, and the price of the 30-
year bond increases to 110.32, a change of 10.32 percent. In the other
direction, if the yield increases by 100 basis points to 11 percent, the
price changes are –7.27 percent and –8.72 percent, respectively. Thus,
the longer-maturity bond is more price sensitive in both cases.

In Exhibit 2-2, we compare Bond C, a 15-year, 2 percent bond
priced at 38.51, with Bond B, the 30-year bond. Both bonds are
priced to yield 10 percent. Now, the price of Bond C changes by
11.63 percent (to a price of 42.99) if the yield drops by 100 basis
points to 9 percent, and falls by 10.15 percent if the yield increases
to 11 percent. In both cases, the percentage change for Bond C, the
shorter bond, is *greater* than the percentage change for Bond B, the
longer bond.

Notice that in Exhibit 2-2, the shorter bond has a much smaller
coupon than the longer bond. Even though the smaller coupon does
indeed have something to do with reversing the order of price sen-
sitivities, making the coupons equal does not always guarantee that
the usual ordering holds. This can be seen in Exhibit 2-3, where we
compare two deep discount bonds, both with a coupon of 1 percent
and both priced to yield 15 percent. Bond D is a 15-year bond with
a price of 17.33, and Bond E is a 30-year bond with a price of 7.88.
The percentage price changes in response to a 100-basis-point drop
in yield are 11.60 percent for the short bond, and 11.04 percent for
the longer bond. If the yield rises to 16 percent, the percentage
changes in price are –10.16 percent and –8.88 percent, respectively.

Exhibit 2-1. Comparison of Price Sensitivity of Two Bonds

			Initial		Final Yield	
	Coupon	Maturity	yield	9%	10%	11%
Bond A:	10%	15 Years	10%	Price:	108.14	100	92.73
			(Percentage change in price):	(8.14%)		(–7.27%)
Bond B:	10%	30 Years	10%	Price:	110.32	100	91.28
			(Percentage change in price):	(10.32%)		(–8.72%)

Exhibit 2-2. Comparison of Price Sensitivity of Two Bonds

	Coupon	Maturity	Initial yield		Final Yield		
					9%	10%	11%
Bond C:	2%	15 Years	10%	Price:	42.99	38.51	34.60
				(Percentage change in price):	(11.63%)		(−10.15%)
Bond B:	10%	30 Years	10%	Price:	110.32	100	91.28
				(Percentage change in price):	(10.32%)		(−8.72%)

Exhibit 2-3. Comparison of Price Sensitivity of Two Deep-Discount Bonds with the Same Coupon and Yield

			Initial yield		Final Yield		
	Coupon	Maturity			14%	15%	16%
Bond D:	1%	15 Years	15%	Price:	19.34	17.33	15.57
				(Percentage change in price):	(11.60%)		(−10.16%)
Bond E:	1%	30 Years	15%	Price:	8.752	7.88	7.18
				(Percentage change in price):	(11.04%)		(−8.88%)

27

Thus, even with equal coupons, the longer bond is actually less price sensitive than the shorter bond.[1]

Thus, the term-to-maturity of a bond alone does not contain enough information to be an indicator of price sensitivity. Its usefulness is severely limited even as a criterion to rank bonds according to sensitivity, much less as a numerical measure.

DURATION DEFINED

As an alternative to using maturity as a risk estimator, Frederick Macaulay, in 1938, derived a measure, which he called *duration*, that blends the information contained in coupon, maturity, and yield into a single number.[2]

Duration can be defined as follows:

If we think of a bond as a series of cash flows, then the Macaulay duration of the bond is the weighted average of the lengths of time prior to the cash flows, the weights being the present values of the corresponding payments.

This is a working definition of duration, that is, it not only describes what duration is, but also tells us how to compute it for any given bond. The discount rate used to compute the present values is usually the yield to maturity of the bond. The weight for the time to any cash flow is obtained by dividing the present value of that cash flow by the total present value of all cash flows, i.e., dividing by the price of the bond (including accrued interest).

An alternative procedure is to first compute the sum of the products of the present value of each cash flow and the time of

---

[1] This phenomenon, in which a longer bond is less price sensitive than a shorter bond with an identical coupon, occurs only in discount bonds, except when they are zero-coupon bonds.

[2] Frederick Macaulay, *Some Theoretical Problems Suggested by Movements in Interest Rates, Bond Yields and Stock Prices in the United States Since 1856* (National Bureau of Economic Research, 1938).

occurrence of that cash flow, and divide this sum by the price of the bond to get the Macaulay duration. Exhibit 2-4 shows how to compute the Macaulay duration of a 5-year, 10 percent coupon par bond using this procedure. In practice, duration is computed using a closed-form formula, shown in the appendix to this book.

As explained in the previous section, the term-to-maturity of a bond represents only the final payment. The final payment represents only a fraction of the security's value. The larger this fraction is, the better maturity is as a risk measure. In other words, the duration of a security for which the final payment represents a substantial portion of value is close to its maturity. Examples of such securities are short-term bonds and low-coupon bonds. The Macaulay duration of a pure discount bond, i.e., a zero-coupon bond, is equal to its maturity. If we think of a bond as a portfolio of zero-coupon bonds, then the weighted average duration of this portfolio equals the duration of the bond. The weightings are of course the market values of the coupons, which in turn are equal to the present values of cash flows generated by the zeros.

Exhibit 2-4. Calculation of Macaulay Duration for a 5-Year, 10% Par Bond

Semiannual period	Time	Cash flow	Present value of cash flow	Present value × time
1	0.5	5	4.7619	2.3810
2	1.0	5	4.5351	4.5351
3	1.5	5	4.3192	6.4788
4	2.0	5	4.1135	8.2270
5	2.5	5	3.9176	9.7941
6	3.0	5	3.7311	11.1932
7	3.5	5	3.5534	12.4369
8	4.0	5	3.3842	13.5368
9	4.5	5	3.2230	14.5037
10	5.0	105	64.4609	322.3044
Totals			100.0000	405.3910

Duration = 405.3910/100 = 4.053910

MACAULAY DURATION AS AN INDICATOR
OF PRICE SENSITIVITY

The price of a bond depends on its yield. Mathematically, we say that price (P) is a function of yield (Y). To estimate how sensitive price is to changes in yield, a technique from calculus can be used. The technique is to compute the "first derivative" of the function (in our case the price function). The first derivative is denoted by dP/dY and measures *the rate of change in price due to change in yield*. As shown in the appendix to this book, the first derivative of the price function is:

$$\frac{dP}{dY} = -\frac{\text{Macaulay duration} \times (\text{Price}/100)}{(1 + \text{Yield}/200)}$$

The negative sign on the right-hand side of the formula means that the change in price will be in the opposite direction of the change in yield. In the formula, we divide yield by 200 first to adjust for semiannual compounding (a factor of 2) and then to convert it to a decimal (a factor of 100).

We can rearrange the last formula as follows:

$$100 \times \frac{dP/dY}{\text{Price}} = -\frac{\text{Macaulay duration}}{(1 + \text{Yield}/200)}$$

The expression on the right-hand side of the equation (i.e., Macaulay duration divided by (1 + Yield/200)) is known as *modified duration*. Exhibit 2-5 illustrates the computation of the modified duration for the bond whose Macaulay duration we computed earlier in Exhibit 2-4.

The left-hand side of the formula represents the percentage change in price for a 100-basis-point change in yield, which we defined to be equal to the price sensitivity of a bond. Therefore, *modified duration* represents the price sensitivity of a bond for a 100-basis-point change in yield.

Thus, Macaulay duration is an *ordinal* measure of price sensitivity; that is, we can use it to rank or order different bonds according to their price sensitivity. Modified duration is a *cardinal* measure;

Exhibit 2-5. Calculation of Modified Duration

Coupon   = 10%
Maturity = 5 years
Price   = 100
Yield   = 10%
Macaulay duration = 4.053910 (see Exhibit 2-4)

$$\text{Modified duration} = \frac{4.053910}{(1 + 10/200)}$$

$$= \frac{4.053910}{1.05}$$

$$= 3.860867$$

that is, it is numerically equal to price sensitivity. Since (1.0 + Yield/200) is very close to 1, it is not incorrect to use Macaulay duration and modified duration interchangeably. Such usage is also justified because, in practice, these measures are approximate anyway.

It should be understood that (modified) duration is a *rate*. By this we mean that if the duration of the bond is 8 and the yield changes by 100 basis points, then the price change will be *approximately* 8 percent. The reason why the price change is not exactly equal to 8 percent is that duration itself changes as yield changes. This situation is similar to saying that a car is traveling at a speed of 55 miles per hour. We do not imply that the car will travel 55 miles in the next hour (unless it maintains its speed for the whole hour). The change in duration as the yield changes is related to the convexity property of the bond, a topic that we discuss in detail in the next chapter.

Often, it is more useful to redefine duration in another way:

Duration of a bond is the maturity of a zero-coupon bond with equal price sensitivity.

Exhibit 2-6 shows the value of a $100 investment in a 12.5 percent coupon, 20-year bond with a Macaulay duration of 8.3, compared with an equal investment in a zero-coupon bond with 8.3 years to maturity. The yield for the two bonds is 11 percent. Since the Macaulay duration of a zero-coupon bond is equal to its matu-

Exhibit 2-6. Value of $100 Investment in a 20-Year, 12.5% and Zero-Coupon Bond with the Same Modified Duration

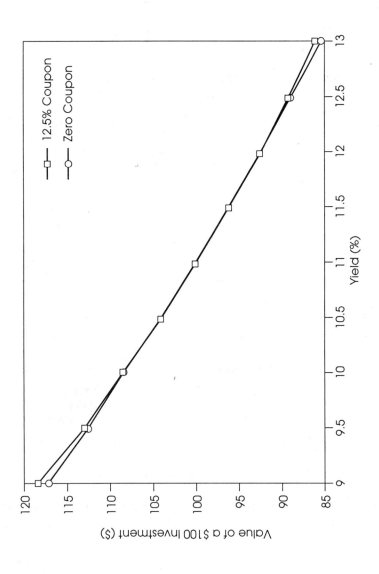

rity, 8.3, it follows that the two positions have equal price sensitivity. As is evident in the exhibit, for small changes in yield, the changes in the two positions are equal in magnitude.

It is useful to think of duration as the maturity of a zero-coupon bond with equal price sensitivity because this definition can easily be extended to securities that are more complex than straight bonds, such as options. For example, an option expiring in one year might have a duration of 150. This simply means that the option has a price sensitivity equal to that of a 150-year zero-coupon bond. In Chapter 7 we discuss the application of the duration concept to options.

Approximating Duration

Since modified duration is a measure of the price volatility of a bond to interest-rate changes, it can be approximated by simply changing yields by a small amount up and down, and then looking at how the price changes. More specifically, modified duration can be approximated using the following formula:

$$= -\frac{P_- - P_+}{2(P_0)\Delta y}$$

where

P_0 = initial price (per $100 of par value)

P_- = price if yield is decreased by x basis points

P_+ = price if yield is increased by x basis points

Δy = x basis points in decimal form

To illustrate this formula for approximating modified duration, consider a 20-year, 7 percent coupon bond selling at 74.26 to yield 10 percent. Suppose we evaluate the price changes for a 20-basis-point change up and down. Then,

P_0 = 74.26

P_- = 75.64

P_+ = 72.92

Δy = 0.002

then substituting into the formula:

$$\frac{75.64 - 72.92}{2(74.26)(0.002)} = 9.16$$

The modified duration for this bond calculated using the formula presented earlier is 9.18.

DOLLAR DURATION

Thus far in this chapter we have focused on price sensitivity in terms of percentage change in price. There is another term that is frequently used in duration analysis:

> *Dollar duration of a bond equals the dollar change in the value of the bond due to a small change in yield.*

As in the case of duration, dollar duration is expressed as a price change for a 100-basis-point change in yield. Since (modified) duration represents the percentage change in price, dollar duration can be obtained by simply multiplying modified duration and price and then dividing the product by 100. Dollar duration, sometimes called *dollar price sensitivity,* is also one hundred times what is known as the *price value of a basis point.*[3]

For example, the dollar duration of the 5-year, 10 percent coupon bond in Exhibits 2-4 and 2-5 is equal to 3.860867. In this case, the dollar duration is equal to the modified duration because the bond is priced at par.

The main advantage of dollar duration is that it is *additive,* and, in most applications, we are most concerned with dollar duration, not Macaulay or modified duration. The dollar duration of an arbitrary par holding of a bond equals the product of the par amount times the dollar duration per bond divided by 100. The dollar duration of a portfolio of bonds is the sum of the dollar durations of the

---

[3] The price value of a basis point is the change in the price of a bond for a change in yield of one basis point.

individual bonds. For example, the dollar duration of $10 million of the bond in Exhibits 2-4 and 2-5 is 0.386 million. This means that if the yield changes by 100 basis points, the total market value of the $10 million holding will change by approximately $386,000 ($0.386 million).

The Price-Yield Curve and Dollar Duration

Exhibit 2-7 shows a plot of the price of a 30-year, 10 percent coupon bond against its yield. The price representing a $100 par value of the bond is plotted along the vertical axis in dollars, and the yield is represented along the horizontal axis, in percentage points. This plot is known as the *price-yield curve*, and provides valuable insight into the behavior of fixed-income securities.

The plot clearly shows that the price and yield are inversely related, i.e., price decreases as yield increases. If we were to draw a tangent to this curve at a given yield level (10 percent in the exhibit), then the slope of this line represents the dollar change in price for a unit change in yield. That is, the slope of the tangent to the price-yield curve represents the dollar duration of the bond at that yield level.

APPLICATIONS OF DURATION ANALYSIS

The Duration Yield Curve

The yield curve is a pictorial representation of the (Treasury) yields as a function of maturity. It is a useful tool to get an intuitive feel for the way different maturity sectors are priced in the market. Within the duration framework, if we are willing to accept duration as a measure of risk and yield to maturity as a measure of reward, we can then plot yield against duration to obtain what is called a *duration yield curve*. This curve represents the trade-off between risk and reward within this context. Exhibit 2-8 shows the usual maturity yield curve and Exhibit 2-9 shows the corresponding duration yield curve.

By examining the different Treasury bonds within the yield-duration framework, we can determine those bonds that appear to have a higher return (yield) for a similar level of risk (duration), or those that appear to have a lower level of risk (duration) for about

Exhibit 2-7. Price-Yield Curve for a 30-Year, 10% Bond

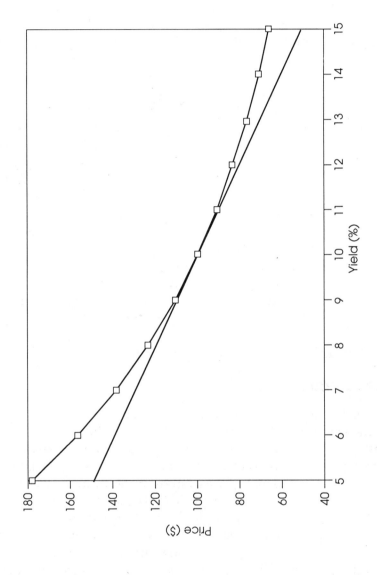

Exhibit 2-8. Maturity Yield Curve for Treasury Bonds (on 10/30/87)

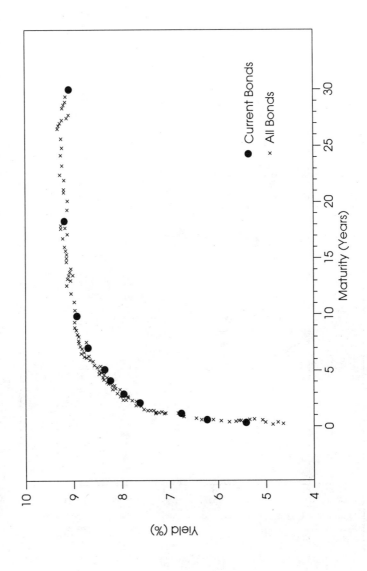

Exhibit 2-9. Duration Yield Curve for Treasury Bonds (on 10/30/87)

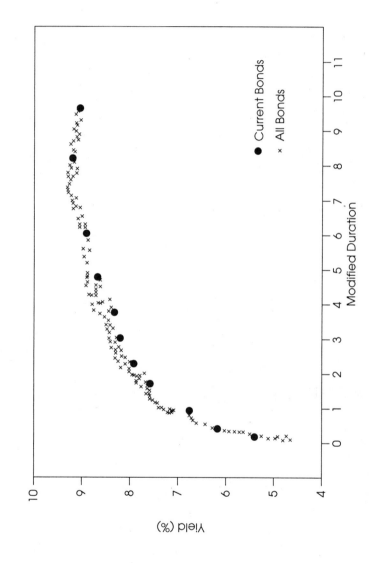

the same return (yield). If this is acceptable, then an investor could sell the lower-yielding (or higher-risk) bonds and purchase the higher-yielding (or lower-risk) bonds.

Examples of bond swaps based on this idea are given below.

Example 1: The following swap transaction based on prices as of October 30, 1987, maintains duration while increasing yield:

Sell:

13.75s of 8/15/04, price: 139 18/32, yield: 9.101, duration: 7.74

Buy:

11.625s of 11/15/04, price: 120 21/32, yield: 9.201, duration: 7.80

Example 2: The following swap, also based on prices as of October 30, 1987, maintains yield while it reduces duration:

Sell:

8.625s of 8/15/97, price: 98.50, yield: 8.854, duration: 6.37

Buy:

11.5s of 11/15/95, price: 115.00, yield: 8.853, duration: 5.16

Barbell-Bullet Analysis

The barbell-bullet analysis takes the yield curve application one step further. A *barbell* is a combination or a portfolio of two bonds where the holdings of the two bonds are determined to satisfy certain criteria. In our application, we select the bonds and their holdings such that the duration of the barbell is equal to that of a third bond, known as the *bullet*. We then compare the yield on the barbell to the yield on the bullet to determine the possibility of a swap.

In the creation of a barbell, there are two unknowns, which are the par holdings of each of the two bonds that comprise it. We need two conditions to determine these two unknowns.

The first condition is that the total dollar duration of the barbell equals that of the bullet. By equating the dollar durations, we equate the interest-rate risk of the two positions. Therefore, we can conclude whether the bullet or the barbell is relatively rich or cheap simply by comparing their yields. A reasonable strategy would be to sell the position (i.e., barbell or the bullet) with the lower yield and purchase the other with the higher yield. This transaction maintains the risk (dollar duration) while increasing the return (yield). A barbell-bullet swap has maturity or yield curve risk, but this can be minimized, if desired, by limiting our analysis to bonds in a narrow maturity sector.

A common second condition is to equate the total market value of the barbell to that of the bullet. The second condition ensures that the proceeds from the sale of the bullet (barbell) can be used to purchase the barbell (bullet) with no need for additional funds, nor is any cash left over after the transaction. Note that since the market values and the dollar durations of the two positions are equal, it follows that the modified durations are equal as well. In computing the yield of the barbell, it is common to use the weighted average yield of the two bonds. The weights used are proportions of the bonds in the barbell, i.e., the market values of each of the bonds divided by the total market value. In Chapter 4, we discuss in more detail the issue of using average yields.

Exhibit 2-10. Barbell-Bullet Analysis Based on Duration and Average Yield

The three bonds used in this analysis:

Bond	Coupon	Maturity (years)	Price plus accrued	Yield	Dollar duration
A	8.50	5	100	8.50%	4.00544
B	9.50	20	100	9.50%	8.88151
C	9.25	10	100	9.25%	6.43409

Bullet: Bond C
Barbell: Bonds A and B
Composition of barbell: 50.2% of Bond A; 49.8% of Bond B
Dollar duration of barbell = $0.502 \times 4.00544 + 0.498 \times 8.88151 = 6.434$
Average yield of barbell = $0.502 \times 8.50 + 0.498 \times 9.5 = 8.998$

Strategy: Sell the barbell and buy the bullet
Yield pickup = Yield on bullet – Average yield of barbell
$\qquad\qquad = 9.25 - 8.998 = 0.252$, or 25.2 basis points

A typical barbell-bullet swap is illustrated in Exhibit 2-10 using three hypothetical bonds. Using average yield, the analysis of the three bonds suggests a strategy of buying the bullet and selling the barbell. Notice that the dollar duration of the bullet equals that of the barbell. The yield on the bullet, however, is greater than the average yield on the barbell by 25.2 basis points. Thus, the strategy will produce a 25.2-basis-point yield pickup.

Thus, within the framework that we have presented, we have seen strategies that appear to increase reward with little or no increase in risk or that decrease risk with little or no decrease in reward. These conclusions about the levels of risk and reward are valid only as long as we accept duration and yield to completely represent the framework. But there is more: The duration/yield framework is only a static framework in the sense that we do not analyze the effect of changes in market levels. Fortunately, as we shall see in the next chapter, we can do better.

Chapter 3

The Second Generation:
Parametric Analysis

In the previous chapter we discussed duration as a measure of interest-rate risk (i.e., price sensitivity) and strategies based on duration. But, duration is not a complete measure of interest-rate risk. In this chapter, we will address this problem by extending the duration concept.

GRAPHICAL PRESENTATION OF DOLLAR DURATION

Let us return to the price-yield curve that we saw in the previous chapter, reproduced in Exhibit 3-1. The curve belongs to a 30-year, 10 percent bond. The tangent to the curve, which represents the dollar duration of the bond, is shown. Since dollar duration is a measure of price sensitivity, it can also be used as an estimator of price change due to a yield change. That is, knowing the starting price, the dollar duration and the yield change, we can estimate the price change, and therefore the new price, as follows:

New price = Initial price + Price change

The price change for a given yield change due to dollar duration is:

Price change ≈ –Dollar duration × Yield change

Exhibit 3-1. Price-Yield Curve for a 30-Year, 10% Bond

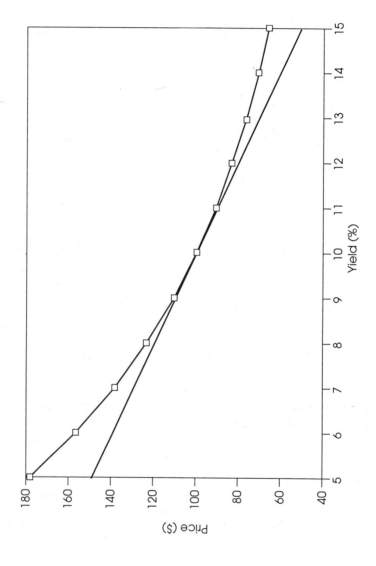

For example, at a 10 percent yield the price of the bond shown in Exhibit 3-1 is 100, and the dollar duration is 9.46. If the yield increases by 100 basis points to 11 percent, then the price change can be estimated by:

Price change = –9.46 × 1 = –9.46

The price change is negative to reflect the inverse relationship between price and yield. The estimated new price is then 90.54, as shown below:

New price = 100 + (–9.46) = 90.54

Similarly, for a decrease in yield, the price change is +9.46, and the estimated new price is 109.46 (100 + 9.46). These estimates are shown graphically in Exhibit 3-2. It is important to note the following three properties of the price-yield curve and tangent line in the exhibit:

1. The estimated prices are on the tangent line drawn at the starting point.

2. How well duration can approximate the actual price depends on the magnitude of the yield change. For small yield changes, the tangent line is very close to the price-yield curve and the approximation is good. For larger changes, the divergence of the price-yield curve from the tangent line increases, and the approximation becomes worse.

3. Regardless of whether yield increases or decreases, the estimated new price is *lower* than the actual new price. In other words, when the market declines, the *actual* drop in price is *smaller* than the *estimated* drop in price, and when the market rallies, the *actual* gain in price is *greater* than the *estimated* gain. Graphically, the entire price-yield curve lies *above* the tangent line.

CONVEXITY

This property can be explained by recognizing that the dollar duration of the bond is not a constant. It changes as the yield of the bond

Exhibit 3-2. Estimated and Actual Price Changes for a 30-Year, 10% Bond

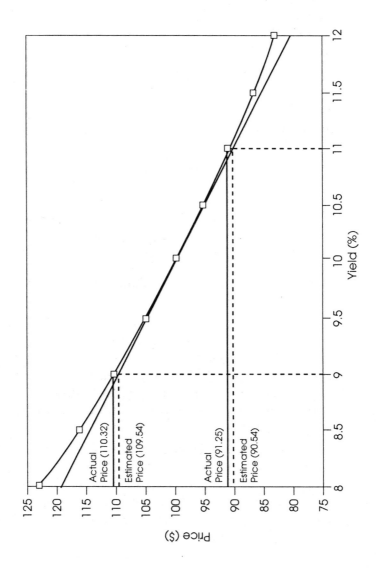

changes. In fact, the curve becomes *flatter* (the dollar duration becomes smaller) at higher yield levels, and becomes *steeper* (the dollar duration becomes larger) at lower yield levels. Therefore, as the market declines, each successive basis-point increase in yield produces a smaller drop in the price of the bond. The cumulative effect of a slow but steady decrease in dollar duration is that the estimated price change, which does not reflect this decrease, overestimates the actual price decrease. Similarly, in a market rally, as the yield decreases, each successive basis-point rally produces a larger gain in price. Therefore, the actual gain is larger than the estimated gain, because the estimate does not incorporate the changing slope of the tangent line, i.e., changing dollar duration.

This property is called *convexity*. As shown later, use of convexity along with duration gives a more accurate indication of how an investment will behave when interest rates change. Convexity can be represented numerically as follows:

> *If a bond is viewed as a series of cash flows, then the convexity of the bond is the sum of the weighted average of the squares of the lengths of time prior to the cash flows and one-half the weighted average of the lengths of time prior to cash flows, the weights being the present values of the corresponding payments.*

The calculation of convexity for a 5-year, 10 percent bond priced at par is shown in Exhibit 3-3.

Note that convexity is given by the sum of the fifth and sixth columns in Exhibit 3-3, divided by the price. A good approximation to convexity can be obtained by omitting the fifth column (as it is small) and simply dividing the sixth column by the price. This simplifies the definition and calculation of convexity.

> *Convexity is approximately equal to the weighted average of the squares of the lengths of time prior to the cash flows, the weights being the present values of the corresponding payments.*

The convexity obtained using this approximation will be slightly lower than the actual convexity. In Exhibit 3-3, the bond's convexity is 18.644281, about 9.8 percent less than the actual value

Exhibit 3-3. Calculation of Convexity for a 5-Year,
10% Par Bond

Semiannual period	Time	Cash flow	Present value of cash flow	Present value × 1/2 × time	Present value × (time)²
1	0.5	5	4.7619	1.1905	1.1905
2	1.0	5	4.5351	2.2676	4.5351
3	1.5	5	4.3192	3.2394	9.7182
4	2.0	5	4.1135	4.1135	16.4541
5	2.5	5	3.9176	4.8971	24.4852
6	3.0	5	3.7311	5.5966	33.5797
7	3.5	5	3.5534	6.2185	43.5292
8	4.0	5	3.3842	6.7684	54.1471
9	4.5	5	3.2230	7.2519	65.2667
10	5.0	105	64.4609	161.1522	1611.5223
Totals			100.0000	202.6955	1864.4281

Convexity = (202.6955 + 1864.4281)/100 = 20.671236

(20.671236). Convexity is similar to Macaulay duration in that it is
an ordinal measure. *Modified convexity* is a cardinal measure and is
obtained by dividing convexity by the factor $(1 + \text{yield}/200)^2$. The
calculation of modified convexity is shown in Exhibit 3-4. We can
define modified convexity as follows:

> *Modified convexity, which is convexity divided by $(1 + \text{yield}/200)^2$,
> is an indicator of the percentage effect on price caused by the change
> in dollar duration resulting from a small change in yield.*

Exhibit 3-4. Calculation of Modified Convexity

Coupon   = 10%
Maturity   = 5 years
Price   = 100
Convexity = 20.671236

Modified convexity = $20.671236/(1.0 + 10/200)^2$
                    = 20.671236/1.1025
                    = 18.749420

Approximating Convexity

In the previous chapter, a formula for approximating modified duration was given. The corresponding formula to approximate modified convexity is given below:

$$= \frac{P_+ + P_- - 2(P_0)}{(P_0)(\Delta y^2)}$$

where

P_0 = initial price (per $100 of par value)

P_- = price if yield is decreased by x basis points

P_+ = price if yield is increased by x basis points

Δy = x basis points in decimal form

For example, consider a 20-year, 7 percent coupon bond selling at 74.26 to yield 10 percent, which we used in the previous chapter to illustrate how to approximate modified duration. Suppose we evaluate the price changes for a 20-basis-point change up and down. Then,

P_0 = 74.26

P_- = 75.64

P_+ = 72.92

Δy = 0.002

Substituting these values into the formula:

$$\frac{75.64 + 72.92 - 2(74.26)}{(74.26)(0.002)^2} = 134.66$$

The modified convexity is equal to 132.08. The approximated modified convexity (134.66) has proven itself to be a good approximation of convexity (132.08).

Dollar Convexity

We can define dollar-weighted or *dollar convexity* (obtained by multiplying modified convexity by price and dividing by 100) as follows:

> *Dollar convexity of a fixed-income security measures the rate of change in dollar duration of the security to changes in yield levels.*

An investor is generally more concerned with the effect of a parameter on a security's value. Because dollar duration is a measure of the actual dollar change in price due to a change in yield, we can also state:

> *Dollar convexity is an indicator of the actual dollar effect on price for a small change in yield of the change in dollar duration resulting from the change in yield.*

Estimating Price Change with Duration and Convexity

We saw that duration can be used to estimate price changes resulting from yield changes:[1]

Price change $\approx$ –Duration $\times$ Yield change

In the role of an estimator, duration treats the price-yield function as though it were along the tangent to the actual price-yield curve. Because of this, duration is sometimes said to provide a *linear* or *first-order* approximation to the price change, and dollar duration is said to be the first derivative of the price-yield function. Since the price-yield relationship is not linear, we can get a better approx-

---

[1] For the equations in this paragraph, the words "duration" and "convexity" can refer to *modified* duration and convexity, in which case the price change is in percentage terms, or *dollar* duration and convexity, in which case the price change is in dollar terms.

imation by using higher-order derivatives. Intuitively, the use of higher-order derivatives simply means that we are actually approximating the curve by higher-order polynomial functions. Convexity represents the second derivative of the price-yield function.

Thus, by including convexity in our estimation process, we obtain a better, second-order approximation:

$$\text{Price change} \approx -\text{Duration} \times \text{Yield change}$$

$$+ \frac{1}{2} \times \text{Convexity} \times \text{Yield change} \times \text{Yield change}$$

The mathematical methods used to obtain these two approximations are detailed in the appendix to this book.

Exhibit 3-5 shows the price-yield curve for a 30-year, 10 percent coupon bond along with the linear or duration estimate and the convexity estimate. It is clear that including convexity improves the estimate significantly. It is interesting to observe that the second-order approximation still underestimates the price gain in a rallying market, but unlike the first-order approximation, it underestimates the price loss in a declining market. The result is that the price estimate is smaller than the actual price if yields decline and greater than the actual price if yields rise.

Higher-Order Components

Convexity is often used interchangeably to represent two close but different concepts. In some cases, it is used to describe the entire curvature, i.e., the complete nonlinearity, of the price-yield function. In other cases, it is used to describe only the *second-order* component of this curvature.

The second-order component accounts for a large portion of the curvature, as shown by Exhibit 3-5. Except for long-term low-coupon bonds, the first- and second-order derivatives explain a large portion of the price change for a wide range of yield changes.

While it is possible to extend the process of estimating price by using terms higher than the second order, little explanatory power is added. Therefore, we will ignore higher-order terms.

Exhibit 3-5. Price-Yield Curve for a 30-Year, 10% Bond with Duration and Convexity Estimates

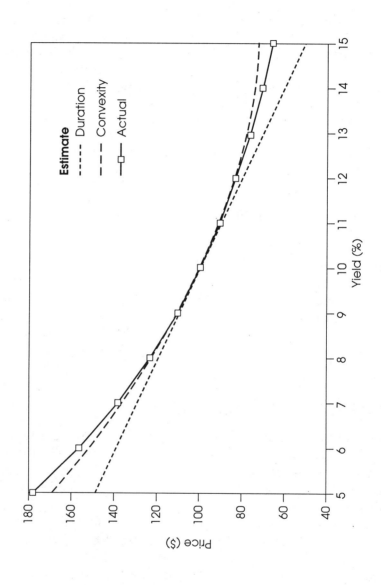

Additional Comments on Convexity

Sometimes convexity is incorrectly interpreted as the effect of changes in Macaulay duration on price. Consider for example a zero-coupon bond for which the duration is constant (equal to its maturity) at all yield levels. The incorrect definition would imply that a zero-coupon bond has zero convexity, as its duration does not change. In fact, zero-coupon bonds are highly convex, since convexity represents the effect of changes in dollar duration, and the dollar duration of a zero-coupon bond changes rapidly as market yields change.

Mathematically, convexity can be thought of as a measure of *spread* or *distribution* of cash flows given a constant duration. In other words, *for a given duration*, the more spread out the cash flows, the greater the convexity. Thus, among equal-duration bonds, the zero-coupon bond has the lowest convexity, since its cash flow is concentrated at maturity.[2] Intuitively, a barbell would have a higher convexity than a bullet bond of equal duration since its cash flows are more spread out.

A few observations can be made from the relationship between price change and duration and convexity. Let us assume for the moment that both dollar duration and dollar convexity are positive, which is true for all option-free bonds. Then, since dollar duration occurs in the equation with a negative sign, it means that if the yield change is positive, i.e., if the yield increases, the price change is negative, i.e., the price decreases, and vice versa. Thus, the effect of dollar duration can be positive or negative depending on whether the yield change is negative or positive, respectively. On the other hand, dollar convexity is multiplied by the square of the yield change. Therefore, the convexity effect for an option-free bond is *always positive*, independent of whether the yield change is positive or negative.

Another observation is that since dollar convexity is multiplied by the square of the yield change, for small yield changes this product becomes very small and can be ignored.[3] That is, for small yield

---

[2] However, the zero-coupon bond has the highest convexity among all bonds of a given *maturity*.

[3] This follows from the fact that the square of a number close to zero is much smaller than the number itself.

changes, the duration estimate is a very good approximation. If the yield changes are very large, then convexity and derivatives of order higher than two will become significant and will improve the approximation.

One key assumption in both duration and convexity analysis is that the yield levels of the different securities under consideration will change by equal amounts. The actual returns obtained can be very different from those indicated by the analysis if the yields change differentially for different bonds. However, higher-convexity bonds do provide some level of protection from adverse yield movements. Exhibit 3-6 illustrates this point further. Here Portfolio A and Portfolio B are compared. They both have a duration equal to 19.05, and at a yield level of 10 percent, both portfolios have a value of $100. Portfolio A has a convexity of 371.88, and B has a convexity of 551.22. If the yield on A rises by 367 basis points, its value drops to $50. On the other hand, Portfolio B can withstand a more extreme rise in rates. Its value drops to $50 for an increase in yield of 493 basis points. A similar effect holds when rates decline. A smaller rally in yield can produce as large a gain in B as a larger rally produces in A.

We can think of duration and convexity along with yield, maturity, and coupon as properties or *parameters* of a bond or a portfolio. Therefore, the analysis that uses these concepts has popularly been called *parametric analysis* of fixed-income securities. There are other parameters, such as the effect of changes in market volatility and the effect of the passage of time; however, a discussion of these parameters is beyond the scope of this chapter.

APPLICATIONS OF CONVEXITY

We have demonstrated that duration is only an approximate estimator of price changes. Two bonds (or portfolios) with equal duration do not necessarily have the same price behavior for large changes in yield. Bonds with higher convexities behave better in the sense that (1) for similar decreases in yield, they gain more than bonds with lower convexities, and (2) for similar increases in yield, they lose less.

Exhibit 3-6. Convexity as a Buffer for Adverse Yield Movements

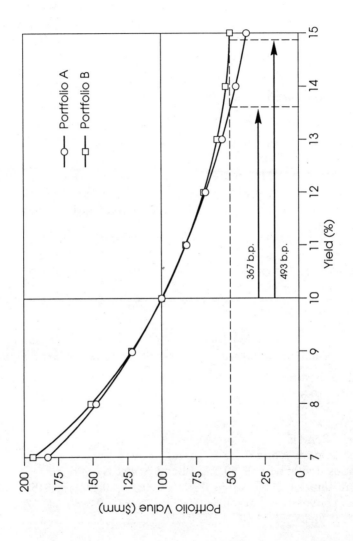

Therefore, if all other things are equal, we should expect bonds of higher convexity to cost more than bonds of relatively lower convexity. Parametric analysis, as opposed to simple duration analysis, acknowledges that any yield pickup achieved in a duration-matched swap might be accompanied by a convexity give-up.

Barbell-Bullet Analysis

Exhibit 3-7 looks at the same barbell-bullet swap that we analyzed in Exhibit 2-10 of Chapter 2. As we saw in Chapter 2, the barbell has a lower yield than the equal-duration bullet. However, the convexity of the barbell is greater than that of the bullet, indicating that the barbell might provide better returns than the bullet under certain market moves. Therefore, the yield spread is in a way the *payment for convexity*.

Exhibit 3-7. Barbell-Bullet Analysis Based on Duration, Convexity, and Average Yield

Three bonds used in analysis:

Bond	Coupon	Maturity (years)	Price plus accrued	Yield	Dollar duration	Dollar convexity
A	8.50	5	100	8.50%	4.00544	19.8164
B	9.50	20	100	9.50%	8.88151	124.1702
C	9.25	10	100	9.25%	6.43409	55.4506

Bullet: Bond C
Barbell: Bonds A and B
Composition of barbell: 50.2% of Bond A; 49.8% of Bond B
Dollar duration of barbell = $0.502 \times 4.00544 + 0.498 \times 8.88151 = 6.434$
Dollar convexity of barbell = $0.502 \times 19.8164 + 0.498 \times 124.1702 = 71.7846$
Average yield of barbell = $502 \times 8.50 + 0.498 \times 9.5 = 8.998$

Strategy: Sell the barbell and buy the bullet
Yield pickup = Yield on bullet – Average yield of barbell
$\qquad$ = $9.25 - 8.998 = 0.252$, or 25.2 basis points

Convexity give-up = Convexity of barbell – Convexity of bullet
$\qquad$ = $71.7846 - 55.4506 = 16.334$

Exhibit 3-7 shows that the same transaction that looked attractive under the duration/yield framework now does not necessarily retain its attractiveness under the parametric framework. The yield pickup was not, after all, free. So far, everything seems to fall into place neatly. Again, all this is reasonable only if we accept the parametric framework. There is more.

Chapter 4

The Other Side of the Equation: Total Return

In the previous chapter, we examined the limitations of duration in representing risk, and we modified it by including convexity. In this chapter, we will focus on the other side of the risk-reward equation—*yield*.

TROUBLE IN PARADISE: YIELD VERSUS AVERAGE YIELD

The measure of reward used thus far in this book, yield or average yield, does not recognize the possibility that the more convex barbell in our last illustration in the previous chapter might perform better under certain conditions. Average yield, used here as an indication of returns from a portfolio of bonds, has a serious theoretical problem as well.

Yield to maturity as generally defined and used in the industry is an *internal rate of return*. That is, it represents a single discounting rate that equates the present value of all cash flows from a bond to its market value. It is a very valuable tool in summarizing the effects of different prices and coupons. However, yield or an internal rate of return is not additive and therefore cannot be averaged. Average yield

---

[1] Unfortunately, average yield is still used, incorrectly, by many practitioners as an equivalent of internal rate of return and is used interchangeably with yield.

is not an internal rate of return and has no useful and correct interpretation.[1]

A proper measure that can be used in this context is the *cash-
flow yield* of a portfolio, which is the discount rate that equates the
sum of the present values of all cash flows from all bonds in the
portfolio to the total market value of the portfolio. Thus, cash-flow
yield is the internal rate of return for the portfolio.

The Barbell-Bullet Analysis Reconsidered

Intuitively, using the barbell example we presented in Chapters 2
and 3, it seems as though the yield on the longer bond must be
weighted by some measure of time since it is earned for a longer
period of time. If we compute the *dollar-duration-weighted yield* of the
portfolio, we get an excellent approximation to the actual cash-flow
yield. That is, instead of weighting by just market value, we weight
by the product of the duration and market value. The duration of
the longer bond in the barbell increases the weight for the yield on
the long bond by just the right amount.

Exhibit 4-1 shows the barbell-bullet swap—but now computing
the dollar-duration-weighted yield (as a proxy for the cash-flow
yield) instead of the average yield. Notice that the yield on the bullet is *greater* than that on the barbell by only 6.3 basis points.

There is a greater surprise in store for us. We intuitively argued
in the previous chapter that the more convex portfolio should cost
more (yield less) than the less convex portfolio. But it is not uncommon to observe in the market situations where a barbell has *both higher
cash-flow yield and greater convexity*. For example, on October 30, 1987,
the yield, dollar duration, and dollar convexity for three actual Treasury issues were as follows (taking into account accrued interest):

Issue	*Yield*	*Dollar duration*	*Dollar convexity*
7.875s of 10/31/89	7.583	1.822	4.284
9.500s of 10/15/94	8.653	5.284	34.088
9.125s of 9/30/91	8.193	3.328	13.446

Exhibit 4-1. Barbell-Bullet Analysis Based on Duration, Convexity, and Dollar-Duration-Weighted Yield

Three bonds used in analysis:

Bond	Coupon	Maturity (years)	Price plus accrued	Yield	Dollar duration	Dollar convexity
A	8.50	5	100	8.50%	4.00544	19.8164
B	9.50	20	100	9.50%	8.88151	124.1702
C	9.25	10	100	9.25%	6.43409	55.4506

Bullet: Bond C
Barbell: Bonds A and B
Composition of barbell: 50.2% of Bond A; 49.8% of Bond B
Dollar duration of barbell $= 0.502 \times 4.00544 + 0.498 \times 8.88151 = 6.434$
Dollar convexity of barbell $= 0.502 \times 19.8164 + 0.498 \times 124.1702 = 71.7846$
Cash-flow yield of barbell* $=$

$$\frac{(8.5 \times 0.502 \times 4.00544) + (9.5 \times 0.498 \times 8.88151)}{6.434} = 9.187$$

Strategy: Sell the barbell and buy the bullet
Yield pickup $=$ Yield on bullet $-$ Dollar-duration weighted yield
$\qquad\qquad = 9.25 - 9.187 = 0.063$ or 6.3 basis points

Convexity giveup $=$ Convexity of barbell $-$ Convexity of bullet
$\qquad\qquad = 71.7846 - 55.4506 = 16.334$

---

* The calculation shown is actually a dollar-duration-weighted yield, a very close approximation to cash-flow yield.

Consider a barbell consisting of 56.5 percent of the first Treasury issue and 43.5 percent of the second Treasury issue. The dollar duration for the barbell is 3.328, which is equal to the dollar duration of the third Treasury issue (the bullet). The cash-flow yield for the barbell is 8.322, which is 12.9 basis points greater than the yield on the bullet (8.193). The dollar convexity of the barbell is 17.248, which is greater than that for the bullet (13.446). Thus, there is *both* a yield *and* convexity pickup!

The explanation that the lower yield of the barbell is due to higher convexity, which looked so simple and even seemed obvious, has disappeared in this situation. This discrepancy can be attributed to the fact that yields or internal rates of return computed over different time periods are not directly comparable. Thus, we cannot conclude that the barbell is a better investment simply because its yield is greater than that of the bullet, notwithstanding the fact that the durations of the two positions are equal and the convexity of the barbell is actually higher. The implication is that it is naive and often incorrect to talk about *cost of convexity* when it is stated in terms of yield differences. Even though convexity is still a desirable property, we must take into account the movement of interest rates in order to address any trade-off that might be involved.

Thus both the duration and the parametric frameworks have proved to be blatantly inadequate for certain uses in portfolio management; they fail to assess correctly relative value. Given their inability to analyze correctly even the simple securities considered here—straight Treasury bonds—it is obvious that their use is even more inappropriate in evaluating more complex securities, such as bonds with call features. A robust, and, most of all, consistent framework is needed; we must re-examine our initial notion of duration as a measure of risk and yield as a measure of reward.

THE TOTAL RETURN CONCEPT

The total return concept can solve most of the problems encountered in the duration and parametric frameworks. In *total return analysis,* total returns are computed to a fixed date, known as the *horizon date,* for all bonds under consideration. Therefore, the total returns, which we also refer to as *horizon returns,* become comparable, unlike yields that are computed to the respective maturities of each of the bonds.

Determining total return involves estimating what will happen to a given investment in a specified security. The result can be stated in dollars or normalized and annualized and expressed as a rate of return.

Total return consists of two components:

Future value of intermediate cash flows. Any cash flows received between the settlement date and the horizon date must be reinvested and brought forward to the horizon date. The sum of the cash flows plus any reinvestment income is known as the *future value* of a cash flow.

Value of the bond at the horizon date. Total return also depends on the price of the bond on the horizon date. This can be viewed as the present value of all cash flows that are scheduled to occur *after* the horizon date.

Therefore, to determine total return we need information about the state of the market in the future. Enough assumptions must be made in order to compute these two components.

Exhibit 4-2 illustrates how the total return for a 7-year bond can be computed assuming a reinvestment rate of 5 percent. Column 2 shows the cash flow in each of the 14 periods. Column 4 shows the future value of each of the cash flows, which is computed by using the following equation:[2]

$$\text{Future value} = \text{Cash flow} \times (1 + \text{Reinvestment rate}/200)^{\text{no. of periods}}$$

In Exhibit 4-2, the total future value is 74.335, which when added to the value of the bond at the horizon date of 100 gives 174.335. On a semiannual basis, the total return is 4.05 percent. On a bond-equivalent basis it is 8.10 percent and on an effective annual yield basis 8.26 percent. The yield to maturity for this bond is 9 percent.

The case where the maturity of the bond is longer than the horizon is similarly handled. For example, if the bond in Exhibit 4-2 is

---

[2] When the interim cash flows are just fixed-rate coupon payments, the future value of all the coupon payments can be calculated by using the following formula:

$$\text{Coupon interest} \times \left[\frac{(1 + \text{Reinvestment rate}/200)^{\text{no. of periods}} - 1}{\text{Reinvestment rate}/200} \right]$$

For our example in Exhibit 4-2:

coupon interest = $4.5
reinvestment rate = 5%
number of periods = 14

$$\$4.5 \left[\frac{(1 + 5/200)^{14} - 1}{5/20} \right] = \$74.335$$

a 10-year bond instead of a 7-year bond and the projected price of the bond at the horizon date is 95 instead of 100, then the total future value is 169.335, and the total return on a bond-equivalent basis is 7.67 percent compared to a yield to maturity of 9 percent.

Exhibit 4-2. Total Return Calculation When the Horizon Date Is the Same as the Maturity Date

Bond:

Years to maturity: 7 (or 14 periods)
Coupon rate: 9%
Current price: 100
Yield to maturity: 9%

Assumptions:

Horizon (in years): 7
Reinvestment rate: 5%

Calculation:

1. *Future value of intermediate cash flows*
   • coupon interest of $4.50 per $100 par every six months for seven years
   • interest earned from reinvesting the semiannual coupon interest payments at 5% (reinvestment rate)

Calculation of future value of intermediate cash flows:

Period	Coupon	Principal	Future value
1	4.5	0	6.203
2	4.5	0	6.052
3	4.5	0	5.904
4	4.5	0	5.760
5	4.5	0	5.620
6	4.5	0	5.483
7	4.5	0	5.349
8	4.5	0	5.219
9	4.5	0	5.091
10	4.5	0	4.967
11	4.5	0	4.846
12	4.5	0	4.728
13	4.5	0	4.613
14	4.5	100	104.500
		Total	174.335

Exhibit 4-2 (Continued).

2. *Bond's price at the horizon date*

bond's price = maturity value = $100

Total dollars at the horizon date: $74.335 + $100 = $174.335

Total return on a semiannual basis

$$\left(\frac{\$174.335}{\$100}\right)^{1/14} - 1 = 0.0405, \text{ or } 4.05\%$$

Total return on an annual bond-equivalent basis

2 × 4.05% = 8.10%

Total return on an effective annual yield basis

$(1.0405)^2 - 1 = 0.0826 = 8.26\%$

Since interest rates can take a large number of different values, it is usual to compute the total return under different sets of assumptions, called *scenarios,* rather than provide just one number that is similar to the yield.

SCENARIO ANALYSIS

Care must be taken in creating scenarios so that the results obtained do not simply mirror the assumptions made, but rather illuminate the true relative values of the securities under consideration. In other

---

[3] The decision as to the degree of simplification used in the analysis depends on two factors. First, one must consider how major a role the assumptions play in the determination of the results. If the results are largely insensitive to the specific assumptions made, there is a greater degree of freedom to simplify. Second, one must consider how much precision is required and how the result of the analysis will be used. Clearly, greater precision is required if an actual transaction is contemplated. However, if the goal of the analysis is simply to gain insight into the general behavior of securities, then a simpler analysis might be justified.

words, erroneous assumptions in creating scenarios will produce erroneous results. We will elaborate on the various factors that need to be considered in making these assumptions in the next chapter. However, even simple[3] scenario analysis can provide some insight into the way total return and, therefore, the value of a security changes with market conditions.

As stated above, total return has two components: reinvestment income and price of the bond at the horizon date. The reinvestment income portion of total return increases as the reinvestment rate increases. This effect is greater for high-coupon bonds, since their sizable cash flows, which are reinvested at the increasingly higher reinvestment rates, cause the bond's return to move upward at a faster rate than in the case of current-coupon bonds. For low-coupon discount bonds a substantial portion of a security's return is locked into the price at the horizon date. In this case, the reinvestment component still increases as rates increase, but does so more slowly. However, a zero-coupon bond whose maturity is equal to or longer than the horizon is immune to the effects of reinvestment rates because it does not make any coupon payments and so there is nothing to reinvest.

In Exhibit 4-3, four bonds are compared, each of 5-year maturity, but with coupons of zero, 5 percent, 10 percent and 15 percent. A horizon period of five years is assumed so that the price of the bond at the horizon date is invariant (equal to face value paid at maturity) and the differences in the reinvestment component are magnified in total return. The initial prices are chosen such that all bonds yield 10 percent to maturity. Exhibit 4-3 illustrates that total returns rise as the reinvestment rate increases and that the increase is more dramatic for higher-coupon securities. The zero-coupon bond has a perfectly horizontal line, showing its immunity to reinvestment rates.

Total return also depends on the time to horizon. In Exhibit 4-4, the total return for a 10-year, 10 percent coupon bond priced at par is examined. The reinvestment rate is varied from zero to 20 percent, and the total return is plotted for 1-year, 5-year, and 10-year horizons. The price of the bond at the horizon date is held constant at the initial price of par; that is, the horizon yield is set equal to the initial

Exhibit 4-3. Total Returns for 5-Year Bonds with Various Coupons

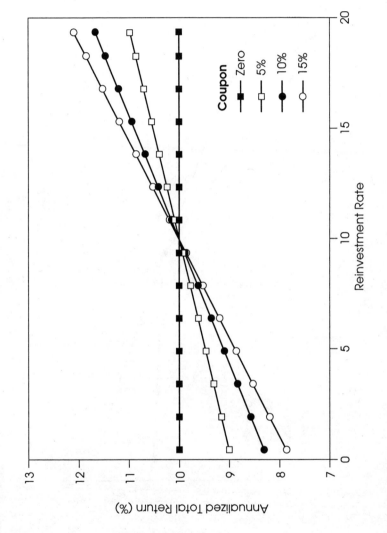

Note: All bonds initially priced to yield 10 percent to maturity.

Exhibit 4-4. Total Returns for a 10-Year, 10% Par Bond at Various Horizons

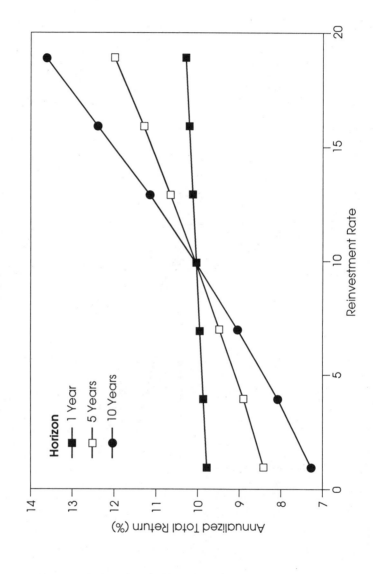

yield of 10 percent. The exhibit illustrates that the reinvestment rate has a greater impact on total return at longer horizons.

The assumptions made in determining a bond's price at the horizon date can significantly influence total returns. An interesting phenomenon occurs if we use, for each scenario, a single interest rate to determine both the horizon yield for the bond and the reinvestment rate, instead of setting the horizon yield to the initial yield of the bond. Exhibit 4-5 shows the total return for the same 10-year, 10 percent-coupon bond with this new assumption for the bond's price at the horizon date. The horizons used are 5, 6.5, and 9 years. For shorter horizons, the bond's price at the horizon date plays a greater role in determining total return, and the impact of reinvestment is small. Therefore, the returns are greater at lower interest-rate levels.[4] For longer horizons, the reinvestment component is a major part of total return and dominates the impact of the bond's price at the horizon date. Therefore, for longer horizons, total return increases with the level of interest rates.

For some particular horizon, approximately 6.5 years for the bond in Exhibit 4-5, the total return is almost constant, independent of the interest rate. This horizon turns out to be equal to the duration of the bond. Thus, duration is the point at which the negative effect of a higher interest rate on the bond's price is exactly balanced by its positive effect on reinvestment returns. Intuitively, if duration is longer, the resultant larger price change requires a longer time for the reinvestment effect to balance it. This also illuminates why duration becomes smaller at higher yield or coupon levels. As coupon or yield levels increase, the time required for the reinvestment effect to catch up with a given price change decreases.

The technique of equating duration to horizon to obtain more stable returns is called *immunization*. For horizons longer than the duration, total return increases with interest rates; for shorter horizons, the return decreases with increases in interest rates.

---

[4] For artificially large interest rates, the reinvestment component can dominate. Under these conditions, total return can increase even for short horizons with further rises in rates.

Exhibit 4-5. Total Returns for a 10-Year, 10% Par Bond at Various Horizons

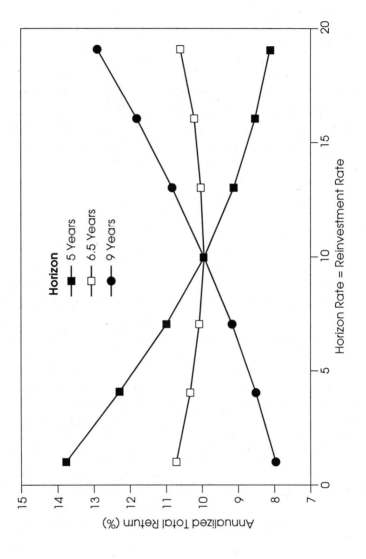

In summary, the behavior of total return depends on the horizon chosen. This dependence arises from the interplay of reinvestment income and capital gains or losses as they react to interest-rate changes. As time passes, the impact of reinvestment income on return intensifies, while the impact of capital gains or losses on return diminishes.

Thus, for short horizons (relative to the duration), the net change in market rates during the holding period generally determines the bond's performance. For long horizons, the average level of interest rates during the holding period is more important. Finally, for intermediate horizons when the holding period is close to the duration of the bond, the two effects neutralize each other. Therefore, the starting yield is more important than either the size or direction of rate changes. This is immunization.

The concept of immunization is based on the assumption that the average level of reinvestment rates and the horizon yield are equal. If we relax this assumption, then the total return will no longer be a constant but will depend on both the level of reinvestment rates and the horizon yield.

APPLICATIONS

Break-Even Reinvestment Analysis

In order to illustrate how the concepts introduced in this chapter can be used in portfolio management, we present a simple comparative analysis. We define:

> *The break-even reinvestment rate between two bonds is the reinvestment rate at which the total returns for two bonds over a given horizon are equal.*

Depending on the maturities, coupons and prices of the two bonds, the total return of one of the bonds is expected to be greater than that of the other if the reinvestment rate is below the break-even rate, and smaller if it is above the break-even rate. Therefore, depending on interest-rate expectations, it is possible to conclude whether one bond is relatively more attractive than another. Confi-

Exhibit 4-6. Break-Even Reinvestment Rate Analysis between Two 5-Year Bonds

	Bond 1	Bond 2
Coupon:	15.000	5.000
Maturity:	5 years	5 years
Price:	120	80
Yield:	9.84	10.21

Total returns:

Reinvestment rate:	8	9	10	11	12	13	14	15	16
Bond 1:	9.41	9.64	9.88	10.12	10.36	10.61	10.86	11.12	11.37
Bond 2:	9.95	10.07	10.18	10.30	10.42	10.55	10.67	10.80	10.93

Break-even rate: 12.49

Note: The horizon is 5 years, the same as the maturity of the bonds.

dence in such a conclusion is especially high if the break-even rate is extreme, i.e., much higher or much lower than current or expected interest rates. Sometimes the break-even rate is within the expected interest-rate band, in which case the analysis may be inconclusive as to the determination of the more attractive bond.

Exhibit 4-6 compares Bond 1, a 5-year, 15 percent bond priced at 120, and Bond 2, a 5-year, 5 percent bond priced at 80, for a horizon of 5 years (the same as the maturity of the bonds). Bond 2 has a greater total return if an 8 percent reinvestment rate is assumed. On the other hand, if a 16 percent reinvestment rate is assumed, Bond 1 would have a higher total return. Both bonds have higher returns as reinvestment-rate assumptions climb, yet they do not increase at the same rate.

Exhibit 4-7 shows a graph of this relationship, which is a sloping curve for each bond with the curve for Bond 1 being steeper. It also illustrates the point at which the two curves intersect. This point is called the *break-even point,* and the corresponding reinvestment

Exhibit 4-7. Break-Even Reinvestment Rate Analysis between Two 5-Year Bonds

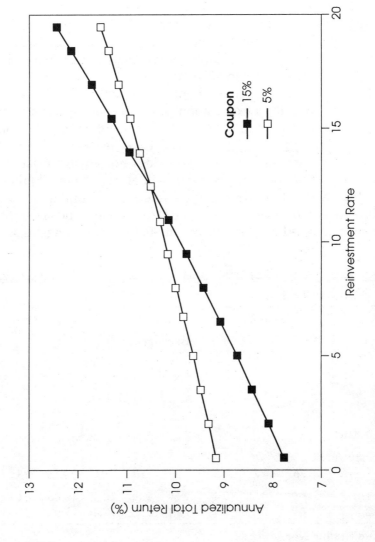

Note: The 15% bond is priced at 120, and the 5% bond is priced at 80.

rate is the *break-even reinvestment rate*. If the expected cash flows from the bonds are reinvested at this rate, both bonds would generate the same total return.

By examining the location of the break-even reinvestment rate between two bonds, one can determine the more attractive bond. If an investor's expectation of future rates is higher than the break-even reinvestment rate, then the 15 percent bond will achieve a greater total return than the 5 percent bond, as shown in Exhibit 4-7. Conversely, if an investor's expectation of future rates is lower than the break-even reinvestment rate, then the 5 percent bond will achieve a greater total return.

A break-even reinvestment rate does not always exist for any two bonds. It may be that one bond will always have a higher total return than another bond for any assumed reinvestment rate. Exhibit 4-8 shows a comparison between the same 5-year bonds as in Exhibit 4-6; however, Bond 2 is now priced at 90. Over any range of selected

Exhibit 4-8. Break-Even Reinvestment Rate Analysis between Two 5-Year Bonds

	Bond 1	*Bond 2*
Calendar:	Treasury	Treasury
Coupon:	15.000	5.000
Maturity:	5 years	5 years
Price:	120	90
Yield:	9.84	7.43

Total returns:

Reinvestment rate:	6	7	8	9	10	11	12	13	14
Bond 1:	8.96	9.18	9.41	9.64	9.88	10.12	10.36	10.61	10.86
Bond 2:	7.28	7.38	7.49	7.61	7.72	7.84	7.96	8.08	8.21

Break-even rate: None

Note: The horizon is five years, the same as the maturity of the bonds.

reinvestment rates, Bond 1 will always generate higher total returns than Bond 2, and therefore no break-even point exists between them. At these prices, Bond 1 is inherently cheaper.

Barbell-Bullet Analysis

Here, we examine how total return analysis can be applied to the barbell-bullet analysis. In previous barbell-bullet analyses, our measure of potential return was yield to maturity for the bullet and average or dollar-duration-weighted yield for the barbell. Exhibit 4-9 shows the performance of the three bonds we used in our previous barbell-bullet illustrations over a six-month horizon, assuming a parallel shift in the yield curve (i.e., the yield for all maturities changes by an equal number of basis points). The first column of the exhibit shows the change in yield, followed by the price of each bond at the corresponding new yield. The fifth and sixth columns show the total dollars at the end of six months (which in our example represents the price plus coupon interest) for the barbell and bullet, respectively. Since the strategy that we first presented in Chapter 2 is to sell the barbell and buy the bullet, the seventh column shows the difference in the total dollars at the end of six months. The last three columns provide the same information based on total return rather than total dollars.

Our total return analysis suggests that if yields change by more than 100 basis points, the barbell will outperform the bullet. This would generate a loss if we pursued a strategy of buying the bullet and selling the barbell. In contrast, a gain would be produced if yields change by 100 basis points or less. The better performance of the barbell for large changes in yield is due to its better convexity.

While we have restricted our analysis thus far to a parallel shift in the yield curve, Exhibits 4-10 and 4-11 show the same information as Exhibit 4-9 for nonparallel shifts. In Exhibit 4-10, we assumed that if the yield on Bond C (the intermediate-term bond) changes, Bond A (the short-term bond) will increase by 25 basis points while Bond B (the long-term bond) will decrease by 25 basis points. Under this scenario, the barbell will always outperform the bullet. In Exhibit 4-11, the nonparallel shift assumes that for a change in Bond C's yield, the yield on Bond A will decrease by 25 basis points while that on Bond B will increase by 25 basis points. In this case, the bullet would

Exhibit 4-9. Barbell-Bullet Analysis Based on Total Return Analysis: Parallel Shift in Yield Curve Assumed

Yield change	Price of Bond			Dollar Value of			Total Return		
	A	B	C	Barbell	Bullet	Difference	Barbell	Bullet	Difference
-5.000	124.90124	169.20719	143.37301	146.96915	143.37301	-3.59613	93.94	86.75	-7.19
-4.750	123.75147	164.71523	141.01688	144.15470	141.01688	-3.13782	88.31	82.03	-6.28
-4.500	122.61503	160.39327	138.71132	141.43162	138.71132	-2.72030	82.86	77.42	-5.44
-4.250	121.49174	156.23402	136.45514	138.79617	136.45514	-2.34103	77.59	72.91	-4.68
-4.000	120.38141	152.23050	134.24717	136.24480	134.24717	-1.99764	72.49	68.49	-4.00
-3.750	119.28389	148.37606	132.08625	133.74412	132.08625	-1.68787	67.55	64.17	-3.38
-3.500	118.19901	144.66438	129.97128	131.38088	129.97128	-1.40960	62.76	59.94	-2.82
-3.250	117.12661	141.08938	127.90117	129.06199	127.90117	-1.16081	58.12	55.80	-2.32
-3.000	116.06652	137.64531	125.87487	126.81448	125.87487	-0.93962	53.63	51.75	-1.88
-2.750	115.01858	134.32665	123.89133	124.63554	123.89133	-0.74421	49.27	47.78	-1.49
-2.500	113.98264	131.12812	121.94956	122.52246	121.94956	-0.57291	45.04	43.90	-1.15
-2.250	112.95854	128.04473	120.04857	120.47267	120.04857	-0.42410	40.95	40.10	-0.85
-2.000	111.94612	125.07160	118.18741	118.48369	118.18741	-0.29628	36.97	36.37	-0.59
-1.750	110.94525	122.20432	116.36515	116.55317	116.36515	-0.18802	33.11	32.73	-0.38
-1.500	109.95576	119.43836	114.58088	114.67886	114.58088	-0.09798	29.36	29.16	-0.20
-1.250	108.97752	116.76960	112.83371	112.85860	112.83371	-0.02489	25.72	25.67	-0.05
-1.000	108.01038	114.19403	111.12279	111.09033	111.12279	0.03245	22.18	22.25	0.06
-0.750	107.05420	111.70785	109.44727	109.37209	109.44727	0.07518	18.74	18.89	0.15
-0.500	106.10883	109.30741	107.80632	107.70198	107.80632	0.10434	15.40	15.61	0.21
-0.250	105.17415	106.98924	106.19916	106.07821	106.19916	0.12095	12.16	12.40	0.24

Yield change	Price of Bond			Dollar Value of			Total Return		
	A	B	C	Barbell	Bullet	Difference	Barbell	Bullet	Difference
0.000	104.25000	104.75000	104.62500	104.49904	104.62500	0.12596	9.00	9.25	0.25
0.250	103.33626	102.58651	103.08308	102.96283	103.08308	0.12025	5.93	6.17	0.24
0.500	102.43280	100.49574	101.57265	101.46799	101.57265	0.10466	2.94	3.15	0.21
0.750	101.53949	98.47477	100.09300	100.01301	100.09300	0.07999	0.03	0.19	0.16
1.000	100.65619	96.52083	98.64342	98.59645	98.64342	0.04698	-2.81	-2.71	0.09
1.250	99.78278	94.63125	97.22323	97.21691	97.22323	0.00632	-5.57	-5.55	0.01
1.500	98.91913	92.80350	95.83174	95.87306	95.83174	-0.04132	-8.25	-8.34	-0.08
1.750	98.06513	91.03515	94.46830	94.56364	94.46830	-0.09533	-10.87	-11.06	-0.19
2.000	97.22065	89.32385	93.13229	93.28741	93.13229	-0.15512	-13.43	-13.74	-0.31
2.250	96.38556	87.66740	91.83207	92.04322	91.82307	-0.22015	-15.91	-16.35	-0.44
2.500	95.55976	86.06366	90.54003	90.82994	90.54003	-0.28991	-18.34	-18.92	-0.58
2.750	94.74312	84.51058	89.28259	89.64650	89.28259	-0.36391	-20.71	-21.43	-0.73
3.000	93.93553	83.00623	88.05017	88.49186	88.05017	-0.44169	-23.02	-23.90	-0.88
3.250	93.13687	81.54872	86.84219	87.36504	86.84219	-0.52285	-25.27	-26.32	-1.05
3.500	92.34704	80.13627	85.65612	86.26510	85.65812	-0.60698	-27.47	-28.68	-1.21
3.750	91.56592	78.76718	84.49742	85.19112	84.49742	-0.69370	-29.62	-31.01	-1.39
4.000	90.79341	77.43979	83.35955	84.14224	83.35955	-0.78268	-31.72	-33.28	-1.57
4.250	90.02939	76.15253	82.24402	83.11761	82.24402	-0.87358	-33.76	-35.51	-1.75
4.500	89.27377	74.90391	81.15032	82.11643	81.15032	-0.96611	-35.77	-37.70	-1.93
4.750	88.52643	73.69248	80.07796	81.13793	80.07796	-1.05997	-37.72	-39.84	-2.12
5.000	87.78727	72.51685	79.02647	80.18138	79.02647	-1.15491	-39.64	-41.95	-2.31

Note: Starting value for each bond is 100.

Exhibit 4-10. Barbell-Bullet Analysis Based on Total Return Analysis: Nonparallel Shift in Yield Curve Assumed

Yield change*	Price of Bond			Dollar Value of			Total Return		
	A	B	C	Barbell	Bullet	Difference	Barbell	Bullet	Difference
-5.000	123.75147	173.87681	143.37301	148.71790	143.37301	-5.34489	97.44	86.75	-10.69
-4.750	122.61503	169.20719	141.01688	145.82165	141.01688	-4.80478	91.64	82.03	-9.61
-4.500	121.49174	164.71523	138.71132	143.02049	138.71132	-4.30917	86.04	77.42	-8.62
-4.250	120.38141	160.39327	136.45514	140.31052	136.45514	-3.85538	80.62	72.91	-7.71
-4.000	119.28389	156.23402	134.24717	137.68801	134.24717	-3.44084	75.38	68.49	-6.88
-3.750	118.19901	152.23050	132.08625	135.14942	132.08625	-3.06316	70.30	64.17	-6.13
-3.500	117.12661	148.37606	129.97128	132.69134	129.97128	-2.72005	65.38	59.94	-5.44
-3.250	116.06652	144.66438	127.90117	130.31054	127.90117	-2.40937	60.62	55.80	-4.82
-3.000	115.01858	141.08938	125.87487	128.00393	125.87487	-2.12906	56.01	51.75	-4.26
-2.750	113.98264	137.64531	123.89133	125.76854	123.89133	-1.87721	51.54	47.78	-3.75
-2.500	112.95854	134.32665	121.94956	123.60156	121.94956	-1.65201	47.20	43.90	-3.30
-2.250	111.94612	131.12812	120.04857	121.50029	120.04857	-1.45173	43.00	40.10	-2.90
-2.000	110.94525	128.04473	118.18741	119.46216	118.18741	-1.27475	38.92	36.37	-2.55
-1.750	109.95576	125.07165	116.36515	117.48469	116.36515	-1.11954	34.97	32.73	-2.24
-1.500	108.97752	122.20432	114.58088	115.56553	114.58088	-0.98465	31.13	29.16	-1.97
-1.250	108.01038	119.43836	112.83371	113.70243	112.83371	-0.86872	27.40	25.67	-1.74
-1.000	107.05420	116.76960	111.12279	111.89324	111.12279	-0.77046	23.79	22.25	-1.54
-0.750	106.10883	114.19403	109.44727	110.13591	109.44727	-0.68864	20.27	18.89	-1.38
-0.500	105.17415	111.70785	107.80632	108.42845	107.80632	-0.62213	16.86	15.61	-1.24
-0.250	104.25000	109.30741	106.19916	106.76900	106.19916	-0.56984	13.54	12.40	-1.14

Yield change*	Price of Bond			Dollar Value of			Total Return		
	A	B	C	Barbell	Bullet	Difference	Barbell	Bullet	Difference
0.000	103.33626	106.98924	104.62500	105.15574	104.62500	–0.53074	10.31	9.25	–1.06
0.250	102.43280	104.75000	103.08308	103.58695	103.08308	–0.50387	7.17	6.17	–1.01
0.500	101.53949	102.58651	101.57265	102.06099	101.57265	–0.48834	4.12	3.15	–0.98
0.750	100.65619	100.49574	100.09300	100.57627	100.09300	–0.48327	1.15	0.19	–0.97
1.000	99.78278	98.47477	98.64342	99.13129	98.64342	–0.48786	–1.74	–2.71	–0.98
1.250	98.91913	96.52083	97.22323	97.72459	97.22323	–0.50136	–4.55	–5.55	–1.00
1.500	98.06513	94.63125	95.83174	96.35479	95.83174	–0.52305	–7.29	–8.34	–1.05
1.750	97.22065	92.80350	94.46830	95.02056	94.46830	–0.55225	–9.96	–11.06	–1.10
2.000	96.38556	91.03515	93.13229	93.72063	93.13229	–0.58834	–12.56	–13.75	–1.18
2.250	95.55976	89.32385	91.82307	92.45378	91.82307	–0.63071	–15.09	–16.35	–1.26
2.500	94.74312	87.66740	90.54003	91.21884	90.54003	–0.67881	–17.56	–18.92	–1.36
2.750	93.93553	86.06366	89.28259	90.01470	89.28259	–0.73212	–19.97	–21.43	–1.46
3.000	93.13687	84.51058	88.05017	88.84029	88.05017	–0.79012	–22.32	–23.90	–1.58
3.250	92.34704	83.00623	86.84219	87.69457	86.84219	–0.85237	–24.61	–26.32	–1.70
3.500	91.56592	81.54872	75.65612	86.57655	85.65812	–0.91843	–26.85	–28.68	–1.84
3.750	90.79341	80.13627	84.49742	85.48530	84.49742	–0.98788	–29.03	–31.01	–1.98
4.000	90.02939	78.76718	83.35955	84.41991	83.35955	–1.06035	–31.16	–33.28	–2.12
4.250	89.27377	77.43979	82.24402	83.37950	82.24402	–1.13548	–33.24	–35.51	–2.27
4.500	88.52643	76.15253	81.15032	82.36324	81.15032	–1.21292	–35.27	–37.70	–2.43
4.750	87.78727	74.90391	80.07796	81.37033	80.07796	–1.29237	–37.26	–39.84	–2.58
5.000	87.05620	73.69248	79.02647	80.40000	70.02647	–1.37352	–39.20	–41.95	–2.75

Note: Starting value for each bond is 100.

* Change in yield for Bond C. Nonparallel shift as follows:

yield change bond A = yield change bond C + 25 basis points
yield change bond B = yield change bond C – 25 basis points

Exhibit 4-11. Barbell-Bullet Analysis Based on Total Return Analysis: Nonparallel Shift in Yield Curve Assumed

Yield change*	Price of Bond			Dollar Value of			Total Return		
	A	B	C	Barbell	Bullet	Difference	Barbell	Bullet	Difference
-5.000	126.06449	164.71523	143.37301	145.31565	143.37301	-1.94264	90.63	86.75	-3.89
-4.750	124.90124	160.39327	141.01688	142.57911	141.01688	-1.56223	85.16	82.03	-3.12
-4.500	123.75147	156.23402	138.71132	139.93038	138.71132	-1.21906	79.86	77.42	-2.44
-4.250	122.61503	152.23050	136.45514	137.36590	136.45514	-0.91076	74.73	72.91	-1.82
-4.000	121.49174	148.37606	134.24717	134.88228	134.24717	-0.63511	69.76	68.49	-1.27
-3.750	120.38141	144.66438	132.08625	132.47627	132.08625	-0.39002	64.95	64.17	-0.78
-3.500	119.28389	141.08938	129.97128	130.14477	129.97128	-0.17349	60.29	59.94	-0.35
-3.250	118.19901	134.64531	127.90117	127.88483	127.90117	0.01635	55.77	55.80	0.03
-3.000	117.12661	134.32665	125.87487	125.69360	125.87487	0.18126	51.39	51.75	0.36
-2.750	116.06652	131.12812	123.89133	123.56840	123.89133	0.32293	47.14	47.78	0.65
-2.500	115.01858	128.04473	121.94956	121.50664	121.94956	0.44291	43.01	43.90	0.89
-2.250	113.98264	125.07165	120.04857	119.50585	120.04857	0.54271	39.01	40.10	1.09
-2.000	112.95854	122.20432	118.18741	117.56368	118.18741	0.62373	35.13	36.37	1.25
-1.750	111.94612	119.43836	116.36515	115.67786	116.36515	0.68729	31.36	32.73	1.37
-1.500	110.94525	116.76960	114.58088	113.84624	114.58088	0.73464	27.69	29.16	1.47
-1.250	109.95576	114.19403	112.83371	112.06676	112.83371	0.76695	24.13	25.67	1.53
-1.000	108.97752	111.70785	111.12279	110.33744	111.12279	0.78534	20.67	22.25	1.57
-0.750	108.01038	109.30741	109.44727	108.65641	109.44727	0.79086	17.31	18.89	1.58
-0.500	107.05420	106.98924	107.80632	107.02184	107.80632	0.78448	14.04	15.61	1.57
-0.250	106.10883	104.75000	106.19916	105.43203	106.19916	0.76714	10.86	12.40	1.53

Yield change*	Price of Bond			Dollar Value of			Total Return		
	A	B	C	Barbell	Bullet	Difference	Barbell	Bullet	Difference
0.000	105.17415	102.58651	104.62500	103.88530	104.62500	0.73970	7.77	9.25	1.48
0.025	104.25000	100.49574	103.08308	102.38008	103.08308	0.70300	4.76	6.17	1.41
0.500	103.33626	98.47477	101.57265	100.91485	101.57265	0.65780	1.83	3.15	1.32
0.750	102.43280	96.52083	100.09300	99.48817	100.09300	0.60484	-1.02	0.19	1.21
1.000	101.53949	94.63125	98.64342	98.09863	98.64342	0.54479	-3.80	-2.71	1.09
1.250	100.65619	92.80350	97.22323	96.74492	97.22323	0.47830	-6.51	-5.55	0.96
1.500	99.78278	91.03515	95.83174	95.42576	95.83174	0.40598	-9.15	-8.34	0.81
1.750	98.91913	89.32385	94.46830	94.13992	94.46830	0.32839	-11.72	-11.06	0.66
2.000	98.06513	87.66740	93.13229	92.88623	93.13229	0.24606	-14.23	-13.74	0.49
2.250	97.22065	86.06366	91.82307	91.66357	91.82307	0.15949	-16.67	-16.35	0.32
2.500	96.38556	84.51058	90.54003	90.47087	90.54003	0.06916	-19.06	-18.92	0.14
2.750	95.55976	83.00623	89.28259	89.30709	89.28259	-0.02450	-21.39	-21.43	-0.05
3.000	94.74312	81.54872	88.05017	88.17125	88.05017	-0.12109	-23.66	-23.90	-0.24
3.250	93.93553	80.13627	86.84219	87.06239	86.84219	-0.22020	-25.88	-26.32	-0.44
3.500	93.13687	78.76718	85.65812	85.97961	85.65812	-0.32149	-28.04	-28.68	-0.64
3.750	92.34704	77.43979	84.49742	84.92203	84.49742	-0.42462	-30.16	-31.01	-0.85
4.000	91.56592	76.15253	83.35955	83.88882	83.35955	-0.52927	-32.22	-33.28	-1.06
4.250	90.79341	74.90391	82.24402	82.87917	82.24402	-0.63515	-34.24	-35.51	-1.27
4.500	90.02939	73.69248	81.15032	81.89230	81.15032	-0.74198	-36.22	-37.70	-1.48
4.750	89.27377	72.51685	80.07796	80.92748	80.07796	-0.84952	-38.15	-39.84	-1.70
5.000	88.52643	71.37571	79.02647	79.98400	79.02647	-0.95752	-40.03	-41.95	-1.92

* Change in yield for Bond C. Nonparallel shift as follows:
yield change bond A = yield change bond C – 25 basis points
yield change bond B = yield change bond C + 25 basis points

outperform the barbell only if the yield on Bond C does not rise by more than 250 basis points or fall by more than 325 basis points.

Thus, total return analysis tells us that by looking at measures such as yield (yield to maturity, average-weighted yield or dollar-duration-weighted yield), duration and convexity can be misleading because the performance of a security or a portfolio of securities depends on the magnitude of the change in yields over some investment horizon and how the yield curve changes.

MERITS OF TOTAL RETURN ANALYSIS

In later chapters, we will describe more complex securities than the plain-vanilla bonds that we used in our illustrations in this chapter. Total return analysis provides a common denominator for comparing complex securities with differing risk and reward characteristics; each security is represented by a return profile that allows for a comparison of disparate securities on a common platform.

Total return analysis:

1. *Encourages comparative analysis.* By summarizing the details, total return analysis focuses on the important aspects. The different features of a security, such as the expiration date of an option or the remaining term of a mortgage, are important only to the extent that they influence the profile. For most analytical purposes, the profile is all that we need to know about a security. Therefore, total return analysis helps us to focus on substance rather than becoming distracted by details. This encourages comparative analysis among disparate securities and helps in the discovery of alternatives.

2. *Isolates investment horizon from investment choice.* For example, total return analysis shows returns from the rolling over of short-term securities to the horizon date or the returns from a longer-maturity investment that is liquidated at the horizon date. This effectively widens the scope of investment decision.

3. *Has the facility to deal with portfolios.* Total return analysis can be applied to portfolios with as much ease as it is applied to individual securities. The key to this facility is that the returns, which when expressed in dollars, are additive. Because it can be applied so easily to portfolios, it is an ideal method for relating assets to liabilities. This is perhaps one of the most important contributions of total return analysis. Since the return profile concept is equally applicable to assets and liabilities, total return analysis helps us monitor the efficacy of an asset portfolio relative to the liabilities and pinpoints any weaknesses.

4. *Provides an objective method of evaluation.* The total return framework frees the analysis from arbitrariness. When new and innovative products are created, the market tries to value them relative to other older products. In order to carry out the valuation effectively, we need a framework that is broad enough to accommodate the new products. The older techniques, which use yield and duration, are at a loss to value consistently some new products with, for example, negative duration such as interest-only stripped mortgage-backed securities, some inverse floaters and CMO residuals.[5]

5. *Helps locate efficient hedge vehicles.* Again, the return profile makes it easy to determine the effectiveness of a hedge candidate.

6. *Facilitates the use of the full array of available securities.* For example, total return analysis can answer such questions as if and how an option on the long bond can be used to enhance returns from a short-term investment. The flexibility it offers in terms of securities also extends to the creation of combinations. Using the return profiles, various desirable profiles can be synthesized by using appropriate combinations of different securities. If the

---

[5] See Chapter 8.

return from one security is weak in one scenario, we can look for another whose return is stronger in the same scenario. Thus, synthetic alternatives and synthetic hedges can be discovered. The additivity of the profiles makes the whole process simple.

7. *Emphasizes the effect of market changes on performance.* Static analytical tools, such as yield to maturity, fail to reveal the sensitivity of performance to market changes. Total return does. With this capability, we are able to incorporate market judgments in investment choice. Since the analysis shows the performance of securities under different scenarios, we can use our knowledge or inclination about the scenarios along with total return analysis to select preferred investments.

8. *Allows for parameters such as duration and convexity to be used.* Such parameters provide an understanding of the results and a way to predict them. Individual parameters are important only for their ability to represent the profile.

CONCLUSION

We have presented a framework based on the concept of total returns. We have demonstrated that the popular duration and convexity ideas are often misused, chiefly because of overzealous application. However, total return analysis is more complicated. Detailed attention should be paid to the various assumptions that must be made. Therefore, the process is unavoidably laborious. There is always the tendency to ignore the analysis, thinking that this discussion is too theoretical. On the contrary, the line separating theory and practice is very thin indeed; theory when properly applied becomes practice. The analysis we propose is useful *now*.

We showed in the barbell-bullet example in Exhibit 2-10 in Chapter 2 that the duration-average-yield method would have recommended purchasing the *bullet* because of a yield pickup. Later, the slightly more computationally intensive duration-cash-flow yield analysis shown in Exhibit 3-7 in Chapter 3, even after including convexity, implied that there was only a small yield pickup. However, it is not uncommon to observe situations such as the one cited in this chapter where a barbell appears to be *cheap* because it has higher yield and higher convexity, and therefore should be purchased and the bullet sold. On the other hand, our total return framework indicates that if the two bonds, which comprise the barbell, are fairly priced, then the barbell is also fairly priced. Thus, the simpler, less tedious methods would have led us into executing the wrong transaction. Admittedly, total return analysis is tedious and computationally expensive. Unfortunately, there is no shortcut to excellence.

Total return analysis, as opposed to static analysis, also addresses a very important criterion for investments—*suitability*. It is very difficult to relate a soft number, such as the yield to maturity of a bond, to our investment goals. In many instances, investments (or assets) are acquired to meet the cash-flow requirements of liabilities. The framework developed here can be used to analyze both asset and liability characteristics. In turn, the analysis can be used to ensure that the assets and liabilities are matched as desired and to apply appropriate controls as needed.

Parametric analysis has several simplifying implied assumptions; total return analysis also needs implicit and explicit assumptions. One might wonder if we are just replacing one set of assumptions with another. We are, but with enormous added value. We can compare the situation to a hedging decision. Usually, when we hedge, market risk is being traded for basis risk. Therefore, we would hedge only if the resulting basis risk is less than the market risk. In the next chapter we develop the minimum set of conditions that a framework must satisfy to be consistent. We believe that consistency is absolutely necessary in any framework. Using an inconsistent framework is similar to computing with a malfunctioning calculator; the theoretical correctness of the calculator is not just a utopian luxury, but a practical requirement.

Chapter 5

Making the Right Assumptions: Internal and External Consistency

In order to compute total returns, we have to make certain assumptions about the course of future interest rates. We minimize the risk that the analysis is merely an opinion about the future by including various scenarios. Yet, as discussed in the previous chapter on scenario analysis, different assumptions lead to dramatically different results, and this in turn impacts buy and sell decisions significantly. Within the total return framework, parameters such as duration, convexity, and yield play only an indirect role and manifest themselves through the total return under various scenarios. As a consequence, assumptions about the evolution of future interest rates are of critical importance. Therefore, we must exercise extreme caution in making assumptions that do not result in mere reflections of our assumptions, but that indicate the true relative values sought.[1]

To illustrate this, let us consider three Treasury bonds of different maturities along the yield curve with coupons of 6 percent, 9 percent and 10 percent. For the sake of simplicity, we assume that all are

---

[1] It is not always true that simple assumptions produce useless results. As we have seen in the section on scenario analysis in the previous chapter, simple assumptions can provide valuable insight, though we would not use the results for actual investment decisions.

priced at par with no initial accrued interest. We wish to compare the 9 percent coupon bond with a barbell consisting of equal amounts of the 6 percent and 10 percent bonds, using a six-month horizon. Now, let us make the assumption that the horizon prices of the three bonds equal their starting price of par. Since there is no cash flow before the horizon date and no capital gain or loss, total returns are determined simply by the coupon paid at the horizon. The return is equal to 9 percent for the bullet and 8 percent for the barbell.

On close examination, we find that the barbell's total return is actually equal to its average yield, a number that we rejected in the previous chapter. Key here is our assumption that all three bonds would be priced at par at the horizon, which we will show later in this chapter to be inconsistent. We gain nothing by varying this biased base case to generate additional scenarios. We will be left with the task of explaining the results by attributing the differences in total returns to the "cost of convexity" and the like.

Given that results and conclusions are very sensitive to the framework chosen, i.e., the assumptions made with regard to interest-rate movements, is there a set of "neutral" assumptions that will not color or bias the results? We state two simple conditions that every acceptable framework must satisfy. The first, *internal consistency*, which is of a theoretical nature, guarantees that the framework is not self-contradictory. The second, *external consistency*, is a practical condition that dictates that the parameters of the framework be consistent with the market. The former addresses the values of the securities and establishes a basic structure; the latter connects the framework to market prices and calibrates it. Both are the subject of this chapter.

INTERNAL CONSISTENCY: THE NO-ARBITRAGE CONDITION

The no-arbitrage condition requires that no *riskless profitable arbitrage* exist among fairly priced securities. It is usually employed in the valuation of options on various securities and was first used in the derivation of the Black-Scholes formula for options on stocks.[2] Risk-

---

[2] Fischer Black and Myron Scholes, "The Pricing of Options and Corporate Liabilities," *Journal of Political Economy* (May–June 1973), pp. 637–659.

less profitable arbitrage refers to the possibility that we can purchase a set of securities and finance this purchase by the sale of another set of securities such that after a specified period of time, we are left with a positive amount of money after satisfying all obligations independent of the direction and magnitude of market moves.[3] That is, we obtain positive profits with zero net investment. Thus, such an arbitrage is both riskless, because no money is being invested, and profitable. The internal consistency condition requires that such arbitrage not be possible within the framework.

As a consequence of the no-arbitrage condition, we normally do not have the freedom to assume how the yields and prices of different securities move relative to one another; they have to maintain a proper relationship among themselves in order to ensure that there is no riskless arbitrage. For example, we cannot assume that yield curve shifts are parallel without violating this condition.[4]

It is possible to express the no-arbitrage condition more intuitively by means of a *closure property:*[5]

A portfolio of short and long positions in fairly priced securities is also fairly priced.

Stated this way, this condition seems to make sense. We should not be able to create a cheap or rich portfolio simply by combining other securities that are neither rich nor cheap. This means that if a portfolio as a whole is cheap (rich), then at least one position in it must be cheap (rich).[6] The closure condition is very simple to understand and is stated more at a logical level than a mathematical one.

---

[3] We include the lending and borrowing of money in purchasing and selling securities.

[4] This is not to say that nonparallel shifts are better. In fact, we cannot assume *any* type of shift for the yield curve that has not been specifically computed to satisfy the consistency condition.

[5] This property is called *closure* because the set of fairly priced securities is a closed one; all combinations of the securities are also members of the fairly priced set.

[6] In this context, a cheap position is a long position in a cheap security or a short position in a rich security. A rich position is defined conversely.

Yet it is a very powerful statement. By making this condition slightly more rigorous, we can make it an exact equivalent of the no-arbitrage condition. Any framework that does not satisfy this condition is self-contradictory.

In summary, the no-arbitrage condition places some restrictions on the assumptions that we can make on the relative yield or price movements of the various securities. Any acceptable framework should ensure that these restrictions are not violated.

The no-arbitrage condition seems to be an obvious necessity, but surprisingly it is violated in most analyses. For example, the duration-cash-flow-yield framework does not satisfy the closure property and therefore is self-contradictory. As we saw in the barbell-bullet analysis, we can start with two fairly priced securities and obtain a portfolio (the barbell) that seems cheap as it has the same duration but a higher cash-flow yield. Including other simple parameters in the analysis does little to help. For instance, the duration-convexity-cash-flow-yield approach is also unacceptable; it may imply that the barbell is cheap as it has the same duration but higher convexity and higher cash-flow yield.

Application 1: The Yield Curve Revisited

In Chapter 2 we concluded that the duration framework as implemented in the duration yield curve, which implies that different bonds of equal duration should have equal yields, produces erroneous results and can lead to inappropriate transactions. It is possible to develop a simple yield curve model that satisfies the no-arbitrage condition. Indeed, such a model can be of practical use in creating accurate trading strategies.

Yield Spreads Do Not Necessarily Indicate Value. Similar-maturity bonds with different coupons trade at different yields, and similar-coupon bonds with different maturities also trade at different yields. However, the yield spread between two bonds does not necessarily indicate the relative cheapness of one bond and the richness of another. Just as the long bond, trading at 300 basis points over the three-month T-bill, is not cheaper than the T-bill, it is possible for two bonds of similar maturities and different coupons to have different yields and yet both be fairly priced. Bonds of equal duration do not necessarily trade at equal yields.

Whether the yield spreads among Treasury bonds of different coupons but similar maturities indicate value can be determined by looking at the building blocks of all bonds—cash flows. If we can value cash flows, we can value bonds. Let's assume for the moment that we know the fair values, or equivalently fair yields, of zero-coupon bonds of all maturities up to a certain maximum. These fair yields for zero-coupon bonds are called *spot rates*. The series of prices of zero-coupon bonds of all maturities is known as the *discount function*. If we consider a coupon bond to be simply a portfolio of zero-coupon bonds whose cash flows correspond to coupon and principal payments, we can determine the fair value of any bond of any coupon within the maturity spectrum under consideration by summing the values of each cash flow as represented by the discount function.

Exhibit 5-1 shows how this is done. Column two shows the hypothetical yields for zero-coupon bonds with maturities from six months to ten years. From this we can determine the present value of one dollar payable at these maturities. This is shown in column three and represents the discount function. Column four shows the cash flow from a 5 percent-coupon bond. These cash flows are discounted at the respective rates in column two, and the corresponding present values are shown in column five.[7] The sum of all the present values in column five is the fair value for the 10-year, 5 percent-coupon bond. This process can be repeated for any bond or for any known and fixed cash flow. Columns six and seven show the computation for a five-year, 10 percent bond.

Once the values of the different bonds are computed, we can plot their yields in the traditional manner against maturity or, if preferred, duration. In plotting the yields, it is more insightful to group bonds by coupon and draw one curve for each coupon. Since all bonds on a given curve have the same coupon, such curves are called *isocoupon* curves (*iso* means "same or equal").

---

[7] The present values can also be obtained by multiplying the numbers in columns three and four.

Exhibit 5-1. Calculation of Fair Value

Time (years)	Spot rates	Present value of $1	Coupon flow 5% bond	Present value	Coupon flow 10% bond	Present value
1.0	6.680	0.9364	2.5	2.341	5	4.682
1.5	6.980	0.9022	2.5	2.256	5	4.511
2.0	7.211	0.8679	2.5	2.170	5	4.340
2.5	7.350	0.8349	2.5	2.087	5	4.175
3.0	7.457	0.8028	2.5	2.007	5	4.014
3.5	7.563	0.7712	2.5	1.928	5	3.856
4.0	7.643	0.7408	2.5	1.852	5	3.704
4.5	7.706	0.7116	2.5	1.779	5	3.558
5.0	7.769	0.6831	2.5	1.708	5	3.416
5.5	7.855	0.6546	2.5	1.637	5	3.273
6.0	7.947	0.6265	2.5	1.566	5	3.133
6.5	8.034	0.5993	2.5	1.498	5	2.997
7.0	8.105	0.5734	2.5	1.434	5	2.867
7.5	8.162	0.5488	2.5	1.372	5	2.744
8.0	8.206	0.5255	2.5	1.314	5	2.628
8.5	8.245	0.5032	2.5	1.258	5	2.516
9.0	8.280	0.4818	2.5	1.205	5	2.409
9.5	8.317	0.4611	2.5	1.153	5	2.306
10.0	8.355	0.4411	102.5	45.213	105	46.316
			Fair value:	78.201	Fair value:	112.291
			Fair yield:	8.243	Fair yield:	8.177

Note: Fair value as employed here includes price plus accrued interest.

Exhibit 5-2 shows the isocoupon curves for zero, 5 percent, 10 percent, and 15 percent coupons. Bonds that fall on any of these yield curves are fairly priced relative to the zero-coupon bonds; that is, the curves represent the *fair yield* for any bond. We find that bonds of different coupons have different fair yields—we actually expect them to—notwithstanding the fact that they have the same maturity or duration. Thus, the coupon yield curves represent the *coupon-adjusted yield* for each bond.

Coupon-Adjusted Yields. Since the isocoupon curves represent fair yields, if the actual market yield of any bond is not on the curve

Exhibit 5-2. Isocoupon Curves for Zero, 5%, 10%, and 15% Coupons

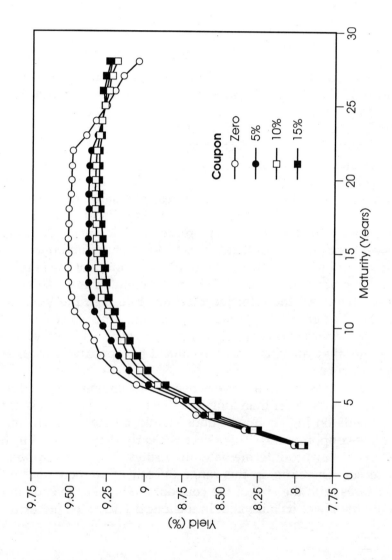

corresponding to its coupon, we can conclude that the bond is either rich or cheap. If the yield is above the curve, a cheap bond is indicated; if it is below, the bond is rich.[8]

Intuitively, coupon spreads occur because the various cash flows from a bond are discounted at different rates according to the discount function. Yield to maturity simply represents a single effective or blended discount rate for all cash flows. The cash-flow characteristics differ from coupon to coupon. High-coupon bonds have larger earlier cash flows, while discount bonds have smaller earlier cash flows. Thus, the effect of different rates at different maturities varies on different bonds.

For example, assume that the zero-coupon curve is positively sloping; that is, shorter maturity rates are smaller than longer maturity rates. (Thus, the earlier coupons are discounted at a smaller rate.) Since the earlier coupons represent a larger fraction of a premium bond, it follows that the yield for a premium bond should be correspondingly low. For a discount bond, more of the bond's value is tied up at maturity, which is being discounted at a relatively larger rate. Therefore, the effective discount rate, i.e., the yield, will be higher. This result is perhaps a surprising one, since we normally expect higher-coupon bonds to trade at relatively higher yields. If they do, they are cheap, in the context of a positively sloping zero-coupon curve.

If the zero-coupon curve is negatively sloping, i.e., shorter maturity rates are greater than longer maturity rates, the effect is reversed; the yields on high-coupon bonds should be greater than the yields on low-coupon bonds. This effect is clearly demonstrated in Exhibit 5-2. For short-to-intermediate maturities, the zero-coupon curve increases. Therefore, in this range the fair or coupon-adjusted yield decreases with the size of the coupon; the higher the coupon on the bond, the lower its fair yield. In the longer end of the maturity range,

---

[8] Of course, the difference between the actual yield and the yield implied by the curve could be due to differences in liquidity, taxes, etc. Therefore, any spread to the curve should be examined to determine if such factors warrant such a spread. We have ignored taxes and other factors in this analysis.

the zero-coupon curve begins to fall. In this range, bonds with higher coupons have relatively higher fair yields.

Although we have not taken tax effects into consideration, it is possible to extend this analysis to include taxes. Such analysis may lead to different conclusions as to the relative cheapness or richness of various bonds.

The reader might wonder why we are using yield to maturity after having demonstrated in the previous chapter that it can be misleading in determining the relative value of different securities. However, there is a significant difference between the usage of yield in the duration framework in Chapter 2 and its use here. In our opinion, the best use for yield to maturity is as a *proxy for price*. That is, since there is a one-to-one correspondence between price and yield for a given security, often it is more advantageous to use yield instead of price. The coupon yield curves are one such occasion. Here, yield has no interpretation as a return but just acts as a representation of price for our convenience.

The coupon-adjusted yield analysis thus acknowledges that a bond is simply a collection of cash flows. Therefore, if we know the value of simple cash flows at different times—i.e., if the value of the zero-coupon curve is known—we can value any bond of any coupon. However, determining an appropriate zero-coupon curve for bond valuation is not easy. There are simply too many choices. An immediate choice is to use Treasury STRIPs data, another is to fit a zero curve to the Treasury coupon bond price data to minimize fitting errors. Here we have a choice of weighting the data on different bonds depending on, among other things, our confidence in the data. For example, we could weight the current-coupon Treasury data more heavily. It is also possible to use historical data along with current data to enhance the fit.

Application 2: Immunization

In our discussion on scenario analysis in the previous chapter, we saw that duration is the horizon at which the positive effect of higher interest rates on reinvestment income is balanced by their negative effect on bond prices. Because the two components of total return balance this way, the return is essentially independent of the course of interest rates. In immunization, the duration of a portfolio is set equal to the horizon and continually adjusted as time and market conditions change in order to achieve stable total returns.

However, in most immunization models, interest-rate movement assumptions do not satisfy the consistency condition. For example, simple immunization models use parallel shifts of the yield curve. As a consequence of this incorrect assumption, the expected returns from a portfolio are overstated.

These models imply that a zero-coupon bond with maturity equal to the horizon has the *minimum* return among all immunized portfolios. This is because the zero-coupon bond has the lowest convexity among all securities with equal duration. Therefore, any immunized portfolio will perform equal to or better than the zero-coupon bond. However, this result is in violation of the no-arbitrage rule, since it allows us to sell a zero-coupon bond and with the proceeds of the sale purchase an immunized portfolio, implying riskless profits due to the gain from convexity as long as interest rates move.

In light of our discussion, we would not conclude that the immunized portfolio would perform better than the zero-coupon bond, but just that the assumptions that led to the result are faulty. We take a lesson from the young astronomer who when he sees canals on the moon, instead of rushing into the street crying "eureka" simply has the sense to have his telescope lens cleaned.

Even the more complicated immunization models are not free from this problem. The bottom line is that immunization is only an *approximate* technique. It does not guarantee that the desired rate of return will be achieved.[9] However, the likelihood of coming close to the target may be within business requirements in many cases. In an immunization context, the strategy generally looks for a zero-risk portfolio. It is unclear that such a low-risk investment is appropri-

---

[9] For a more rigorous derivation of this result, see T. Barnhill and W. Margrabe, "A Theory of Complete Immunization for Default-Free Bonds Under Arbitrary Changes in the Term Structure," Seminar on the Analysis of Security Prices, Center for Research in Security Prices, University of Chicago, May 1986.

ate for all participants; perhaps a higher-risk portfolio strategy with a possibility of a higher return would be better. The total return concept helps us explore such ideas.

EXTERNAL CONSISTENCY: CALIBRATING THE MODEL

In a framework, the assumptions made about the movements of interest rates *imply* the values of securities. The prices of these securities in the market may not be equal to these implied values. The external consistency condition requires that the model be tuned or calibrated so that actual market prices and implied model values are in agreement. Usually, the model has certain parameters, such as interest-rate volatility and drift, that can be varied to bring about the desired agreement. Depending on the number of parameters available for tuning, the agreement between values and prices can be tight or loose; the larger the number of parameters, the more prices can be matched. The calibration process can be modified by our view that only a subset of the market is fairly priced; that is, we can assume that the value-price equality holds only for a selected group of securities. For example, only current-coupon Treasury bonds could be used for calibration. Another valid assumption is to postulate that the market, *on the average*, is fairly priced though individual securities may not be. In this case, we would first determine the average, for example by a statistical fit to the market data, and then use it to compute the values of the parameters of the model.

Calibration connects the model to the market. It is a practical requirement, but not a theoretical necessity. Without calibration, the model can still be internally consistent, though it would not be useful in practical applications. Some practitioners assume a random process for interest-rate movements without tuning the model. The result is shown in Exhibit 5-3, which plots the yield curve implied by the assumption that short-term interest rates follow a lognormal distribution with no drift. The actual yield curve is shown along with implied curves at high and low assumed volatilities. As can be seen, the longer bonds, because of their higher convexity, tend to be more valuable in volatile markets, and therefore their implied yields are low. The higher the volatility, the greater this effect. If this model is used without calibration, then all long-term bonds will *incorrectly*

Exhibit 5-3. Implied Yield Curves Assuming Zero Drift: High and Low Volatilities

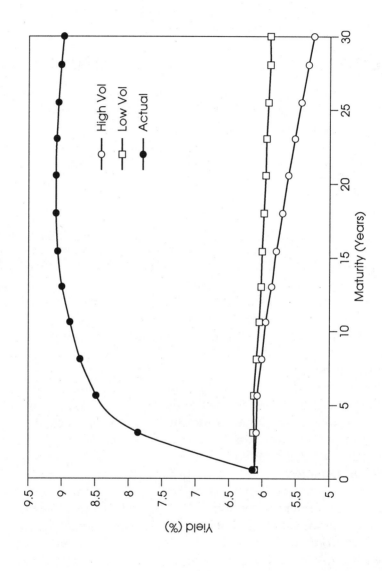

appear cheaper in the market. To avoid this problem, we have to allow interest rates to drift slowly upward in the proper manner until the negative effect of higher rates brings down the value of the longer bonds in line with market prices. This is an example of how we attempt to balance the positive effect of convexity and volatility by the negative effect of duration and higher rates.

MAKING ASSUMPTIONS VERSUS PREDICTING INTEREST RATES

It is important to distinguish between making *assumptions* about interest-rate movements and *forecasting* or *predicting* interest rates. Within the framework developed here, assumptions are made about rate movements to evaluate securities today. We might have specific views on the market, but they do not change the values of the securities we wish to buy; they merely change our preferences for them. In the valuation of securities it is best to keep bullish or bearish views external to the framework. For example, when considering the purchase of a long-duration bond, we would not pay more than it is worth simply because our outlook is bullish. Intuitively, assumptions about interest rates can *imply* a certain amount of forecasting. Most often, the existence of such a predictive element is latent but becomes clear when we apply the concepts developed here. For example, a parallel shift assumption predicts high volatility, thereby making barbells more attractive than bullets. A zero-drift interest-rate process implies a decline in rates, making the longer bonds appear overly attractive. However, an unbiased analysis should neither contain nor imply any type of forecasting. The framework developed here guarantees objectivity in this sense:

> *Assumptions that satisfy the internal and external consistency conditions do not contain any predictive element; they are truly neutral.*

This statement appears to be logical: if the assumptions imply a prediction, then we could establish an arbitrage that could exploit the prediction. Since consistent assumptions are made so as not to create an arbitrage opportunity, it follows that there are no implied predictions. We can view the market as exhibiting its own expectations about the future through the shape of the yield curve, for example. In this context we broaden the statement above:

> *Consistent assumptions contain no predictions beyond what is manifested in the market as a whole.*

Thus, the consistency conditions help create an impartial, objective framework in which to analyze fixed-income securities. Within this framework we can make assumptions about the future, without the need to know it. We can postulate interest-rate movements without making specific predictions. We believe that this quality of the framework makes the details of implementation, such as the actual statistical distributions chosen, less important than its major characteristics: internal and external consistency.

TOTAL RETURN APPLICATION

Here, we examine the results of applying our framework to the barbell-bullet swap. We simplify our discussion by assuming a flat yield curve[10] at 10 percent, that is, bonds of all coupons and maturities yield 10 percent. We compare a barbell consisting of a 10-year, 10 percent bond and a 30-year, 10 percent bond to a 20-year, 10 percent bullet. All bonds are priced at par to yield 10 percent. The modified durations of the bonds in the barbell are 6.2311 and 9.4646 and 8.5795 for the bullet. To create an equal-duration barbell, we use $27.37 worth of the 10-year bond and $72.63 worth of the 30-year bond for every $100 worth of the bullet.

Static analysis: Based purely on yield to maturity, the barbell and the bullet both have the same yield and therefore appear relatively fairly priced. Thus, static analysis indicates no transaction.

Naive total return analysis: Using a five-year horizon, we make the following assumptions:

---

[10] Besides simplicity, another reason for using a flat yield curve is to avoid the temptation to explain away errors in the analysis by calling the discrepancies "payment for convexity."

1. The reinvestment rate and the horizon yield are the same.

2. The horizon yield for all three bonds is the same for each scenario, that is, the yield shifts are parallel.

These two assumptions are usually found in most total return analysis models. The results are shown graphically in Exhibit 5-4. The exhibit plots the difference (in dollar returns) between the barbell and the bullet over the five-year horizon. Because of the effect of its higher convexity, the barbell outperforms the bullet under the assumptions made. Thus, naive total return analysis indicates that the bullet should be sold and the barbell bought.

Total return analysis under the consistent framework: The total returns for the barbell and the bullet computed within a consistent framework are shown numerically in Exhibit 5-5. To obtain these, we have used a model whose interest-rate process is internally consistent—providing the appropriate relative yield shifts of the three bonds at the horizon—and externally consistent with the starting flat yield curve. Reinvestment is in the short-term rate. The differences between the returns (in dollars) of the barbell and the bullet are shown graphically in Exhibit 5-6.

We can make two observations from Exhibit 5-6:

1. One's intuition that the barbell is more convex and therefore likely to benefit more from a large move in rates is confirmed. Such intuition is apparent even in the naive analysis. The barbell performs better than the bullet when rates move significantly. Conversely, the barbell underperforms when rates are stable. This is why being long a barbell is considered being long volatility.

2. The model used also provides a numerical representation of the probability of each scenario being realized, as in Exhibit 5-5. This information can be used for scenario analysis or simulation to determine suitability of or preference for a proposed transaction.

The conclusion is that the barbell and bullet are both fairly priced. Therefore no transaction based in relative value is indicated. We would

Exhibit 5-4. Relative Performance of Barbell over Bullet, Parallel-Shift Assumption

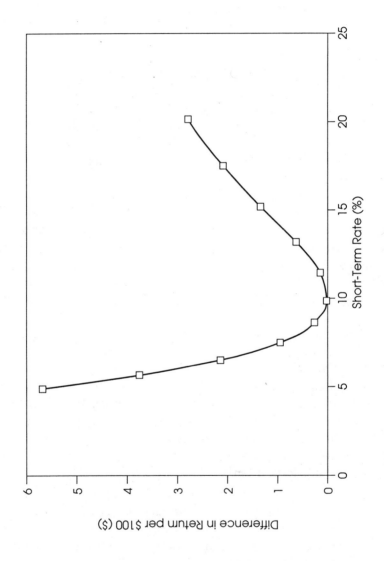

Exhibit 5-5. Relative Performance of Barbell over Bullet, Arbitrage-Free Assumption

Short rate	Probability	Bullet returns	Barbell returns	Difference
4.814	0.001	208.358	209.859	1.527
5.563	0.010	199.364	199.915	0.550
6.425	0.044	190.066	189.940	–0.126
7.419	0.117	180.596	180.115	–0.481
8.564	0.205	171.112	170.597	–0.515
9.883	0.246	161.794	161.537	–0.258
11.402	0.205	152.835	153.071	0.237
13.152	0.117	144.427	145.317	0.890
15.168	0.044	136.756	138.365	1.608
17.489	0.010	129.986	132.282	2.296
20.164	0.001	124.247	127.114	2.868

buy the bullet or the barbell only if we sought, for whatever reason, the return profile generated by the corresponding position.

Without attaching much meaning to it, observe that the conclusion of the static analysis agrees with that of the consistent analysis.

RETURN TO PARAMETRICS

So far, we have clearly demonstrated how such parameters as duration, convexity, and yield fail to provide a consistent or even useful framework. However, the goal here is not to imply that the parameters themselves are useless. On the contrary, parameters are *summary attributes* and provide succinct information about bonds and portfolios. The fact remains that longer-duration bonds can be considered more volatile. Higher-convexity portfolios still do better when interest-rate volatility is higher. It is better to buy a bond at a higher yield and sell it at a lower yield.

On average, the market *seems to know* that the parameters do not describe securities completely. That is why we find differences in the prices and yields among securities and portfolios that are parametrically similar. These differences produce the *illusion* of profitable transactions when completeness is attributed to the parameters.

Exhibit 5-6. Relative Performance of Barbell Over Bullet, Arbitrage-Free Assumption

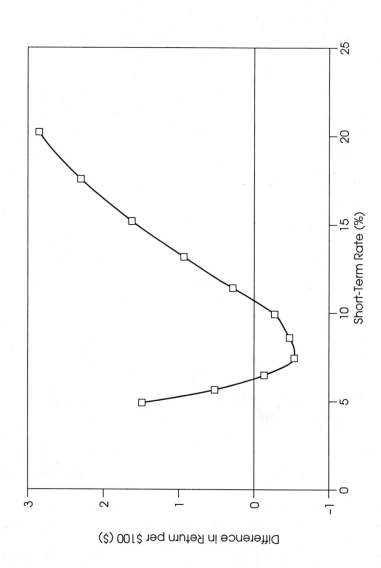

Duration, convexity, and yield are mathematical concepts and as such are factual. It is in the popular interpretation of these parameters, for example, duration as risk and yield as reward, that we find the weakness. Our measurements are more precise than the ideas and interpretations that they represent. The major problem occurs when we attribute more precision to these parameters than they merit. These parameters by themselves cannot constitute a complete, consistent framework. We would not, for example, compute duration to several decimal places; the resulting precision is purely academic. In most cases it is not even worth distinguishing between Macaulay duration and modified duration as measures of portfolio risk. We would not do barbell-bullet swaps just to pick up a few basis points in yield. These parameters are merely *approximate indicators* of the real thing: the total return.

However, the parameters can still be used to set broad strategic goals and to implement specific objectives. Since the parameters represent the summary attributes of portfolios, they can be powerful and necessary tools in situations in which simple characterizations of portfolios are essential. Two immediate examples are hedging applications and asset/liability management. When used properly, the parameters can provide an excellent *handle* on the portfolio or strategy. For example, if the goal is to be aggressively bullish on the market and build a high-risk portfolio, we would look for bonds of high duration. Similarly, if we are trying to match a specific liability in the future, we would set up a portfolio whose duration is approximately equal to that of the liability. The parameters provide a good starting point in developing a satisfactory portfolio that is consistent with our goals.

Chapter 6

Measuring and Controlling Yield Curve Risk

Several years of use of the duration concept has imparted the ability to most financial institutions to all but eliminate market risk via prudent hedging activities. As a result of this, other residual risks have gained prominence. Some of these risks can be dominant in many situations, and, among them, as we noted in Chapter 1, the most important is *yield curve risk*, and it deserves a detailed treatment. In particular, yield curve risk can be significant in portfolios containing options, some mortgage derivatives, and most exotic securities.

As usually stated, the duration of a fixed-income asset (or liability) is the price sensitivity relative to its own yield. Therefore, when we use duration for hedging purposes, we are implicitly assuming that the yield levels of the various assets and liabilities move in parallel, that is, in equal amounts. We demonstrated this in Chapter 4. In fact, however, different credit, coupon, or maturity sectors of the market move differently in terms of their yield. This difference is known as the *basis risk* among the sectors. Basis risk with

Reprinted, with permission, from *Financial Analysts Journal*, forthcoming 1995. Association for Investment Management and Research, Charlottesville, VA. All rights are reserved. (The title of the published article is "The Risk Point Method for Measuring and Controlling Yield Curve Risk." The authors have revised and expanded portions of the original article for this book.)

respect to different maturity sectors is also known as *yield curve risk* and represents changes in the yield curve that are not parallel shifts. These include the so-called reshaping shifts, e.g., twists, pivoting moves, steepening, and flattening.

In general, basis risk is difficult to measure and hedge.[1] Most hedging vehicles address market risk,[2] e.g., changes in the Treasury rates, not basis risk. It is possible to take the view that only market risk is hedgeable and treat basis risk as a prudent business risk that an institution has to take. This is the only approach in dealing with certain types of basis risk, e.g., credit risk.[3]

A risk measure can be considered more complete compared to a simple measure such as duration if we can incorporate some of the important basis risks. Fortunately, it is possible to address yield curve risk in many acceptable ways. By necessity, such a broader risk measure will be more than just one number. In this chapter we develop an approach that we believe is useful in measuring yield curve risk.

THE BASKET AND CASH-FLOW BUCKET METHODS

One method is to divide assets and liabilities into smaller maturity baskets, and analyze each basket separately. If each basket covers a sufficiently small maturity range, then we can assume that the yield curve risk is acceptably small within that range. In a hedging application, we would use hedging instruments suitable for that maturity range to match dollar durations. In an asset/liability context, if each basket or sector is matched, using appropriate hedges as required, then the assets and liabilities are matched as a whole because of the

---

[1] Actually, in practice, basis risk refers to any risk that is not hedgeable or is not hedged. If a risk can be quantified and acceptably managed, e.g., yield curve risk in our case, then that risk is no longer a part of the generic basis risk.

[2] This makes sense because a hedging instrument, in order to ensure its wide usage, should represent the broad market rather than a specific security or too narrow a sector. Otherwise, it would suffer a severe lack of liquidity and the cost of hedging would be unacceptably high.

[3] Recently, however, derivative instruments for managing certain types of credit risk are being developed.

additivity property of dollar duration. To the extent that the yields of all assets and liabilities as well as the hedging instruments used within a sector move in step, this approach is satisfactory.

There is a problem, however. It turns out that an asset of a given maturity might react to changes in rates in another maturity. Consider, for example, a 10-year bond with a coupon of 10 percent. The cash flow from this bond occurs every six months throughout its life. Since the value of a bond is simply the sum of the present values of the individual cash flows, it stands to reason that the value of the 10-year bond could be influenced by rate changes not just in the 10-year maturity but also in all shorter maturities representing the cash flows.

In this context, it is appropriate to clarify what we mean by a "rate." In fixed-income analysis, we use two types of reference interest rates: full-coupon rates and spot or zero-coupon rates. Full-coupon rates are analogous to the yield to maturity on bonds trading at or close to par, e.g., the yield on an on-the-run (current coupon) Treasury. The spot rate for a given maturity, on the other hand, is the yield on a zero-coupon bond with that maturity. As we explained in the previous chapter, when dealing with individual cash flows, e.g., for discounting, it is appropriate to use spot rates; when dealing with bonds trading near par, full coupon rate can be used.

Since a bond is just a collection of cash flows, its yield is a complex blend of the individual spot rates corresponding to the coupon and principal flows. Given the spot rate curve, we can easily determine the coupon yield curve. Conversely, a given spot rate is a complex blend of all coupon rates. Given the coupon rate curve, we can determine the spot rate curve. In summary, a given spot rate depends upon all intermediate coupon rates; a given coupon rate depends upon all intermediate spot rates.

The value of a 10-year par bond, then, responds to all intermediate spot rates, but depends only on the 10-year coupon rate. Thus, to hedge a 10-year par bond, all that we need is another 10-year bond, e.g., the current 10-year Treasury. If we wish to use zero-coupon bonds for hedging, then a 10-year, zero-coupon bond and smaller amounts of all intermediate-maturity zero-coupon bonds will be required for hedging. Similarly, a single cash flow occurring in the tenth year can be efficiently hedged by a 10-year, zero-coupon bond. On the other hand, if we wish to use current coupon Treasuries for hedging, then, in addition to the 10-year Treasury, we will also need shorter maturity Treasuries.

If the bond we are hedging is not priced at par, then it behaves like the combination of a 10-year, full-coupon bond and a 10-year, zero-coupon bond. For example, a $100 million holding of a 9 percent bond selling at 90 can be viewed as the sum of $90 million of a 10 percent par bond and $10 million of a zero-coupon bond. This is because in both cases, there is an annual cash flow of $9 million and a payment at maturity of $100 million. Thus the sensitivity of the 10-year discount bond is the sum of that of each of its components. The hedge for a bond not near par, therefore, is a blend of the hedges for a zero- and that for a full-coupon bond.[4]

In summary, then, an asset (or a liability) of a given maturity might respond to spot or coupon rate changes in other shorter maturities. Therefore, we need to do more than simply group the assets and liabilities in maturity sectors.

One way to handle this problem is to first break down each asset and liability into its cash-flow components. Then the individual cash flows can be grouped into maturity buckets. Now, the price sensitivity of each sector is more clearly defined, at least with respect to spot rates corresponding to each sector.

The cash-flow approach provides valuable insight into the relative natures of the assets and the liabilities. However, it represents risk in terms of spot rate, that is, in terms of zero-coupon bonds, which are rarely used for hedging. A more sophisticated approach is the *risk point method*, discussed in the remainder of this chapter.[5]

---

[4] Similarly, a 10-year premium bond can be decomposed into a slightly larger amount of a par bond and a short position on the zero-coupon bond.

[5] Other approaches are suggested in literature. See, for example, D. Chambers, and W. Carleton, "A Generalized Approach to Duration," in *Research in Finance*, Vol. 7 (1988); Thomas S. Y. Ho, "Key Rate Durations: Measures of Interest Rate Risks," *Journal of Fixed Income* (September 1992); C. Khang, "Bond Immunization When Short-Term Rates Fluctuate More Than Long-Term Rates," *Journal Financial and Quantitative Analysis* (1979), pp. 1085–1090; R. Litterman and J. Scheinkman, "Common Factors Affecting Bond Returns," *Journal of Fixed Income* (June 1991), pp. 54–61; Robert Reitano, "Non-Parallel Yield Curve Shifts and Durational Leverage," *Journal of Portfolio Management* (Summer 1990), pp. 62–67.

(continued on facing page)

THE RISK POINT CONCEPT

Since risk is a measure of change in value, it stands to reason that risk management and security valuation ought to be closely related. Therefore, it is advantageous to use a model that integrates these two aspects. The risk point method attempts such integration. It also has the practical advantage that it measures risk relative to available hedging instruments.

Risk Point Defined

We define the *risk point* of a security or portfolio with reference to a specific hedge instrument. For this reason, it can also be called *relative dollar duration*.[6] It represents the change in the value of the security or portfolio due to a one-basis-point change in the yield of the hedge. If we divide the risk point by the dollar duration or PVBP of the hedge, we get the dollar amount of the hedge instrument to be used as a hedge. This hedge amount will protect the portfolio against risk from small changes in the market sector represented by the hedge instrument.[7]

The discussion of the risk point concept here builds on the following works: Ravi E. Dattatreya, "A Practical Approach to Asset Liability Management," Sumitomo Bank Capital Markets Report, 1989; Ravi E. Dattatreya, "A Practical Approach to Asset Liability Management," in F. Fabozzi and Atsuo Konishi, eds., *Asset Liability Management* (Chicago: Probus Publishing, 1991); Ravi E. Dattatreya, Raj E. Venkatesh and Vijaya E. Venkatesh, *Interest Rate and Currency Swaps* (Chicago: Probus Publishing, 1994); Ravi E. Dattatreya and Raj S. Pundarika, "Interest Rate Risk Management: The Risk Point Method," in Ravi E. Dattatreya and Kensuke Hotta, eds., *Advanced Interest Rate and Currency Swaps* (Chicago: Probus Publishing, 1994); and Ravi E. Dattatreya and Scott Peng, *Structured Notes* (Chicago: Probus Publishing, 1994).

[6] We prefer, however, the former terminology. In the context of modern financial markets, the temporal meaning of duration is no longer relevant.

[7] In defining the framework for risk measurement, we focus more on hedge instruments than on specific market segments or yield curve sectors. The reason for this is that it is of little use to look at risk for which there is no tool for hedging or management. In addition, there is no loss of generality in our approach because almost all major sectors that are sources of risk are well represented by hedge instruments.

Unlike PVBP or dollar duration, which measures the *total* interest-rate risk, the risk point measures only one component of the total risk. This component represents the risk due to a change in rates in a given maturity sector. Thus, to determine a complete risk or hedge, we need a full set of risk points, relative to a set of hedge instruments. From this set of risk points we can determine the portfolio of hedge instruments that will hedge a given portfolio.

Steps in the Risk Point Method

The risk point method consists of three main steps:

1. List the hedge vehicles that are acceptable to employ.
2. Apply a model that values the assets and liabilities relative to the prices of the hedge vehicles.
3. Change the yield or price of one of the hedge instruments by a small amount, keeping all other yields and prices the same. With the new yield, revalue the portfolio again. The change in its value (expressed as dollars per one-basis-point[8] change) is the risk point of the portfolio. This gives the amount of the hedge instrument needed for hedging by simply equating the PVBP of the hedge to the risk point of the portfolio.[9]

This procedure is explained more fully in the next section.

AN IMPLEMENTATION OF THE RISK POINT METHOD

The essential part of the risk point method is a model that values the assets and liabilities relative to the hedge instruments chosen. In

---

[8] One basis point could refer to any other appropriate small unit, e.g., 1 tick for Eurodollar futures, 1 percent for volatility in the case of options, etc.

[9] It is also possible to express the risk point as a *hedge-equivalent*, i.e., the actual amount of the hedge required. The vector of risk points, then, would simply be the hedging portfolio. Representation of the risk point as a relative dollar duration has the advantage that alternative hedge instruments can be easily substituted.

order to be able to deal with a variety of assets and liabilities, the set of hedges chosen must also be broad. An example of a practical implementation of the method follows.

Hedge Instruments

For our example, we include all the current coupon Treasury bonds and notes in the set of hedge instruments that we consider. Treasury bills are included to handle cash flows occurring in the short term.

Valuation Model

We will use a simple but effective valuation model. The procedure will be to value each financial instrument as the sum of the discounted present values of the cash flows generated by the instrument. We must first determine the *discount function,* i.e., all the discount factors that will be used for this procedure. This is a two-step process.

In the first step, to obtain appropriate spreads to evaluate cash flows from corporate bonds, we include spreads from the interest-rate swap market.[10] (This market will be discussed in Chapter 10.) The composite rate, i.e., the sum of the Treasury yield and the spread, is called the *par bond yield* (see Exhibit 6-1).[11,12] It represents the yield on par bonds of the credit quality represented by the spreads used. We then use linear interpolation[13] to generate the *par curve,* i.e., par bond yields at all maturities (see column 3 of Exhibit 6-2).

---

[10] By setting the spreads to zero, we can use the results of the Treasury market. Spreads from other markets (e.g., single-A corporate bonds) can be used if necessary.

[11] The Treasury yields and swap spread used are obtained from market data as of 3.00 PM New York time on May 9, 1994. Each data point is represented on a semiannual pay, 30/360 basis. Note that the familiar 7-year Treasury is absent because they are no longer planned to be issued.

[12] Alternatively, in the short end, it is possible to use LIBOR to determine the composite rate directly. In this case, care should be taken to ensure that the day count conventions are handled correctly.

[13] We could use more sophisticated interpolation. However, linear interpolation gives acceptable results and is used widely in the interest-rate swap market.

Exhibit 6-1. The Hedging Instruments with Yields

Maturity (years)	Treasury yield	Spread (b.p.)	Total
0.5	4.932	28	5.212
1	5.520	29	5.810
2	6.234	31	6.544
3	6.563	35	6.913
5	7.074	32	7.394
10	7.466	41	7.876

Exhibit 6-2. Bootstrapping: Getting the Zero Curve from the Par Curve

Maturity (years)	Par yields	Interpolated par yields	Discounted factor	Cumulative factor	Zero rates
0.5	5.212	5.212000	0.974602	0.974602	5.212000
1.0	5.810	5.810000	0.944257	1.918859	5.818712
1.5		6.177000	0.912552	2.831411	6.194689
2.0	6.544	6.544000	0.878608	3.710019	6.576629
2.5		6.728500	0.846701	4.556720	6.768333
3.0	6.913	6.913000	0.814349	5.371069	6.964043
3.5		7.033250	0.783565	6.154633	7.091448
4.0		7.153500	0.752934	6.907567	7.221785
4.5		7.273750	0.722504	7.630071	7.354956
5.0	7.394	7.394000	0.692321	8.322392	7.490986
5.5		7.442200	0.665550	8.987942	7.541282
6.0		7.490400	0.639435	9.627377	7.593429
6.5		7.538600	0.613973	10.241350	7.647266
7.0		7.586800	0.589156	10.830505	7.702698
7.5		7.635000	0.564977	11.395483	7.759674
8.0		7.683200	0.541431	11.936914	7.818175
8.5		7.731400	0.518511	12.455425	7.878204
9.0		7.779600	0.496207	12.951632	7.939786
9.5		7.827800	0.474514	13.426147	8.002961
10.0	7.876	7.876000	0.453423	13.879569	8.067783

The second step is to determine the zero curve, or, equivalently, the discount factors, from the par curve. Discount factors can be derived sequentially from the par curve one after another. This process is called *bootstrapping*. This procedure builds the zero curve in a step-by-step or inductive manner. For each maturity, it uses the fact that the price of a bond is the sum of the present values of all the cash flows (coupon and principal) from the bond. It is best illustrated using algebraic notation.

Suppose we have already determined the first n semiannual discount factors, $f1, f2, \ldots, fn$. Then the discount factor for the next period, $f(n + 1)$, is determined using the following relationship:

$$1 = c \times f1 + c \times f2 + \cdots + c \times fn + (1 + c) \times f(n + 1)$$

where the left-hand side, 1, represents the price of par, c is the semiannual coupon payment (one-half of the par rate) and $(1 + c)$ represents the final payment with principal and interest for a par bond maturing at the end of the $(n + 1)$th period. Each of the factors of the form $(c \times f1)$ represents the present value of a cash flow. The relationship simply says that the sum of the present values of all cash flows is equal to the price of the bond. The required discount factor, $f(n + 1)$, is therefore given by:

$$f(n+1) = \frac{\left[1 - \left(c \times f1 + c \times f2 + \cdots + c \times fn\right)\right]}{(1+c)}$$

Or,

$$f(n+1) = \frac{\left[1 - c \times \left(f1 + f2 + \cdots + fn\right)\right]}{(1+c)}$$

Thus, given the par curve, if we know the first discount factor, we can compute all other discount factors sequentially. The first discount factor is easy to determine because the six-month par rate is also a six-month zero rate, since a six-month (semiannual) bond has just one cash flow.

From the discount factors, it is easy to compute the zero rates. The nth zero rate, zn, is related to the nth discount factor, fn, via the relationship:

$$fn \times (1 + zn/2)^n = 1$$

assuming semiannual compounding. The interpolated par curve (column 3), the discount function (column 4), and the zero rates (column 6) are all shown in Exhibit 6-2.[14]

Once the discount function or the spot rate curve is known, the value of any security is simply the sum of the present values of its cash flows, discounted at the appropriate spot rate. This is shown in Exhibit 6-3 for a 10-year bond with a coupon of 10 percent. Each present value (column 5) is simply the product of the cash flow (column 4) and the corresponding discount factor (column 2). The total PV, 114.740102, is the value of the bond.

Determination of Risk Points

To determine the risk point corresponding to a given hedge, the following steps are taken: First, the yield on the hedge instrument is changed by one basis point. Then the spot rates are recomputed using this new price for the particular hedge instrument, keeping the prices (and yields) for all other hedges the same as before. The value of the asset (or liability or portfolio) is now recomputed. The change in the value of the asset due to the change in the yield of the hedge gives us the risk point of the asset relative to that hedge instrument. This procedure is repeated for all hedge instruments in the set of hedges chosen. The risk point relative to a hedge can be used to determine the amount of the hedge to be bought (or sold) to hedge it against changes in the price of that hedge.

---

[14] The reader can obtain useful insight into the concepts and procedures by actually working out a number of examples. To facilitate this, we have also shown the intermediate values of the cumulative discount factors for ease of computation. In addition, we have provided all the values to several decimal places so that the reader can verify the calculations.

Exhibit 6-3. Value of a 10%, 10-Year Bond

Maturity (years)	Discount factor	Zero rates	Cash flow	Present value
0.5	0.974602	5.212000	5.00	4.873009
1.0	0.944257	5.818712	5.00	4.721286
1.5	0.912552	6.194689	5.00	4.562759
2.0	0.878608	6.576629	5.00	4.393041
2.5	0.846701	6.768333	5.00	4.233503
3.0	0.814349	6.964043	5.00	4.071745
3.5	0.783565	7.091448	5.00	3.917823
4.0	0.752934	7.221785	5.00	3.764668
4.5	0.722504	7.354956	5.00	3.612519
5.0	0.692321	7.490986	5.00	3.461606
5.5	0.665550	7.541282	5.00	3.327749
6.0	0.639435	7.593429	5.00	3.197177
6.5	0.613973	7.647266	5.00	3.069864
7.0	0.589156	7.702698	5.00	2.945778
7.5	0.564977	7.759674	5.00	2.824887
8.0	0.541431	7.818175	5.00	2.707157
8.5	0.518511	7.878204	5.00	2.592553
9.0	0.496207	7.939786	5.00	2.481037
9.5	0.474514	8.002961	5.00	2.372570
10.0	0.453423	8.067783	105.00	47.609370
			Total PV	114.740102

To illustrate this procedure, let us increase the yield on the 10-year Treasury from 7.466 percent (from Exhibit 6-1) by one basis point to 7.476 percent. The composite rate changes from 7.876 percent to 7.886 percent. The new discount functions and zero rates are recomputed as in Exhibit 6-4 (compare with Exhibit 6-2[15]). The computation of the new value of the 10 percent bond under study is shown in Exhibit 6-5 (compare with Exhibit 6-3). The value of the bond has fallen from 114.740102 to 114.667571, that is, by 0.072531. This number is the change in dollars for every $100 par holding of

---

[15] Note that the change in the 10-year rate impacts the discount function and the zero rates only beyond year 5.

Exhibit 6-4. New Zero Curve After Incrementing 10-Year Yield

Maturity (years)	Par yields	Interpolated par yields	Discounted factor	Cumulative factor	Zero rates
0.5	5.212	5.212000	0.974602	0.974602	5.212000
1.0	5.810	5.810000	0.944257	1.918859	5.818712
1.5		6.177000	0.912552	2.831411	6.194689
2.0	6.544	6.544000	0.878608	3.710019	6.576629
2.5		6.728500	0.846701	4.556720	6.768333
3.0	6.913	6.913000	0.814349	5.371069	6.964043
3.5		7.033250	0.783565	6.154633	7.091448
4.0		7.153500	0.752934	6.907567	7.221785
4.5		7.273750	0.722504	7.630071	7.354956
5.0	7.394	7.394000	0.692321	8.322392	7.490986
5.5		7.443200	0.665506	8.987898	7.542511
6.0		7.492400	0.639344	9.627243	7.595897
6.5		7.541600	0.613830	10.241072	7.650990
7.0		7.590800	0.588957	10.830029	7.707698
7.5		7.640000	0.564721	11.394750	7.765973
8.0		7.689200	0.541114	11.935864	7.825799
8.5		7.738400	0.518130	12.453994	7.887182
9.0		7.787600	0.495762	12.949756	7.950151
9.5		7.836800	0.474003	13.423759	8.014749
10.0	7.886	7.886000	0.452845	13.876605	8.081033

the bond. This is the risk point for the 10 percent bond relative to the 10-year Treasury.

The risk point is usually computed for a given par holding of a security. In analytical situations where the par holding is hypothetical, it is convenient to express it as dollars per $10,000 par holding.[16] This makes the risk point number roughly comparable to duration or dollar duration. The risk points for this bond relative to all the other hedges are shown in Exhibit 6-6 (column 5) on this basis, i.e., for a $10,000 par holding. Also shown here are a few other

---

[16] Change in value for a 1-b.p. move on a $10,000 par holding is equal to 100 times the change in value for a 1-b.p. move on a $100 holding. The latter represents the PVBP or dollar duration.

Exhibit 6-5. Change in the Value of the 10%, 10-Year Bond

Maturity (years)	Discount factor	Zero rates	Cash flow	Present value
0.5	0.974602	5.212000	5.00	4.873009
1.0	0.944257	5.818712	5.00	4.721286
1.5	0.912552	6.194689	5.00	4.562759
2.0	0.878608	6.576629	5.00	4.393041
2.5	0.846701	6.768333	5.00	4.233503
3.0	0.814349	6.964043	5.00	4.071745
3.5	0.783565	7.091448	5.00	3.917823
4.0	0.752934	7.221785	5.00	3.764668
4.5	0.722504	7.354956	5.00	3.612519
5.0	0.692321	7.490986	5.00	3.461606
5.5	0.665506	7.542511	5.00	3.327532
6.0	0.639344	7.595897	5.00	3.196721
6.5	0.613830	7.650990	5.00	3.069148
7.0	0.588957	7.707698	5.00	2.944785
7.5	0.564721	7.765973	5.00	2.823603
8.0	0.541114	7.825799	5.00	2.705569
8.5	0.518130	7.887182	5.00	2.590650
9.0	0.495762	7.950151	5.00	2.478812
9.5	0.474003	8.014749	5.00	2.370017
10.0	0.452845	8.081033	105.00	47.548774
			New PV	114.667571
			Old PV	114.740102
			Change:	–0.072531

results that should be of interest to risk managers. Column 6 shows the fraction (as a percentage) of the total risk represented by any given sector. For example, approximately 95.4 percent of the risk in this bond is in the 10-year sector. Column 6 expresses the risk point as a percentage of the total value of the bond. The numbers in this column are similar to duration. These two columns, along with the risk points themselves, form a more complete picture of the risk in the 10 percent bond under consideration. Exhibit 6-7 shows a graphical depiction of the risk points. We call the collection of risk points the *risk profile* or the *risk point profile*.

Exhibit 6-6. Risk Points for the 10% Bond

Maturity (years)	Treasury yield	Spread (b.p.)	Total	Risk point	Percent of total risk	Percent of total PV
0.5	4.932	28	5.212	–0.002566	0.033757	–0.002236
1.0	5.520	29	5.810	–0.009118	0.119968	–0.007947
2.0	6.234	31	6.544	–0.021308	0.280349	–0.018571
3.0	6.563	35	6.913	–0.055563	0.731037	–0.048425
5.0	7.074	32	7.394	–0.258960	3.407101	–0.225693
10.0	7.466	41	7.876	–7.253094	95.427787	–6.321324
			Totals:	–7.600610	100.000000	–6.624196

Exhibit 6-7. Risk Point Profile of a Constant Maturity Swap Rate Note

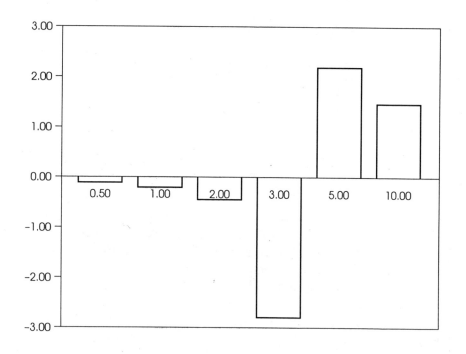

Exhibit 6-8. Risk Points with a Smaller Set of Hedges

Maturity (years)	Treasury yield	Spread (b.p.)	Total	Risk point	Percent of RP	Percent of PV
0.5	4.932	28	5.212	–0.002584	0.033865	–0.002251
1.0	5.520	29	5.810	–0.009182	0.120353	–0.007999
2.0	6.234	31	6.544	–0.021457	0.281247	–0.018692
3.0	6.563	35	6.913	–0.242119	3.173593	–0.210917
5.0						
10.0	7.466	41	7.876	–7.353835	96.390943	–6.406137
			Totals:	–7.629176	100.000000	–6.645995

Properties of Risk Points

Exhibit 6-6 also shows the sum of all the risk points, called the *total risk*.[17] This number, 7.600610, is similar[18] to the PVBP for the bond as it represents the change in the value of the bond due to a parallel move up of the yield curve by one basis point. If this is expressed as a percentage of total value of the bond (Exhibit 6-6, column 7, last row), then we get a number similar to the duration of the bond.

At first blush, it seems as though total risk will increase or decrease based upon the selection of hedge instruments. However, the risk point method is quite robust, and under most conditions handles arbitrary selection of hedge instruments well. For example, let us delete the 5-year Treasury from the hedge instrument list, and recompute the par curve, the zero curve, and the risk points. Exhibit 6-8 shows the new risk points and total risk. Note how the risk in the 7-year sector has been redistributed between the 3-year and the 10-year sectors.

---

[17] Note, however, since some risk points can be negative and some positive, the magnitude of total risk does not always indicate the risk level of an instrument. See, for example, the discussion of the CMS note later in the chapter.

[18] Similar, but not exactly equal, since the PVBP computation starts with a flat yield curve.

The risk points have another interesting property. Consider again the 10 percent coupon, 10-year bond above. The collection of risk points actually represents a portfolio of hedging Treasuries, called the *hedge portfolio*. This portfolio has the property that its risk is the same as that of the bond. When a portfolio is designed so as to match the risk of another, then the former is called an *immunizing* or *duration-matching* portfolio. In addition, the cash flow from this portfolio is close to that of the cash flow from the bond. When a portfolio is designed so that its cash flows match that of another, the former is called a *dedicated* portfolio. The hedge portfolio is always immunizing or duration matching. The larger the number of hedge instruments, the closer the hedge portfolio comes to a fully dedicated portfolio.

There is one difference between the dedicated portfolio in this context and the one used in structured investments. In the latter, only positive holdings are considered, whereas in our hedging portfolio, negative holdings, i.e., short positions, are quite common.

Finally, risk points are additive, in two ways. The risk point in any sector for a portfolio can be computed easily by simply adding the risk points in that sector of all bonds in the portfolio. In addition, we can quickly compute the risk point for a broader sector by adding the risk points for all the smaller sectors within.

Exhibits 6-9 and 6-10 show[19] the risk points for various common fixed-income investments.

It is interesting to look at the risk profile for an exotic structure.[20] In Exhibit 6-11, we show the profile for a 3-year note that pays coupons equal to the 5-year swap rate less a fixed spread. Such a note is called a CMS note or constant maturity swap rate note. The coupon on the note is reset semiannually. Simple duration analysis will treat the note essentially as a floating-rate instrument, implying

---

[19] The data in Exhibit 6-10 for mortgage-backed securities were computed by Thomas Ho of Global Advanced Technology Corporation, New York.

[20] The risk point analysis of exotic securities is covered in detail in Ravi E. Dattatreya and Scott Peng, *Structured Notes* (Chicago: Probus Publishing, 1994).

Exhibit 6-9. Risk Points Profile of Some Common Investments

Maturity (years)	10-year par bond	10-year 3% bond	10-year 15% bond	10-year 0% bond	14.50% annuity	5-year par bond	3-year par bond	3, 10 barbell
0.5	0.000000	0.005890	−0.008606	0.009514	−0.017515	0.000000	0.000000	0.000000
1	0.000000	0.020933	−0.030583	0.033812	−0.062249	0.000000	0.000000	0.000000
2	0.000000	0.048917	−0.071469	0.079013	−0.145466	0.000000	0.000000	0.000000
3	0.000000	0.127555	−0.186362	0.206034	−0.379316	0.000000	−2.685351	−1.753771
5	0.000000	0.594487	−0.868566	0.960251	−1.767856	−4.160751	0.000000	0.000000
10	−6.938302	−6.215646	−7.994128	−5.771025	−2.148999	0.000000	0.000000	−2.406980
Totals:	−6.938302	−5.417864	−9.159714	−4.482402	−4.521401	−4.160751	−2.685351	−4.160751

Chapter 6

Exhibit 6-10. Risk Points for Mortgage-Backed Securities

Maturity (years)	Sequential PO	Sequential IO	PAC bond	Companion bond	Z-PAC bond
1	2.712990	−1.067860	−0.087954	−0.227987	0.084370
2	0.105150	−0.751634	−0.312604	−0.462619	0.176150
3	−0.881439	0.727920	−1.991636	−0.900864	0.408440
5	−0.791930	−0.190383	−8.828908	−0.149317	1.440020
10	−8.551698	6.211113	−10.083130	0.164040	−17.569742
Totals:	−8.137903	5.143436	−26.806461	−1.725013	−14.650842

Exhibit 6-11. Risk Points for a CMS Note

Maturity (years)	Treasury yield	Spread (b.p.)	Total	Risk point
0.5	4.932	28	5.212	−0.058520
1.0	5.520	29	5.810	−0.208950
2.0	6.234	31	6.544	−0.484468
3.0	6.563	35	6.913	−2.831432
5.0	7.074	32	7.394	2.280450
10.0	7.466	41	7.876	1.512276
			Total:	0.209356

a small duration or risk. The risk point profile (Exhibit 6-11, column 5), however, reveals that the CMS note has negative and positive risks. In fact, the note is bullish on rates up to three years and bearish on rates beyond that. In particular, the note has risk in the 5- and 10-year maturities even though it only has a 3-year maturity.

APPLICATIONS OF THE RISK POINT METHOD

The risk point method, being a more complete and comprehensive measure of interest-rate risk, can be used wherever other simple measures such as duration are currently being used. We provide here a brief review.

Hedging

This is the most common use of duration, and therefore, of risk points. Common duration analysis not only gives us just a crude approximation for the hedge, but it also fails to provide critical information as to which hedge instruments are optimal to use. On the other hand, the risk point method correctly identifies the major risks in a portfolio and directly generates the portfolio of hedge instruments best suited for the hedging task. Since the starting point for the risk point method is the selection of hedge instruments, we have full control over which hedge instruments will be considered for hedging from the outset.

The par amount of any hedge instrument required to hedge a portfolio can be determined by dividing the risk point of the portfolio by the PVBP[21] of the hedge instrument. For example, consider the 10 percent coupon bond again. For every $100 of the bond, we need $104.5370 (7.253094/6.938302) of the 10-year Treasury as a component of the hedge.

Indexing

As a structured portfolio methodology, indexing is quite common. Indexing requires one to manage a portfolio in such a way that the returns from the portfolio track that from a given bond index, e.g., various Lehman Brothers indexes or the Merrill Lynch Government Bond Index. A common technique is to purchase, as far as possible, the same bonds as in the index in the same proportions. The effectiveness of this technique is limited because indexes almost always have too many bonds in them and most of these are not available at fair prices in the quantities required. An alternative is to manage the portfolio duration to match the published duration of the index as

---

[21] Note that the PVBP of a hedge is equal to its risk point relative to itself. For example, from Exhibit 6-9, the PVBP of the 10-year Treasury is $6.938302. Note that this PVBP is slightly different from the traditional definition. One reason is that the latter starts out with a flat yield curve rather than the actual yield curve.

closely as possible. This technique allows the manager to pick bonds that are relatively cheap for the portfolio.

For example, suppose a portfolio manager is running an indexed fund tied to an index with a duration of five years. Given the bearish mood of the market, the manager decides to keep the duration of the fund short, at 4.5 years. Rates do climb. However, the manager finds that the fund has barely kept up with the index and has not out-performed the index as expected. Further analysis reveals that the yield curve has steepened as the rates rose. The fund holds a relatively large amount of 10-year bonds, which have suffered a loss. Thus duration matching in normal situations, and using a shorter duration in a bearish market, provides no guarantee that expected results will be obtained. The reason is that duration is an oversimplification.[22]

A superior way to index is to first determine[23] the full risk point profile of the index and then manage the fund against this profile as a guide. Then the manager will know what types of yield curve bets are implied in the fund's portfolio.

Immunization and Dedication

Another popular application of duration is in immunization. If we are managing a portfolio in order to meet a specific liability in the future, immunization calls for balancing the portfolio so that the duration of the portfolio equals the duration of the liability. This procedure is based on a parallel shift assumption for yield curve moves. Therefore, it is subject to the same types of surprises suffered by the index fund manager above.

---

[22] In this context, we can compare duration to the mean of a distribution. A normal distribution with small variance can be represented satisfactorily by its mean. This is an ideal situation. If the variance is large, or if the distribution is skewed, then we need more parameters to describe or represent the situation. The farther the distribution from the ideal, the less meaningful the mean. Similar is the case with duration.

[23] In the absence of published information on the risk points for an index, the profile can be estimated by looking at a simplified portfolio representative of the index.

A more robust approach is to determine the risk point profile of the liability and match this to the risk profile of the portfolio. In this sense, immunization is not much different from index fund management.

In dedicated portfolios, a common strategy is to cash-match in the early years and use immunization in later years. Again, this strategy can be made more robust by using risk point matching rather than just duration matching in the back years.

Benchmarking

In many industrial corporations, the performance of the liability portfolio is measured against a benchmark portfolio. In many ways, this procedure resembles indexing. Again we recommend use of the risk point profile for managing the liabilities. Perhaps the creation of the benchmark portfolio itself can benefit from this method.

Scenario Analysis

One use of duration is in scenario analysis. Under parallel shift assumptions, we can quickly determine the change in the value of a portfolio from its duration. This use of duration is limited to parallel shifts, and it fails to reveal risks due to reshaping shifts of the yield curve. Using the risk point profile of the portfolio, it is easy to carry out scenario analysis including yield curve twists and other reshaping shifts. For example, in the case of the 10 percent coupon bond above (Exhibit 6-6), if the 10-year rate moves up by 10 b.p., and the 5-year rates move up by 5 b.p., and the other rates are unchanged, then the change in the value of a $10,000 holding can be estimated to be $73.825740 (10 × $7.253094 + 5 × $0.258960).

Bond Swap Transactions

A common bond swap transaction is to swap a bond (a bullet) for a pair of bonds (the barbell) in such a way that the duration of the barbell is equal to that of the bullet. Even though it is difficult to match the risk point profiles of the bullet and the barbell, the profiles provide accurate clues as to where the risks and bets in the transaction might be.

EXTENSIONS

The application of the risk point method is not limited to securities with simple, known and fixed cash flows. It is in fact a general approach and can be used to hedge virtually all instruments. As long as a security can be valued relative to a set of hedge instruments, the method is applicable. For example, suppose that we are considering an option on a 10-year, zero-coupon bond. Then, we can easily determine the risk point for the option by first determining the change in the price of the zero relative to the current 10-year Treasury. Secondly, we determine the corresponding change in the price of the option due the change in the zero price. This directly gives us the risk point of the option relative to the current 10-year Treasury.[24]

The concept can also be extended to include risks other than interest-rate risk. For example, suppose that we would like to hedge the option on the 10-year, zero-coupon bond against changes in volatility. We would choose a hedge instrument that responds to volatility, such as an option on the current 10-year Treasury. To determine the risk point, called the *volatility risk point,* which can be defined in various ways, we compute the change in the value of the hedge as well as the option on the zero per unit change in the volatility. The ratio of the two represents the risk point of the option relative to the hedge with respect to volatility. This number is the number of units of the hedge instrument required to hedge the option on the zero to protect against changes in volatility.

In addition to volatility risk, we can similarly define risk points for stock market risk, exchange rate risk, commodity price risk,

---

[24] The risk point for the option relative to the 10-year Treasury is the product of (1) the risk point of the option relative to the zero and (2) the risk point of the zero relative to the 10-year. Mathematically, we can restate this relationship as follows: $d(\text{option})/d(\text{10-year UST}) = [d(\text{option})/d(\text{zero})] \times [d(\text{zero})/d(\text{10-year UST})]$.

Exhibit 6-12. Convexity Points—I

Maturity (years)	Treasury yield	Spread (b.p.)	Total	Risk point	Convexity points
0.5	4.932	28	5.212	–0.002566	0.000011
1.0	5.520	29	5.810	–0.009118	0.000043
2.0	6.234	31	6.544	–0.021308	0.000118
3.0	6.563	35	6.913	–0.055563	0.000405
5.0	7.074	32	7.394	–0.258960	0.003621
10.0	7.466	41	7.876	–7.253094	0.137062
			Totals:	–7.600610	0.141261

credit risk, etc. The two key factors in such extensions are the availability of appropriate hedge instruments and a valuation model.

Convexity

We can also extend the idea of duration-like risk point to convexity. Convexity basically measures the nonlinear relationship between the cause (change in the reference rate) and the effect (value or price of a security). One way to measure the nonlinearity is to look at the difference between a linear estimate and the actual value. In Exhibit 6-12, we show the difference between the change in the value of the 10 percent bond for a 10-basis-point change in the yield of a hedge (column 6) and 10 times the change in value for a 1-basis-point change in yield (i.e., the risk point, column 5). The result, column 7, can be called the *convexity points.*

There is another way to determine convexity, as in Exhibit 6-13. We can move the entire yield curve[25] by a small amount (10 basis points), and recompute the risk points. The difference between the risk points computed before (column 5) and after (column 6) the parallel shift represents a type of convexity points.[26]

---

[25] There are a number of degrees of freedom in selecting the type and magnitude of the yield curve shift. The actual shift chosen is influenced by specifics of any particular situation.

[26] This set of convexity points is considered more useful in certain circumstances.

Exhibit 6-13. Convexity Points—II

Maturity (years)	Treasury yield	Spread (b.p.)	Total	Risk point before	Risk point after	Change or convexity
0.5	5.032	28	5.312	–0.002566	–0.002420	0.000145
1.0	5.620	29	5.910	–0.009118	–0.008604	0.000514
2.0	6.334	31	6.644	–0.021308	–0.020116	0.001192
3.0	6.663	35	7.013	–0.055563	–0.052492	0.003072
5.0	7.174	32	7.494	–0.258960	–0.245042	0.013919
10.0	7.566	41	7.976	–7.253094	–7.205489	0.047605
			Totals:	–7.600610	–7.534163	0.066447

It is difficult to pinpoint exactly how the convexity points ought to be used, as convexity itself is a second-order effect. Nonetheless, we recommend their use, even for just monitoring purposes, by the risk manager. This is especially so when exotic securities are involved.

CONCLUSION AND SUMMARY

In this chapter, we have presented the risk point concept as a more complete measure of interest-rate risk than other commonly used measures such as duration. The concept adds value in almost all situations where duration is used, including hedging, immunization, dedication, indexation, bond swapping, and scenario analysis. The risk point concept is especially valuable in the management of portfolios including options and most of the complex modern financial instruments. We recommend that the risk point method be used as an integral part of a comprehensive risk management program.

In risk management, as in most important situations, our policy is to reject the black box approach. By providing more insight into the nature of risk, the risk point method takes us one step away from the black box, one step closer to our ideal.

Chapter 7

Options and Their Parametric Characteristics

Even though exchange-traded options on debt securities have come into existence only since 1984, option-like features have been common in fixed-income markets for decades. Most of the longer corporate bonds have a call feature in them, providing the issuer the option, i.e., the right but not the obligation, to redeem the bonds before maturity according to the schedule in the indenture. The area of mortgage-backed securities is pervaded by the effect of the option held by the homeowner to prepay the mortgage at any time. Many new securities are being created by varying the option-like features of older ones. Because of such pervasiveness, the valuation of options is considered to be of paramount importance in fixed-income analysis.

In addition to the valuation of securities with option-like characteristics, an understanding of options and how they are valued is important in the measurement of the interest-rate risk of these securities. The increased complexity that the option features add to the proper determination of risk exposure means that for securities with such features, traditional approaches, such as duration analysis, are of little practical use without further enhancement by the application of option models.

The purpose of this chapter is to describe the investment characteristics of options on fixed-income instruments, referred to as interest-rate options. Parameters such as duration and convexity can also be defined for interest-rate options. The characteristics of options that we present in this chapter will be applied in the next two chapters to extend our total return framework to callable bonds and mortgage-backed securities. In Chapter 10, we describe how to use options in active total return management.

WHAT IS AN OPTION?

An option is an agreement in which the seller of the option grants the buyer of the option the right to purchase from or sell to the writer a designated instrument at a specified price within a specified period of time. The writer, also referred to as the seller,[1] grants this right to the buyer in exchange for a certain sum of money called the *option price* or *option premium*. The price at which the underlying instrument may be bought or sold is called the *exercise* or *strike price*. The date after which an option is void is called the *expiration date*. An *American option* may be exercised any time up to and including the expiration date. A *European option* may only be exercised on the expiration date.

An option can be classified as either a call option or a put option, depending on whether the buyer of the option has the right to buy or the right to sell the underlying instrument to the writer of the option. When an option grants the buyer the right to purchase the underlying instrument from the writer, it is called a *call option*. When the option buyer has the right to sell the underlying instrument to the writer (seller), the option is called a *put option*.

RISK AND RETURN FOR OPTIONS

At the expiration date, the profit or loss on an option position depends on the price of the underlying instrument. Since our focus is on options in which the underlying instrument is a fixed-income security, the profit or loss will depend on the market interest rate at the expiration date. Exhibit 7-1 summarizes the risk and return profile at

---

[1] We use the words *writing* and *selling* interchangeably. However, the former is preferred since an option writer is creating the option rather than just selling what he already has.

Exhibit 7-1. Profit/Loss at Expiration on Four Simple Option Positions

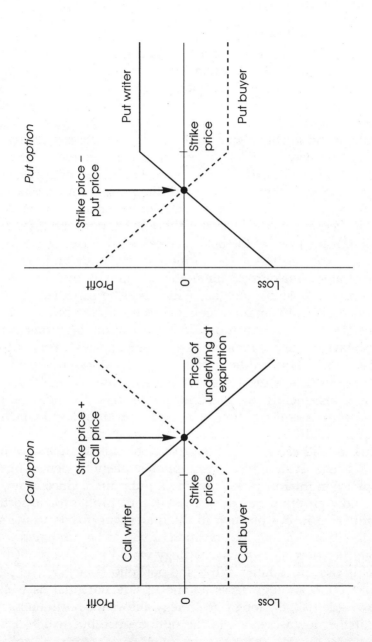

the expiration date for the following four simple option strategies: (1) buy a call option, (2) sell (write) a call option, (3) buy a put option, and (4) sell (write) a put option. These strategies are referred to as simple strategies because no position is taken in another option or bond.

The most straightforward option strategy for participating in the market is to buy a call option. Exhibit 7-2 compares the long call strategy and the long bond strategy. This comparison clearly demonstrates the way in which an option can change the risk-return profile available to portfolio managers. For a portfolio manager who takes a long position in the bond, the portfolio realizes a profit[2] of $1 for every $1 increase in the price of the bond as the market yield falls. However, as the market yield rises the portfolio loses dollar for dollar. If the price of the bond decreases significantly, the long bond strategy can result in a loss of more than the option price. The long call strategy, in contrast, limits the loss to only the option price but retains the upside potential, which will be less than for the long bond position by an amount equal to the option price.

The risk and return profile of the call option writer is the mirror image of the call option buyer, as in Exhibit 7-1. That is, the profit (loss) of the short call position for any given price of the bond at the expiration date is the same as the loss (profit) of the long call position. Consequently, the maximum profit that the short call strategy can produce is the option price; the maximum loss is only limited by how high the price of the bond can increase (i.e., how low the market yield can fall) by the expiration date, less the option price.

The most straightforward option strategy for benefiting from an increase in interest rates is to buy a put option. Once again, we can see how an option alters the risk-return profile for a portfolio by comparing it to a position in the underlying fixed-income security. In the case of a long put position, it would be compared to a short bond position, since such a strategy would realize a profit if market yields rise (price falls). While the portfolio manager who pursues a short bond strategy faces all the upside potential as well as the downside risk, the long put strategy allows the portfolio manager to limit the downside risk to the option price but will still maintain

---

[2] Here we ignore the time value of money for simplicity.

Exhibit 7-2. Comparison of a Long Call and Long Position in the Underlying Bond at Option Expiration Date

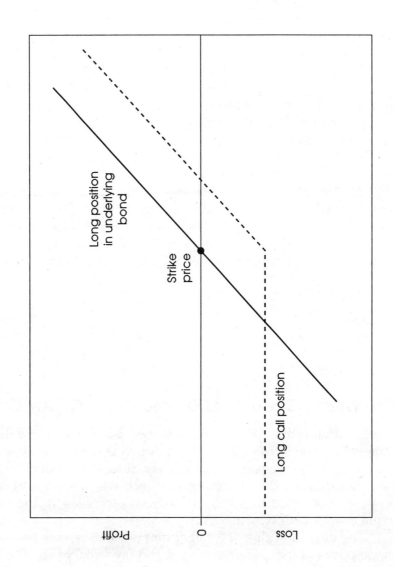

upside potential. However, the upside potential is less than for a short put position by an amount equal to the option price. This is demonstrated in Exhibit 7-3.

The short put strategy is employed if the portfolio manager expects interest rates to fall or stay flat so that the price of the underlying fixed-income security will increase or stay the same. The risk and return profile for a short put option is the mirror image of the long put option. The maximum profit from this strategy is the option price. The maximum loss is only limited by how high the price of the bond can rise by the expiration date less the option price received for writing the option.

To summarize, long calls and short puts allow the portfolio manager to gain if fixed-income security prices rise (interest rates fall). Short calls and long puts allow the portfolio manager to gain if bond prices fall (interest rates rise). A portfolio manager would want to use each strategy under the following circumstances:

Circumstance	*Strategy*
very bullish	buy call
slightly bullish	write put
slightly bearish	write call
very bearish	buy put

THE INTRINSIC VALUE AND TIME VALUE OF AN OPTION

We can divide the option price into two parts: intrinsic value and time value. The *intrinsic value* of an option is the economic value of the option if it is exercised immediately. Since the buyer of an option need not exercise the option, and, in fact, will not do so if there is no economic value that will result from exercising it, the intrinsic value cannot be less than zero.

The intrinsic value of a call option is the difference between the market price of the underlying bond and the strike price. When a call option has intrinsic value, it is said to be "in the money." When the strike price of a call option exceeds the price of the underlying bond, the call option is said to be "out of the money" and has no intrinsic value. An option for which the strike price is equal to the underlying bond price is said to be "at the money" and has no intrinsic value.

Exhibit 7-3. Comparison of Long Put and a Short Position in the Underlying Bond at Option Expiration Date

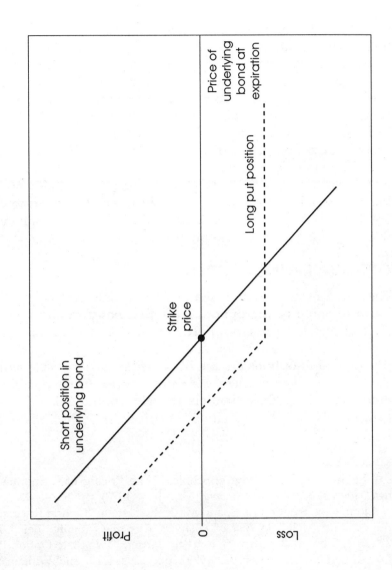

For a put option, the intrinsic value is equal to the amount by which the strike price exceeds the price of the underlying bond. A put option is out of the money when the price of the underlying bond is higher than the strike price. A put option is at the money when the strike price is equal to the price of the underlying bond.

The time value of an option is the amount by which the option price exceeds the intrinsic value. The option buyer hopes that at some time prior to expiration, changes in the market yield will increase the value of the rights conveyed by the option. For this prospect, the option buyer is willing to pay a premium above the intrinsic value. For example, if the price of a call option on a bond with a strike price of $100 is $7 when the price of the bond is $103, the time value of this option is $4 ($7 minus the intrinsic value of $3). If the bond price is $90 instead of $103, then the time value of this option is $7, since the option has no intrinsic value.

OPTION-PRICING MODELS

The value of an option at the expiration date will be equal to the intrinsic value of the option. To implement portfolio and trading strategies, it is necessary to estimate the price of an option at any time prior to the expiration date. The two most popular models for pricing equity options are the *Black-Scholes option pricing model*[3] and the *binomial option pricing model based on price distribution*.[4] The limitations of using these models to value options on fixed-income instruments have been well documented.[5]

---

[3] Fischer Black and Myron Scholes, "The Pricing of Corporate Liabilities," *Journal of Political Economy* (May–June 1973), pp. 637–659.

[4] John Cox, Stephen Ross, and Mark Rubinstein, "Option Pricing: A Simplified Approach," *Journal of Financial Economics* (September 1979), pp. 229–263; Richard Rendleman and Brit Bartter, "Two-State Option Pricing," *Journal of Finance* (December 1979), pp. 1093–1110; and William Sharpe, *Investments* (Englewood Cliffs, NJ): Prentice Hall, 1981), Chapter 16.

[5] See, for example, Lawrence J. Dyer and David P. Jacob, "Guide to Fixed Option Pricing Models," in Frank J. Fabozzi, ed., *The Handbook of Fixed Income Options* (Chicago: Probus Publishing, 1989), pp. 81–82.

An alternative approach is to develop a binomial option-pricing model based on yield distribution. While this is a superior approach to the binomial option-pricing model based on price distribution, it still has a theoretical drawback. All option-pricing models to be theoretically valid must satisfy the internal and external conditions described in Chapter 5. The problem with the binomial model based on yield distribution is that it does not satisfy these conditions. It violates the relationship in that it fails to take into consideration the yield curve and does not calibrate to the market, thereby allowing arbitrage opportunities.

There are more elaborate models that can be used to construct an interest-rate tree that takes the yield curve into consideration and as a result does not permit arbitrage opportunities. These models are referred to as *yield curve option-pricing models* or *arbitrage-free option-pricing models*. The first such model was developed by Ho and Lee in 1986.[6] The basic Ho-Lee model has been extended by other researchers and market practitioners. These include the Black-Derman-Toy model,[7] the Heath-Jarrow-Morton model,[8] the Hull-White model,[9] the Jamshidian model,[10] and the Dattatreya-Fabozzi model.[11]

---

[6] Thomas S. Y. Ho and S. B. Lee, "Term Structure Movements and Pricing Interest Rate Contingent Claims," *Journal of Finance* (December 1986), pp. 1011–1129.

[7] Fischer Black, Emanuel Derman, and William Toy, "A One-Factor Model of Interest Rates and Its Application to Treasury Bond Options," *Financial Analysts Journal* (January–February 1990), pp. 24–32.

[8] D. Heath, R. Jarrow, and A. Morton, "Bond Pricing and the Term Structure of Interest Rates: A New Methodology," Working paper, Cornell University, October 1987.

[9] John Hull and Alan White, "Pricing Interest-Rate Derivative Securities," *Review of Financial Studies* 3 (1990), pp. 573–592.

[10] Farshid Jamshidian, "An Exact Bond Option Pricing Formula," *Journal of Finance* (March 1989), pp. 21–25.

[11] Ravi Dattatreya and Frank J. Fabozzi, "A Simplified Model for Valuing Debt Options," *Journal of Portfolio Management* (Spring 1989), pp. 64–73.

INPUTS INTO OPTION-PRICING MODELS

All option-pricing models use the following five variables as input to determine the theoretical or *fair* option price: (1) current price of the underlying instrument; (2) strike price; (3) time to expiration; (4) coupon rate; and (5) volatility of the underlying instrument over the life of the option. Of these five variables, the only one not known is volatility. In addition, as just noted, it is necessary to model the yield curve and incorporate it into the option-pricing model.

Exhibit 7-4 shows the theoretical price for a call option on a futures contract as a function of the price of the underlying. Since the more active interest-rate options are for options on bond futures (called *futures options*) we have used this option in our illustration.[12] The call option shown in Exhibit 7-4 has one year to maturity and a strike price of 90. The theoretical price is based on an assumed volatility of 10 percent.

The line from the origin to the strike price on the horizontal axis is the intrinsic value of the call option when the price of the underlying futures contract is less than the strike price of 90, since the intrinsic value is zero. The 45-degree line extending from the horizontal axis is the intrinsic value of the call option once the price of the Treasury bond futures contract exceeds the strike price of 90. The reason for this is that the intrinsic value of the call option will increase by $1 each time the price of the underlying instrument increases by $1. Thus, the slope of the line representing the intrinsic value after the strike price of 90 is reached is 1. The theoretical call option price is shown by the curved line. The difference between the theoretical call option price and the intrinsic value at any given price for the underlying instrument is the time value of the option.

Exhibit 7-5 compares the theoretical call option price for different terms to expiration, holding all other factors constant. As can be seen from the exhibit, the shorter the term of the option, the lower its price. The implication of this investment characteristic is that all other factors constant, the option price declines as it approaches the expiration date. Since we have assumed that the price of the under-

---

[12] Options on futures are discussed in Chapter 10.

Exhibit 7-4. Theoretical Value of a Call Option as a Function of Underlying Security Price

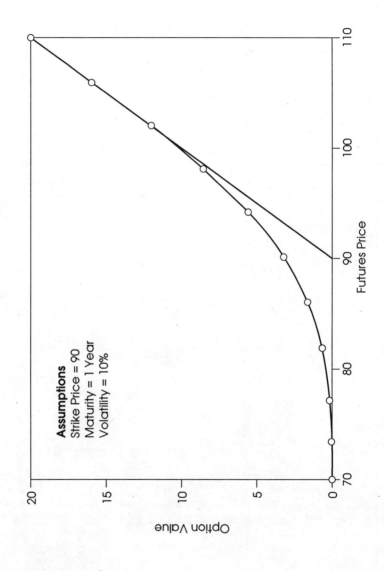

Assumptions
Strike Price = 90
Maturity = 1 Year
Volatility = 10%

Option Value

Futures Price

Exhibit 7-5. Theoretical Value of a Call Option as a Function of Term to Expiration

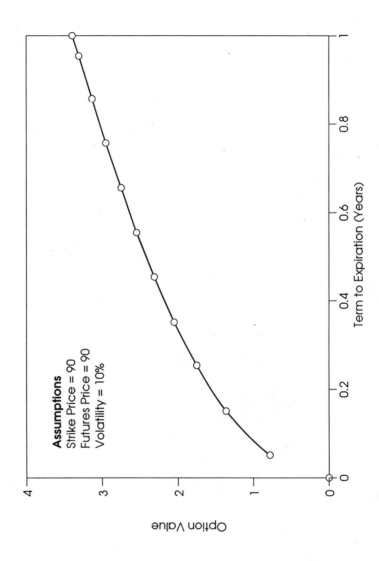

lying futures is unchanged, the intrinsic value of the option is unchanged as the option approaches the expiration date. This means that the component of the option price that is declining is the time value. This decline in the time value of the option, commonly referred to as *time decay*, works to the advantage of the option writer and to the disadvantage of the option buyer. The rate of time decay varies from option to option. Given an option pricing model, the rate of time decay can be measured.[13]

Exhibit 7-6 compares the theoretical call option price as a function of volatility, holding all other factors constant. The higher the assumed volatility, the higher the option price. For options that are deeply out of the money, the option is not significantly affected by the volatility assumption.

Implied Volatility

An option model, in effect, maps or relates a *given* volatility to a unique option value.[14] Similarly, if the option price is known, we can use the same model to determine the corresponding volatility. This is known as *implied volatility,* and it has numerous applications in strategies employing options. The simplest application would be to compare an estimate of volatility (either computed using historical volatility or through an alternative technique) with the implied volatility. If we are confident about our estimate of volatility, and it is greater than the implied volatility, then the option is underpriced; otherwise, it is overpriced.

The more important role of implied volatility is for performing relative value analysis of different options on the same underlying security. For example, suppose the price of an 82 put option (i.e., strike price is 82) is $2.75 with an implied volatility of 0.145. The cor-

---

[13] Mathematically, the rate of time decay is the first derivative of the option price with respect to time. This measure is popularly referred to as the *theta* of an option.

[14] In this context, we can compare option theory to duration theory where the price change can be estimated *given* the yield change, but the question of what the actual yield change will be is left unanswered.

Exhibit 7-6. Theoretical Value of a Call Option as a Function of Volatility

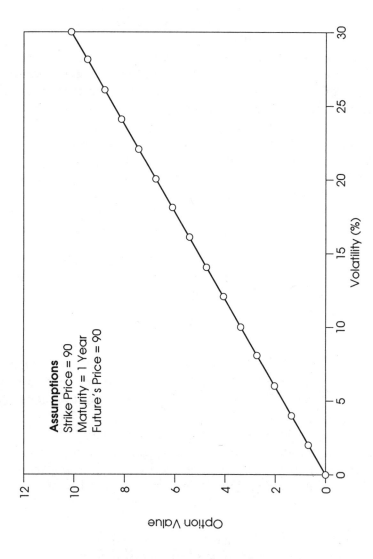

Assumptions
Strike Price = 90
Maturity = 1 Year
Future's Price = 90

responding values for the 84 call option are \$0.95 and 0.183, respectively. It is difficult to assess how the options are relatively priced by simply examining the prices of the options because the strike prices are different and one is a put and the other is a call. The prices, therefore, are not directly comparable. The implied volatilities, in contrast, are, and indicate in this example that the put is cheaper, relatively speaking, than the call. The option with the lower implied volatility is cheaper.

Implied volatility is not only a common yardstick to measure and compare different options, it also democratizes different option models. In a relative value analysis, the difference between the various models is less significant than in absolute pricing of options. Given that the valuation of options is so much dependent on the volatility estimates, the implied volatility approach is the saving grace of option theory.

PUT-CALL PARITY AND EQUIVALENT POSITIONS

A well-known and strong relationship, known as *put-call parity*, exists between the price of put and call options with the same expiration date and strike price and written on the same underlying security. For example, the sale of a call option and the purchase of a put on a nondividend-paying stock would be equivalent to a *synthetic forward sale* of the stock. Thus, this position, combined with a share of the stock would have a total value equal to the present (discounted) value of the strike price. That is,

Put price + Price of underlying security – Call price
= Present value of strike price

However, the above parity relationship between the put and the call option holds only for European options. For American options, in general, the parity relationship does not hold.

For options on bond futures, the parity relationship is slightly different and can be restated as:

Put price – Call price = Present value of futures price
– Present value of strike price

The put-call parity relationship should hold for any option pricing model.

Equivalent Positions

The put-call parity can be used to identify positions that provide similar (but not necessarily identical) payoffs.[15] For example, ignoring the time value of money, the put-call parity suggests the following equivalent positions:

long the security   + short call = short put

short the security + short put = short call

long the security   + long put   = long call

short the security + long call   = long put

long call   + short put = long the security

long put   + short call = short the security

The first and second equivalent positions are commonly referred to as a *conversion* and *reversal*, respectively.

For traders, the put-call parity and the equivalent positions can be used to design portfolios to take advantage of any mispricing. For portfolio managers, these relationships are helpful in understanding the performance characteristics of a portfolio or a security with an embedded option. For example, in the next two chapters we will show how to combine the properties of option-free bonds and options to assess the relative value of bonds with embedded options. For example, a popular strategy employing options is a covered call strategy. This involves selling a call option on a security held in a portfolio. The portfolio manager employing a covered call strategy is then long the security and short a call, which from the first equivalent position above is the same as a short put position. Thus the risk and return profile will be similar to a short put position. As another example, consider the position of the owner of a callable

---

[15] The payoffs may not be identical if American-type options are involved.

bond. As explained in more detail in the next chapter, this position is equivalent to a long position in a noncallable bond and a short position in a call option on that noncallable bond. Once again, the first relationship (the conversion) shows that this is equivalent to a short put position. Thus, the risk-return profile of the owner of a callable bond will be similar to that of a short put position—limited upside potential when interest rates decline but relatively much larger downside potential.

PARAMETERS OF OPTIONS

In earlier chapters of this book we focused on the duration and convexity of option-free bonds and their role as a summary measure of interest-rate risk exposure. To extend these parameters to securities with embedded options and portfolios with options, comparable measures of duration and convexity for options must be defined. An option-pricing model is required to obtain these measures.

The Delta and Duration of an Option

In addition to its role in option pricing, the hedge ratio, or as it is more popularly known, *delta*, plays an important role in assessing the performance of bonds with embedded options and portfolio strategies employing options. The delta of an option represents the dollar change in the value of the option in response to a dollar change in the price of the underlying instrument. For example, if the delta of an option is 0.40, this means that if the price of the underlying instrument increases by $1, the price of the option will increase by $0.40.[16]

Since the price of a call option increases as the price of the underlying instrument increases, the delta of a call option is positive and will range between 0 (for deep out-of-the-money call options) and 1 (for deep in-the-money call options). The delta for a put option is negative, since the price of a put option decreases as the price of the underlying instrument increases.

---

[16] Mathematically, delta is the first derivative of the option price with respect to a change in price of the underlying instrument.

The meaning of delta can be seen from Exhibit 7-7, which is the same as Exhibit 7-4 but includes a tangent line. The slope of the tangent line to the theoretical call option price at a given price for the underlying futures shows how the theoretical price will change for small changes in the price of the underlying instrument. Thus, the slope of the tangent line is the delta. The steeper the slope of the tangent line, the greater the delta. When an option is deep out-of-the-money, the slope of the line is relatively flat. This means a delta close to 0. For a call option that is deep in-the-money, the delta will be close to 1. That is, the call option price will increase almost dollar for dollar with an increase in the price of the underlying instrument. In terms of Exhibit 7-4, the slope of the tangent line approaches the slope of the intrinsic value line after the strike price. The slope of that line is 1. This agrees with what we stated earlier: the delta for a call option ranges from 0 (for deep out-of-the-money options) to 1 (for deep in-the-money call options). The delta for an at-the-money option is approximately 0.5. This also can be seen in Exhibit 7-8, which shows the delta for the call option for a range of futures prices. Exhibit 7-8 also shows the delta for a put option on the same futures contract.

In addition to the price of the underlying instrument, the other five variables that determine the price of an option also influence its delta. Exhibit 7-9 shows how the delta of call options struck at different exercise prices changes as the expiration day comes closer assuming the futures price and volatility are unchanged. The delta of an option that is in-the-money starts at a value below 1, and slowly increases to 1 as the option nears expiration. For an option that is out-of-the-money, the delta is less than 1 and slowly decreases to 0.

The effect of volatility on the delta is shown in Exhibit 7-10. For options that are in the money, delta slowly decreases as the volatility increases, and for options that are out-of-the-money, it slowly increases. For options that are very deeply in- or out-of-the-money, the effect of volatility on the delta is insignificant.

Thus far we have looked at the relationship between the effect of a change in the price of the underlying instrument on the price of the option. But the price of a futures contract in which the underlying for the futures contract is a bond will depend on the interest

Exhibit 7-7. Theoretical Value of a Call Option as a Function of Underlying Security Price (with Tangent Line)

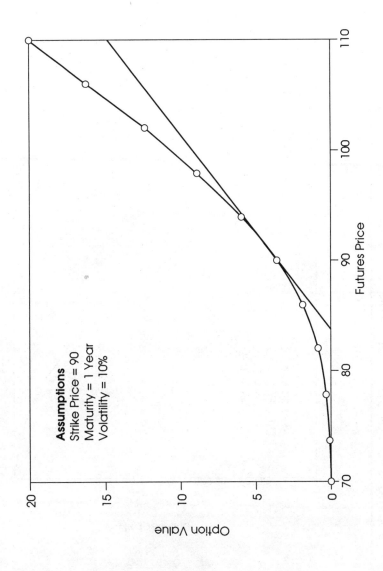

Assumptions
Strike Price = 90
Maturity = 1 Year
Volatility = 10%

Option Value

Futures Price

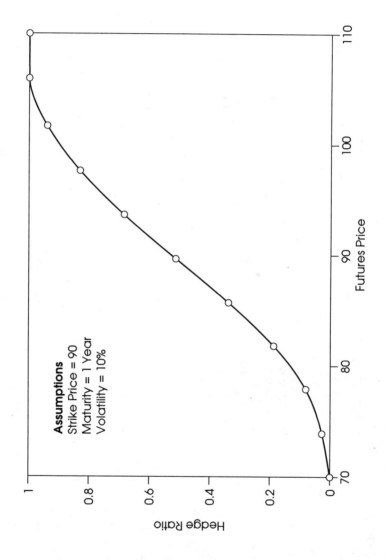

Exhibit 7-8. Delta of a Call Option as a Function of Underlying Security Price

Assumptions
Strike Price = 90
Maturity = 1 Year
Volatility = 10%

Hedge Ratio

Futures Price

Exhibit 7-9. Delta as a Function of Time Expiration

Assumptions:

Futures price = 90
Volatility   = 10%
Short rate   = 8%

Strike = 85		Strike = 90		Strike = 95	
Time to expiration	Delta	Time to expiration	Delta	Time to expiration	Delta
0.05	0.99916	0.05	0.50299	0.05	0.00761
0.10	0.96902	0.10	0.50345	0.10	0.04456
0.15	0.93333	0.15	0.50353	0.15	0.08228
0.20	0.90238	0.20	0.50342	0.20	0.11502
0.25	0.87637	0.25	0.50320	0.25	0.14292
0.30	0.85442	0.30	0.50290	0.30	0.16438
0.35	0.83566	0.35	0.50255	0.35	0.18405
0.40	0.81874	0.40	0.50216	0.40	0.19979
0.45	0.80469	0.45	0.50174	0.45	0.21276
0.50	0.79276	0.50	0.50129	0.50	0.22532
0.55	0.78106	0.55	0.50083	0.55	0.23625
0.60	0.77046	0.60	0.50036	0.60	0.24570
0.65	0.76107	0.65	0.49987	0.65	0.25397
0.70	0.75267	0.70	0.49938	0.70	0.26127
0.75	0.74510	0.75	0.49887	0.75	0.26778
0.80	0.73822	0.80	0.49837	0.80	0.27364
0.85	0.73192	0.85	0.49785	0.85	0.27945
0.90	0.72613	0.90	0.49734	0.90	0.28484
0.95	0.72021	0.95	0.49682	0.95	0.28975
1.00	0.71461	1.00	0.49630	1.00	0.29424

rate. What the portfolio manager is ultimately interested in is the sensitivity of the option price to a change in interest rates.

The relationship between the price of the underlying instrument and the option price shown in Exhibit 7-4 can be mapped into Exhibit 7-11, which shows the relationship between the price of the option and the market interest rate. Recall that the modified duration of a bond is an indicator of it price sensitivity to changes in

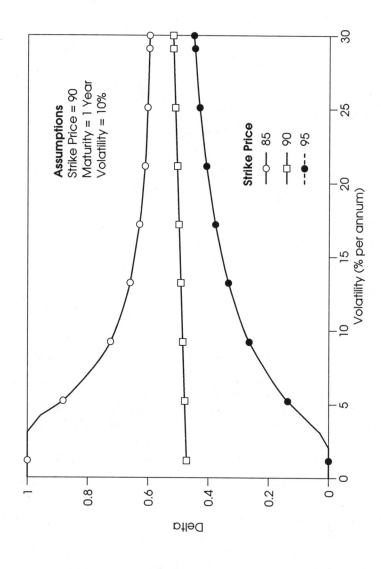

Exhibit 7-10. Delta as a Function of Volatility

Exhibit 7-11. Theoretical Value of a Call Option as a Function of Interest Rates

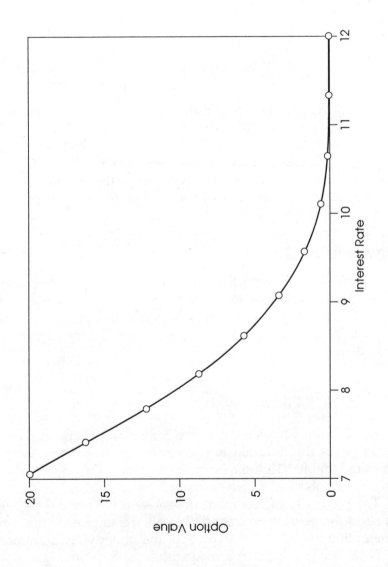

interest rates. We can similarly define a modified duration for an option as follows:

Modified duration for an option =

$$\left(\begin{array}{l}\text{Modified duration of}\\ \text{underlying instrument}\end{array}\right) \times \text{delta} \times \left(\frac{\text{Price of underlying instrument}}{\text{Price of option}}\right)$$

Therefore, the modified duration for an option depends on three factors: (1) the modified duration of the underlying instrument, (2) the delta of the option, and (3) the ratio of the price of the underlying instrument to the price of the option. This last factor can be thought of as a measure of the "leverage" in the option.

The factors that affect the delta of an option and the price of an option will also affect the duration of an option.

Convexity of Options

The relationship between the theoretical call option price and the futures price, as shown in Exhibit 7-4, is convex. The convexity shows the rate of change of the delta and in options parlance is called the *gamma* of the option. More specifically, the gamma of an option is defined as:

$$\text{Gamma} = \frac{\text{Change in delta}}{\text{Change in price of underlying security}}$$

Recall from Chapter 3 that the convexity of a bond measures the change in the duration to changes in interest rates. As can be seen from Exhibit 7-11, the relationship between the option price and interest rates also has a convex shape.

The convexity of an option depends on the same three factors that affect the modified duration of a call option plus (1) the gamma of the option and (2) the convexity of the underlying instrument.

Now that the reader is armed with an understanding of options and their parametric characteristics, the next three chapters explain how to apply these concepts to securities with embedded interest-rate options and how to use these instruments for interest-rate risk control.

Chapter 8

Analysis of Callable Bonds

Most of the longer corporate and agency bonds issued today contain call features that often can have a significant impact on their prices as well as on their performance in changing interest-rate environments. Callability is attractive to issuers as it gives them flexibility in controlling financing costs if and when interest rates move downward. Investors in turn are compensated by means of higher coupon rates when the bonds are issued. The call feature, along with credit risk, is the major factor in the perceived yield spread between corporate and Treasury bonds. Because of the trade-off between the coupon rate or yield and flexibility, proper evaluation of the call feature is important to investors. Inasmuch as different market segments such as corporate callable bonds and Treasuries exert influence on one another, a good understanding of how callable bonds behave and can be valued is helpful even if there is no intention to deal directly with them.

Because the analysis of callable bonds can be complex, market participants have developed some simple procedures to determine value. These procedures, which could perhaps be justified in the stable, calm markets of decades ago, seem almost arbitrary in the volatile interest-rate environment of today. In this chapter, we briefly mention the simple methods and their limitations, and develop a more rational approach to callable bond evaluation using the option principles that we discussed in the previous chapter.

DESCRIPTION OF THE CALL FEATURE

Most corporate bonds provide the issuer with some rights to redeem the bonds early under various circumstances. Here, we are mainly concerned with the provision that allows the issuer to *refund* a bond, i.e., to redeem the bond, before its stated maturity, with funds raised at a lower interest rate. This right is the issuer's call or refunding option. Normally, bonds are call-protected for an initial period of time after issuance. During this period, a bond cannot be refunded, even though redemption due to noninterest-rate related reasons might be allowed. More specifically, if a bond is noncallable, it provides the investor with absolute call protection against the bond being called prior to maturity, except in the case where it may be called to satisfy a sinking-fund requirement. In contrast, if a bond is nonrefundable, the bond may be called if the source of funds comes from other than lower-cost money. Cash flow from operations, proceeds from a common-stock sale, and funds from the sale of property are examples of such sources.

In addition to the protection afforded to the investors by the restricted call timing, a second feature of the bonds often requires the issuer to pay at the time of call an amount referred to as the *call price*, which can be at a premium over par. This premium is generally proportional to the coupon of the bond, but slowly declines to zero in the later years. Intermediate- and short-term bonds are usually callable at par.

Corporate bond indentures may require the issuer to retire a specified portion of an issue each year. This is referred to as the *sinking-fund* requirement. Usually the sinking-fund call price is the par value. When issued at a price in excess of par, the call price generally starts at the issuance price and scales down to par as the issue approaches maturity. Many corporate bond indentures include a provision that grants the issuer the right to retire more than (in rare circumstances more than double) the amount required under the mandatory sinking-fund schedule. This accelerated sinking-fund provision is also a type of call. Clearly, the likelihood of the accelerated sinking-fund option being exercised by the issuer is greater when interest rates are lower than the issue's coupon rate. Hence it can be characterized as a call option.

CLASSICAL ANALYSIS

Because of the call feature, the effective maturity of a callable bond can be anywhere between the first call date and its stated maturity. This uncertainty in the maturity of the bond defeats the popular measure of value, yield to maturity (or simply, yield) which requires a fixed maturity for computation. To accommodate this requirement, traditionally, callable bonds are evaluated by assuming that the bond will be called if the price of the bond is above a certain threshold value, and that it will not be called otherwise. Presumably, if the bond price is high and interest rates are low, this increases the likelihood of call; if the bond price is low and rates are high, then there is a lower probability of call. Once the effective maturity is assumed fixed, the yield can then be easily computed. Depending upon whether the call is assumed or not, we get the yield to call (YTC) or yield to maturity (YTM).

The threshold price used is usually par or the first call price. Sometimes a value known as the *crossover price*[1] is used. This is the price above which the yield to maturity is greater than the yield to call. The implication is that the issuer will behave, with respect to calling the bond, in such a way that the investor receives the minimum yield, and hence the name *minimum yield method* for this approach. Even though the crossover yield or minimum yield analysis appears reasonable on the surface, it breaks down totally under several common situations, indicating that its application is not appropriate except under extreme circumstances.

For example, consider an inverted yield curve environment,[2] where the 5-year rate is at 16 percent and the 30-year rate is 12 percent. Suppose that a 30-year, 12.25 percent coupon bond callable in

---

[1] The crossover price can be easily computed: First we compute the crossover yield, which is the yield at which the price of the bond on the first call date is the call price. Crossover price is the price of the bond today computed at the crossover yield.

[2] Unless otherwise stated, the yield curve represents yield levels of noncallable bonds of the appropriate credit. This can be obtained by adding quality spreads to the Treasury yield curve.

5 years at 105 7/8 is priced at a slight discount to par at 98 2/32, with a YTM of 12.50 percent. The YTC is 13.65 percent, so that the YTM is below the YTC. An investor, using the minimum yield method would ignore the call, treating the bond as a straight 30-year bond. That is, he or she would compare the yield to maturity of the callable bond to the long end of the yield curve to determine value. The bond price looks reasonable until we observe that the YTC itself is 234 basis points below the 5-year rate. We can therefore do better by simply purchasing a straight 5-year bond at a yield of 16 percent.

There are subtle theoretical problems as well with the minimum yield method. The yield or total return computed to call and to maturity are very different in sensitivity to interest-rate changes, the level of uncertainty, or variability in the actual returns obtained, etc., and thus are not directly comparable, nor is there an acceptable procedure to make them so.[3] When the magnitude of the difference between the yields computed to call and to maturity is large, the two yields will imply vastly different reinvestment rates for the same coupon stream. This again is commonly ignored in bond research, but can be handled by using a fixed reinvestment rate and computing the total return rather than the yield.

The usual methods are flawed even when the yield curve is not inverted. They imply an abrupt change at the crossover point when the assumption of call switches over to no-call. One of the reasons for these drawbacks is that these methods use the price (or yield) of the callable bond itself for valuation, whereas the bond, in fact, is responding to changes in the market levels. Therefore, market variables should be used to drive any viable model for callable bonds.

---

[3] However, such direct comparisons between yields to different maturities are deeply entrenched in fixed-income analysis. For example, as we explained in Chapter 2, the average yield is typically used in barbell-bullet analysis even though the maturities of the three bonds involved are disparate. Another common example is the duration-based yield curve discussed in Chapter 5. Here, for example, the yield of a 9-year, zero-coupon bond is treated on the same basis as that of a 30-year, current-coupon bond, since both have almost equal durations. Because of such widespread usage, we do not expect the discrepancy mentioned here to be objectionable to more than a few.

The likelihood of call does not depend on whether the callable bond is selling above par or the call price or even the crossover price but at what rate the redemption can be financed, i.e., on the new issue market. For example, consider a bond that is callable at par immediately. In this case, we do not expect the bond to trade above the call price, and the minimum yield method will treat the bond as noncallable.

Some practitioners improve upon the basic YTM/YTC analysis by making additional adjustments to reflect call. This adjustment, in practice, is usually arbitrary. When a bond is callable immediately, the method breaks down completely, as the YTC is then undefined. Even computing the actual yield realizable under various investment rate assumptions provides only a marginal improvement over the standard analysis, and still retains the major problems.

A better procedure, perhaps, than the minimum yield method is what can be called the *maximum yield method*. Here, the investor demands that the yield computed to any possible call date is higher than a corresponding call-free yield. How much higher the yield should be is still the unknown factor.

The intention of the examples presented above is not to say that such gross errors are made frequently, but only that there is a potential for their occurrence. Most market participants can be expected to make amendments, though not scientific, in the traditional methods as they realize the possibility of mispricing. What is required is a systematic method to determine the price of callable bonds, the development of which is the goal of this chapter.

MARKET RESPONSE OF CALLABLE BONDS

We can obtain useful insight into the valuation of a callable bond by estimating its price behavior in the market. In this context, it helps to view the callable bond as responding to changes in the noncallable yield levels rather than treating the yield (or price) of the callable bond as a fundamental, independent variable. Let us therefore look first at the price behavior of a noncallable bond as a function of interest rates. For simplicity of exposition, we assume a flat yield curve in this section.

Exhibit 8-1 shows the price-yield curve of a 30-year, 10.75 percent noncallable bond. The horizontal axis represents the change in the yield of the bond and the vertical axis the corresponding prices.

A shorter maturity bond is shown in Exhibit 8-2. Specifically, the bond is a 5-year, 10.75 percent noncallable bond. This is a normal bond, except that at maturity it pays 105 instead of the usual 100.[4] The price-yield curve for this bond has the same fundamental characteristics as the one for the 30-year bond. The curve is not as steep, i.e., the dollar duration is smaller. Also, this slope changes less as the yield is varied, i.e., the convexity is smaller. For high yield levels, the long bond price is less than the price of the shorter bond. For lower yield levels, the short bond price is lower.

Consider now a 30-year, 10.75 percent bond, callable in year 5 at 105. In year 5, if the rates are low, the issuer may decide to call the bond, leaving the investor with the unattractive task of investing the proceeds in a low-coupon (or low-yielding) bond. Thus, the callable bond is less attractive to an investor than the noncallable long bond which will continue to pay the 10.75 percent coupon even if rates drop.

Similarly, the callable bond is less attractive to an investor than the short maturity bond of Exhibit 8-2. Because, if the rates rise, the bond will not be called, and the investor loses the opportunity to invest in high-coupon (or high-yielding) bonds. On the other hand, the short bond matures, providing the attractive reinvestment opportunity.

Thus the callable bond is worth less than both the long bond and the short bond. Therefore, we can obtain an upper bound on the price of the callable bond by looking at the lower of the prices of the long and short bonds. This upper bound is shown in Exhibit 8-3. Sometimes this upper bound is called the price-to-worst, and the corresponding yields are called yield-to-worst. However, these are only bounds, and the actual value of the callable bond is *below* the price-to-worst.

The price-yield curve for the callable bond, then, is a curve that is bounded above by the curves for the short and the long bonds.

---

[4] The reason for selecting a maturity payment not equal to par will become clear shortly.

Exhibit 8-1. 10.75%, 30-Year Noncallable Bond Price-Yield Relationship

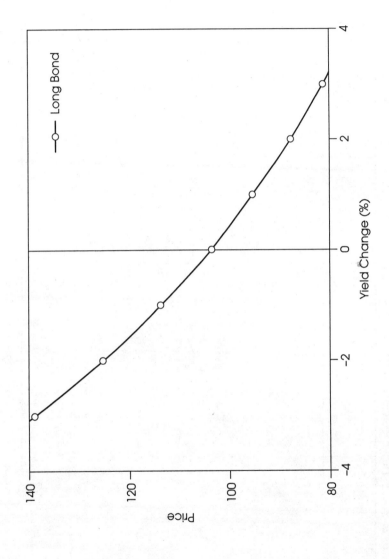

Exhibit 8-2. Price-Yield Relationship for a 10.75%, 5-Year Noncallable Bond (Short Bond)

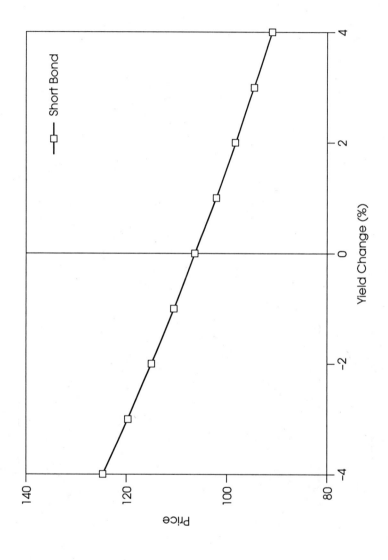

Exhibit 8-3. Upper Bound for the Value of a Callable Bond

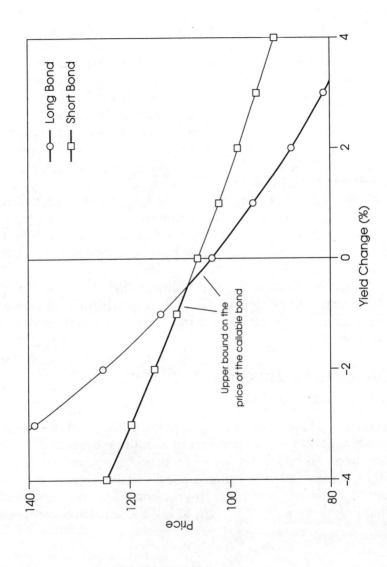

For very low yield levels, the likelihood of call is high, and investors would be willing to pay almost the same for either the short bond or the callable bond. Similarly, at very high yield levels, the likelihood of call is low, and we can expect the value of the callable bond to be close to that of the long bond. For intermediate yield levels, the curve represents a smooth, continuous transition from the long bond to the short bond. This is shown in Exhibit 8-4.

A few additional observations can be made. For very high yield levels, the callable bond behaves much like a long noncallable bond in terms of its duration and convexity. Again, for very low yield levels, the callable bond behavior is close to that of the short bond in its duration and convexity. Thus, as rates fall, the duration of the callable bond falls from that of the long bond to that of the short bond, i.e., it decreases. This property is opposite to that of noncallable bonds, for which the duration increases as rates fall. The callable bond is therefore said to have *negative convexity*[5] in the intermediate yield range.

Finally, the actual price is lower than the so-called price-to-worst, and the discrepancy is small only when the rate levels are in the extreme. In the normal operating range, the difference can be significant.

THE OPTION APPROACH TO PRICING CALLABLE BONDS

The most natural way to analyze a callable bond is to treat it as a combination of a long position in a call-free bond and a short position in a call option on the same bond.[6] For example, consider our 10.75 percent, 30-year callable bond callable in 5 years at 105. The investor effectively owns a 30-year bond and has sold a call option that grants the issuer the right to call the bond in 5 years at an exer-

---

[5] Geometrically, a curve is concave or negatively convex if it lies below the tangent drawn at that point.

[6] Compare this with the covered-call writing or "buy/write" technique, where the investor buys a bond and writes (sells) a call option on the same bond.

Exhibit 8-4. Market Performance of a 10.75%, 30-Year Bond Callable at 105 Compared to a 30-Year Long Bond and 5-Year Short Bond

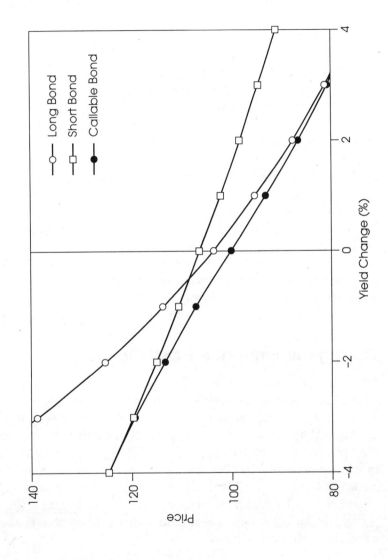

cise price of 105. Therefore, the price of a callable bond is equal to the price of the call-free bond *minus* the value of the option. That is,

Callable bond price = Call-free bond price – Call option price

The reason for subtracting the call option price is that the bond-holder has sold an option to the issuer. Notice that the higher the call option value, the lower the value of the callable bond.

Two approaches can be used to determine if the market price of a callable bond is fair. The first approach is to use a valuation model to determine the call-free bond's value and to use an option-pricing model to determine the theoretical value of the embedded call option. The difference between the two values is then the theoretical value of the callable bond, which can then be compared to the market price. The second approach is to use one model that values the callable bond, taking into account the call option granted to the issuer.[7] Both approaches give identical results if the models used to value the call-free bonds and the embedded call option are properly developed. More specifically, the models must be such that they satisfy the internal and external consistency conditions that we set forth in Chapter 5.

Valuing the Embedded Call Option

The idea of decomposition is not new. Some researchers have attempted to model the implicit option as a European option expiring on the first call date and used the Black-Scholes model to determine its value. Unfortunately this approach substantially underestimates the option value, and therefore, is of little practical value as it leads to inconsistent results. For example, such a model would conclude incorrectly that a bond callable in one year is more valuable than an identical bond callable in two years. This is because the one-year European option is worth less than a two-year option. It also fails for bonds callable immediately.

---

[7] For an explanation of this approach, see Andrew J. Kalotay, George O. Williams, and Frank J, Fabozzi, "A Model for the Valuation of Bonds and Embedded Options," *Financial Analysts Journal* (May–June 1993), pp. 35–46.

The embedded option in a callable bond has many complexities in addition to those that are already present in the more standard, exchange-traded options on bonds, as discussed below. Only by including all of the complex features of the option in our model can we make the decomposition approach a useful one.

European-American Effect.   The implicit option in callable bonds combines the exercise features of both European and American options by providing for a period of call protection during which the option cannot be exercised. The bond is callable at any time after this period.

Strike Price.   Usually, the strike price of an exchange-traded option is held constant until expiration. However, the call price for a typical callable bond starts at a price above par (usually around par plus half the coupon) and declines steadily year by year until it reaches par. Subsequently, the bond is callable at par until maturity. We could include in the strike price the costs associated with the call and perhaps the cost of financing the call by a new issue.

Yield-Price Distribution.   To evaluate an option on a security, we have to make an assumption about the behavior of the price movement of the security. The popular stock option models assume that the price of the stock moves according to a lognormal distribution, which implies that the price of the security can increase or decrease indefinitely. Because a bond's price approaches par as it nears maturity, its price volatility eventually decreases, making this assumption inappropriate for describing bond price movements. It is relatively much easier to develop a consistent assumption for the movement of interest rates and then derive the price movement of bonds. This is the proper approach to take.[8]

Volatility.   The value of an option depends on the way in which the underlying security moves. Option models usually define a

---

[8] However, if the time to expiration of an option is significantly shorter than the time to maturity of the underlying bond, variations of the price-based stock option models can be used to get reasonable estimates of option value.

property called volatility, which measures the rate and range of up and down movements of the price of the security. Usually, the standard deviation (or variance) of the assumed distribution is used as the volatility measure.

In general, the value of an option increases with volatility. An estimated volatility, admittedly an easier task to produce than a prediction of the market direction, nevertheless remains an opinion about the future. The uncertainty in this input variable, more than anything else, keeps option pricing something of an art. Most models assume that the (yield) volatility is constant throughout the life of the option, which in the case of a callable bond is its stated maturity. One can include in the model a varying volatility, making the model more complex. We feel that the additional precision gained, if any, is marginal, in light of the relatively gross approximations made in other input variables. Furthermore, the user would then face the unenviable task of guessing how the volatility varies.

Each of the factors discussed above highlights a shortcoming of popular stock-option models, such as the celebrated Black-Scholes model, in evaluating callable bonds. We use the more flexible binomial model with extensive modifications incorporating the factors discussed above as well as those below. Most modern option models, including the two mentioned here, are based on the same central concept. They price the option so as to remove any possible riskless arbitrage between the option and the underlying security, rather than use an expectation of how the market might move. This is the correct way to value options.

The Interest-Rate Process. In stock models, we can assume, without any internal contradiction, that the price of the stock is independent of the level of interest rates. This allows us complete freedom in selecting the stock-price distribution and the interest-rate distribution. For simplicity, most stock models assume a constant interest rate. However, this degree of freedom is not available in bond option models because the interest-rate levels and the bond prices are not independent. Behavior of short-term rates influences the level of longer-term rates. Any interest-rate process assumption will imply corresponding prices of various securities.

The interdependence of interest rates of different maturities results in the internal and external consistency conditions that must be satisfied by an assumed interest-rate process.[9] Both of the consistency conditions are extremely important in developing a viable model to value callable bonds. If the internal consistency condition is violated, we get meaningless, self-contradictory results. If the external consistency condition is not satisfied, many securities in the market can appear, incorrectly, cheap or rich.

VALUATION

As noted earlier, a callable bond can be valued by either (1) valuing the call-free bond and the embedded option, and then calculating the difference, or (2) valuing the callable bond with one valuation model that recognizes the issuer's call option.

There are several ways of implementing an interest-rate process that satisfies the internal and external conditions for all of these valuation models. A reasonable yet relatively simple approach assumes that the entire yield curve at any point in time can be fully determined by knowing the value of one independent variable called the *factor*. In many models, known as *one-factor models*, the independent variable can be interpreted as the short-term rate.

A stochastic (random) process that is in line with market experience for the short rate is assumed. The consistency conditions are used to calibrate the model and to determine the full yield curve at any point in time as required.

The approach used to value a callable bond is the *binomial lattice method* or simply, *binomial method*. In this approach, the short-term rate is assumed to take on one of two possible values and generate a *tree* of future short-term interest rates. The interest-rate tree is ultimately used to value all bonds (callable and call-free) and options. That is, the interest-rate tree provides the appropriate discount rates at which to discount cash flows. The interest-rate tree is constructed such that (1) when the interest-rate tree is used to value the on-the-run Treasuries, the value produced is identical to the market price for those issues, and (2) it is consistent with the volatility

---

[9] See Chapter 5.

assumption. The interest-rate tree constructed in this fashion is said to be an *arbitrage-free interest-rate tree*.

Adjustment for Quality Spread

To use this interest-rate tree to value corporate bonds, we have to make an adjustment since the interest-rate tree is generated using Treasury price data. Therefore, the rates on the tree are suitable for discounting only Treasury cash flows. If we use these rates to discount cash flows from non-Treasury securities such as corporate bonds, then the resulting value will be an overestimate. We have to correspondingly use a higher discounting rate to reflect a corporate bond's lower quality.

A simple mechanism to incorporate quality difference is to add a small constant (i.e., a spread) to each rate on the tree and then use it for discounting corporate cash flows.[10] Note that this spread is over the short-term rate and therefore is not the same as the yield spreads normally quoted.

Incorporating the Embedded Call Option

When one is seeking to value a callable bond using one valuation model, adjustments to the cash flow must be made to take into account the right of the issuer to call the bond. To do this, a rule for when the issuer will call in the bond must be incorporated into the valuation model. It is the call rule that is used to adjust the cash flows in determining the value of a callable bond.

OPTION-ADJUSTED SPREAD

The valuation model gives the theoretical value of a bond. For example, if the market price of a callable bond is $102, and the theoretical value taken from the binomial model is $102.5, this means that

---

[10] A constant spread can be added to the short-term rates on the tree. We could, if desired, make the spread a function of the maturity of the bond, i.e., of time and/or level of rates. However, the marginal improvement in valuation might not warrant the additional complexity.

this bond is cheap by $0.5, according to the valuation model. Bond market participants, however, prefer to think not in terms of a bond's price being cheap or expensive in dollar terms but rather in terms of a yield's spread—a cheap bond trades at a higher yield spread and an expensive bond at a lower yield spread.

The market convention is to think of a yield spread as the difference between the yield to maturity on a particular bond and the yield on a comparable-maturity Treasury. However, this is inappropriate because, as we have explained, there is not one rate at which all cash flows should be discounted but a set of spot rates. Given that this is the correct procedure for discounting, market participants determine the spread over the issuer's spot rate curve. In terms of the interest-rate tree, it is the constant spread that when added to all the tree rates will make the theoretical value equal to the market price. The constant spread that satisfies this condition is called the *option-adjusted spread* (OAS). The spread is referred to as an "option-adjusted" spread since the spread takes into consideration the option embedded in the issue.

It should be noted that not all dealers and vendors of analytical systems will calculate the OAS from a binomial model in the same way. Thus, the interpretation of the OAS can vary. Some dealers and vendors use the interest-rate tree without an adjustment for the quality spread to calculate the OAS. That is, the OAS is defined as the spread over the Treasury interest-rate tree that will make the model's value equal to the market price. In this case, the OAS is accounting for three things: (1) the quality spread, (2) the liquidity risk, and (3) any mispricing. In contrast, if the binomial interest-rate tree adjusted for the quality spread is used, then the OAS is accounting for just (1) the liquidity risk and (2) any mispricing. Ignoring liquidity risk, a fairly priced corporate bond should have an OAS equal to zero if the binomial interest-rate tree adjusted for the quality spread is used to calculate the OAS. In either case, the OAS has taken out the option risk.

EFFECTIVE DURATION AND EFFECTIVE CONVEXITY

Modified duration is a measure of the sensitivity of a bond's price to interest-rate changes, *assuming that the expected cash flow does not change with interest rates.* Consequently, modified duration may not be an appropriate measure for bonds with embedded options because the expected cash flows change as interest rates change.

While modified duration may be inappropriate as a measure of a bond's sensitivity to interest-rate changes, there is a duration measure that is more appropriate for bonds with embedded options. Since duration measures price responsiveness to changes in interest rates, the duration for a bond with an embedded option can be estimated by letting interest rates change by a small number of basis points above and below the prevailing yield, and seeing how the prices would change. On page 33 of Chapter 2, we provided a formula for calculating the approximate duration.

The two prices in the formula are those derived from the binomial method. This is done by shifting the yield curve by a small number of basis points up and down and then recalculating the interest-rate tree. The OAS is added to the new interest-rate tree. This adjusted tree is then used to determine the theoretical value if yields change and to provide the prices used in the formula.

When duration is calculated in the manner just describe, it is called an *effective duration* or *option-adjusted duration.* Thus, unlike modified duration, which assumes that cash flows will not change when interest rates change, effective duration recognizes the impact of rate changes on cash flows and price. Exhibit 8-5 summarizes the distinction between modified duration and effective duration.

Similarly, the convexity measure that appropriately adjusts for the embedded call option can be calculated. This is done by using the formula on page 49 of Chapter 3 for determining the approximate convexity. The same prices used in the effective duration formula can be used in the convexity formula. The resulting convexity measure is called *effective convexity* or *option-adjusted convexity.*

PORTFOLIO AND ASSET/LIABILITY MANAGEMENT IMPLICATIONS

The price performance characteristics of callable bonds must be understood by portfolio managers in order to effectively implement any portfolio strategy. Several examples are given below.

Exhibit 8-5. Modified Duration Versus Effective Duration

```
┌─────────────────────────────────────────────────────────┐
│                        Duration                          │
│  Interpretation: Generic description of the sensitivity  │
│  of a bond's price (as a percent of initial price) to a  │
│  parallel shift in the yield curve                       │
└─────────────────────────────────────────────────────────┘
```

Modified Duration	**Effective Duration**
Duration measure in which it is assumed that yield changes do not change the expected cash flow	Duration measure in which recognition is given to the fact that yield changes may change the expected cash flow

Indexing

An indexing strategy seeks to match the performance of a bench-mark portfolio. Because of the large number of issues in a typical bond index, an indexed portfolio is constructed using a small sub-set of the issues in the index rather than all the issues. In the strat-ified sampling (or cell) approach, the index is partitioned into cells on the basis of features such as market sector, duration, quality, etc. Issues are then selected for each cell so as to match the characteris-tics of the index. Because the indexed portfolio is not identical to the index, the performance of the two will not be identical. The dif-ference between the performance of the two is called *tracking error*. The objective is to construct a portfolio with minimum tracking error.

Constructing an indexed portfolio that matches the perfor-mance of the U.S. government bond sector is not difficult, because of the lack of a call feature for most issues in this sector.[11] In contrast to the small tracking error for Treasuries, the embedded option in callable corporate bonds makes it more difficult to construct a portfolio to track this sector. To reduce the likelihood of large tracking error for the corporate bond sector, the characteristics used to create the cells should include the duration and convexity of the issues in this sector. More specifically, the effective duration and effective convexity should be matched.

Active Strategies: The Importance of the Benchmark

The performance of portfolio managers is evaluated relative to some benchmark index or bogey. The objective is to outperform the market in any interest-rate environment. The plan sponsor determines the benchmark index, presumably based on its liability structure. Since the performance of the index will depend on its composition, particularly with respect to the proportion of noncallable to callable bonds, the portfolio manager must understand the performance characteristics of the benchmark index.

Typically, active bond portfolio managers hold a large portion of their portfolio in nongovernment bonds. The nongovernment bond sector is comprised primarily of corporates and mortgage-backed securities. The securities in these market sectors are characterized by issues that have embedded call options—as we have seen in the case of corporates in this chapter and mortgage-backed securities in the next chapter.

When interest rates are declining and volatility is increasing, callable corporate bonds (as well as mortgage-backed securities) will underperform U.S. government bonds because (1) negative convexity "kicks in" as interest rates decline sufficiently and (2) the value of the embedded call option increases, thereby decreasing the price of a callable bond as volatility increases. In an environment of increasing interest rates and decreasing volatility, callable bonds will outperform U.S. government bonds. Exhibit 8-6 summarizes the

---

[11] While there are some callable U.S. government bonds outstanding, the Treasury no longer issues callable bonds.

Exhibit 8-6. Expected Performance Characteristics for Callable and Noncallable Bonds under Different Market Environments

Performance Expectations
Relative to Comparable-Duration
Government Securities Portfolios
Direction of Interest Rates

	Increase in Rates	No Change	Decrease in Rates	
NC	+	+	⊕	Increase
C	Amb	–	⊖	
NC	O	O	+	No Change
C	+	O	⊖	
NC	+	O	+	Decrease
C	⊕	+	–	

(volatility changes)

Performance Expectations
Callable vs. Noncallable
Nongovernment
Direction of Interest Rates

	Increase in Rates	No Change	Decrease in Rates	
NC	Amb	+	⊕	Increase
C	Amb	–	⊖	
NC	O	O	⊕	No Change
C	+	O	–	
NC	O	O	+	Decrease
C	⊕	+	–	

(volatility changes)

⊕ Big Winner	Amb Ambiguous	NC Noncallable Portfolio
	+ Winner	C Callable Portfolio
⊖ Big Loser	– Loser	

Source: Chris P. Dialynas, "The Active Decisions in the Selection of Passive Management and Performance Bogeys," in Frank J. Fabozzi and T. Dessa Garlicki-Fabozzi, eds., *Advances in Bond Analysis and Portfolio Strategies* (Chicago: Probus Publishing, 1987), Exhibit 1, p. 22.

expected relative performance of callable bonds and noncallable bonds in various market environments.

Active portfolio decisions, therefore, should be made on the basis of not only the anticipated direction of interest rates, but also (1) the nature of the benchmark index and (2) expected interest-rate volatility.

Immunization

The objective of immunization, both single-period and multiperiod, is to lock in a target rate of return that will be sufficient to satisfy a liability or liability stream. A necessary condition is that the dollar duration of the assets equals the dollar duration of the liabilities.

Typically, an immunized portfolio is constructed using corporate bonds. The theory of immunization is that as interest rates decline, the lower reinvestment income due to lower reinvestment rates would be more than offset by capital appreciation of the portfolio due to lower interest rates. In the case of a callable corporate bond, the offsetting capital appreciation is truncated due to their negative convexity. The standard duration (modified duration) of a bond portfolio that includes callable corporate bonds is not a good measure of its interest-rate sensitivity.

In addition, not only is there the requirement that the dollar duration of the assets and liabilities must be equal, but there is the requirement that the convexity of the assets be greater than or equal to the convexity of the liabilities. It is the effective convexity that should be considered in satisfying this requirement.

To eliminate or mitigate call risk, the immunized portfolio can be restricted to only noncallable bonds. Or if callable bonds are included, the universe can be restricted to deep-discount callable bonds (i.e., bonds where the call option is deep out-of-the-money). However, restricting the universe of acceptable bonds to noncallable bonds and/or deep-discount callable bonds raises the cost of an immunized portfolio because they offer a lower yield than callable bonds.

If there are no restrictions placed on callable bonds that may be included in the immunized portfolio, the optimization program used to create the portfolio should recognize the value of the embedded call option. After the initial portfolio is created, more frequent monitoring of the portfolio during declining interest-rate and high interest-rate volatility environments is essential. This will permit the swapping of any callable corporate bonds for other bonds before a substantial negative impact on the immunized portfolio due to negative convexity is realized.

Surplus Hedging for Corporate Pension Plans

The Financial Accounting Standards Board in December 1985 issued Statement of Accounting Standards No. 87. This statement, referred to as FASB 87, established reporting standards for defined-benefit pension plans. Basically, FASB 87 requires that for fiscal years beginning after December 15, 1988, companies recognize on the balance sheet certain pension liabilities if the market value (present value) of the liabilities exceeds the market value of the pension assets.

Corporate pension-fund portfolio strategies have focused on protecting the surplus (market value of fund assets minus market value of fund liabilities). Prior to FASB 87, if a fund held long-term bonds and interest rates declined, the value of the fund assets increased and the fund was deemed to be considerably better off. Under FASB 87, whether a fund is better off depends on what happens to the market value (present value) of the pension liabilities. Since under FASB 87 the present value of pension liabilities will be discounted at a market interest rate, in a declining interest-rate environment, their value will increase. The surplus may either increase, decrease, or fall. Similarly, in a rising interest-rate environment, the market value of the fund assets will fall but so will the present value of the pension liabilities.

What happens to the surplus will depend on the dollar duration of the fund assets and dollar duration of the pension liabilities, as well as their convexities. If the dollar durations are matched and the convexity of the fund assets exceeds that of the pension liabilities, the value of the surplus should be protected (immunized) against a change in interest rates. When the fund assets include a large portion of callable corporate bonds, the problem of negative convexity must be considered.

Hedging

To hedge a portfolio's value against adverse interest-rate movements, an offsetting position in some instrument (either Treasury securities, Treasury futures, or options) can be taken. The objective of the hedge is to offset any change in the portfolio value with an equal dollar change in the short position. To determine the amount of the position in the hedging vehicle to hedge a portfolio's value, a hedge ratio is typically calculated using the following formula:[12]

$$\text{Hedge ratio} = \frac{\text{Dollar duration of portfolio}}{\text{Dollar duration of hedging vehicle}}$$

For callable bonds, the drawback of determining the hedge ratio in this fashion is that it ignores the convexity of the instruments involved. While cash Treasuries and futures have positive convexity, callable bonds exhibit negative convexity. Consequently, a more appropriate procedure for hedging callable bonds is to use cash Treasuries and futures to hedge price changes due to duration but buy call options and/or long zero-coupon bonds to hedge price changes due to convexity.

---

[12] More precisely, the ratio of the dollar durations should be multiplied by a yield beta that measures the relative interest-rate movements of the portfolio and the hedging vehicle. Regression analysis is used to estimate the yield beta.

Chapter 9

Analysis of
Mortgage-Backed Securities

In this chapter we look at the analysis of mortgage-backed securities (pass-throughs, stripped mortgage-backed securities, and collateralized mortgage obligations). The major difficulty in the analysis of mortgage-backed securities is the uncertainty of cash flows, because the mortgagors can prepay their loans at any time prior to maturity without a prepayment penalty. The mortgage-backed security investor would then receive the scheduled payment, which consists of the coupon interest and the principal amortization, plus any additional prepayment of principal in the pool. The main issue in the analysis of mortgage-backed securities, therefore, is how to treat the uncertain cash flows and how to explicitly evaluate the premium that an investor should demand as fair compensation for the extra risk from prepayments.

MORTGAGES

To understand mortgage-backed securities, an understanding of the cash-flow characteristics of the underlying collateral is necessary. Therefore, we begin this chapter with a review of mortgages.

A mortgage is a loan secured by the collateral of some specified real estate property that obliges the borrower to make a predetermined series of payments. The mortgage gives the lender (*mortgagee*) the right, if the borrower (the *mortgagor*) defaults (i.e., fails to make the contracted payments), to "foreclose" on the loan and seize the property in order to ensure that the debt is paid off. The interest rate on the mortgage loan is called the *mortgage rate*. When the lender makes the loan based on the credit of the borrower and on the collateral for the mortgage, the mortgage is said to be a *conventional mortgage*. The lender also may take out mortgage insurance to guarantee the fulfillment of the borrower's obligations.

The types of real estate properties that can be mortgaged are divided into two broad categories: residential and nonresidential properties. The first category includes houses, condominiums, cooperatives, and apartments. Residential real estate can be subdivided into single-family (one- to four-family) structures and multifamily structures (apartment buildings in which more than four families reside). Nonresidential property includes commercial and farm properties. Our focus in this chapter is on residential mortgage loans.

A borrower can select from many types of mortgage loans. These include level-payment, fixed-rate, fully amortized mortgages; adjustable-rate mortgages; graduated-payment mortgages; growing-equity mortgages; balloon mortgages; two-step mortgages; fixed-rate, tiered-payment mortgages; and fixed/adjustable-rate mortgage hybrids. Below we describe just the first mortgage design in order to demonstrate the basic principles that will be encountered in a pool of mortgages.[1]

Fixed-Rate, Level-Payment Mortgage

The basic idea behind the design of the level-payment, fixed-rate mortgage (or simply level-payment mortgage) is that the borrower pays interest and repays principal in equal installments over an agreed-upon period of time, called the maturity or term of the mortgage. Thus at the end of the term, the loan has been fully amortized.

For a level-payment mortgage, each monthly mortgage payment is due on the first of each month and consists of: (1) interest

---

[1] The other mortgage designs are discussed in Frank J. Fabozzi and Lynn Edens, "Mortgages," Chapter 23 in Frank J. Fabozzi and T. Dessa Fabozzi, eds., *The Handbook of Fixed Income Securities* (Burr Ridge, IL: Irwin Professional Publishing, 1994).

of 1/12th of the fixed annual mortgage rate times the amount of the outstanding mortgage balance at the beginning of the previous month, and (2) a repayment of a portion of the outstanding mortgage balance (principal). The difference between the monthly mortgage payment and the portion of the payment that represents interest equals the amount that is applied to reduce the outstanding mortgage balance. The monthly mortgage payment is designed so that after the last scheduled payment is made, the amount of the outstanding mortgage balance is zero (i.e., the mortgage is fully repaid).

The portion of the monthly mortgage payment applied to interest declines each month and the portion applied to reducing the mortgage balance increases. The reason for this is that as the mortgage balance is reduced with each monthly mortgage payment, the interest on the mortgage balance declines. Since the monthly mortgage payment is fixed, an increasingly larger portion of the monthly payment is applied to reduce the principal in each subsequent month.

To illustrate a level-payment, fixed-rate mortgage, consider a 30-year (360-month), $100,000 mortgage with an 8.125 percent mortgage rate. The monthly mortgage payment would be $742.50. Exhibit 9-1 shows for selected months how each monthly mortgage payment is divided between interest and repayment of principal. At the beginning of month 1, the mortgage balance is $100,000, the amount of the original loan. The mortgage payment for month 1 includes interest on the $100,000 borrowed for the month. Since the interest rate is 8.125 percent, the monthly interest rate is 0.0067708 (0.08125 divided by 12). Interest for month 1 is therefore $677.08 ($100,000 times 0.0067708). The $65.41 difference between the monthly mortgage payment of $742.50 and the interest of $677.08 is the portion of the monthly mortgage payment that represents repayment of principal. This $65.41 in month 1 reduces the mortgage balance.

The mortgage balance at the end of month 1 (beginning of month 2) is then $99,934.59 ($100,000 minus $65.41). The interest for the second monthly mortgage payment is $676.64, the monthly interest rate (0.0066708) times the mortgage balance at the beginning of month 2 ($99,934.59). The difference between the $742.50 monthly mortgage payment and the $676.64 interest is $65.86, representing

Exhibit 9-1. Amortization Schedule for a Level-Payment, Fixed-Rate Mortgage

Mortgage loan: $100,000
Mortgage rate: 8.125%
Monthly payment: $742.50
Term of loan: 30 years (360 months)

Month	Beginning mortgage balance	Monthly payment	Monthly interest	Sch. princ. repay.	Ending mortgage balance
1	100,000.00	742.50	677.08	65.41	99,934.59
2	99,934.59	742.50	676.64	65.86	99,868.73
3	99,868.73	742.50	676.19	66.30	99,802.43
4	99,802.43	742.50	675.75	66.75	99,735.68
25	98,301.53	742.50	665.58	76.91	98,224.62
26	98,224.62	742.50	665.06	77.43	98,147.19
27	98,147.19	742.50	664.54	77.96	98,069.23
74	93,849.98	742.50	635.44	107.05	93,742.93
75	93,742.93	742.50	634.72	107.78	93,635.15
76	93,635.15	742.50	633.99	108.51	93,526.64
141	84,811.77	742.50	574.25	168.25	84,643.52
142	84,643.52	742.50	573.11	169.39	84,474.13
143	84,474.13	742.50	571.96	170.54	84,303.59
184	76,446.29	742.50	517.61	224.89	76,221.40
185	76,221.40	742.50	516.08	226.41	75,994.99
186	75,994.99	742.50	514.55	227.95	75,767.04
233	63,430.19	742.50	429.48	313.02	63,117.17
234	63,117.17	742.50	427.36	315.14	62,802.03
235	62,802.03	742.50	425.22	317.28	62,484.75
289	42,200.92	742.50	285.74	456.76	41,744.15
290	41,744.15	742.50	282.64	459.85	41,284.30
291	41,284.30	742.50	279.53	462.97	40,821.33
321	25,941.42	742.50	175.65	566.85	25,374.57
322	25,374.57	742.50	171.81	570.69	24,803.88
323	24,803.88	742.50	167.94	574.55	24,229.32
358	2,197.66	742.50	14.88	727.62	1,470.05
359	1,470.05	742.50	9.95	732.54	737.50
360	737.50	742.50	4.99	737.50	0.00

the amount of the mortgage balance paid off with that monthly mortgage payment. Notice that the last mortgage payment in month 360 is sufficient to pay off the remaining mortgage balance. When a loan repayment schedule is structured in this way, so that the payments made by the borrower will completely pay off the interest and principal, the loan is said to be *fully amortizing*. Exhibit 9-1 is then referred to as an *amortization schedule*.

As Exhibit 9-1 clearly shows, *the portion of the monthly mortgage payment applied to interest declines each month and the portion applied to reducing the mortgage balance increases*. The reason for this is that as the mortgage balance is reduced with each monthly mortgage payment, the interest on the mortgage balance declines. Since the monthly mortgage payment is fixed, an increasingly larger portion of the monthly payment is applied to reduce the principal in each subsequent month.

Prepayments and Cash-Flow Uncertainty

Our illustration of the cash flow from a level-payment, fixed-rate mortgage assumes that the homeowner does not pay off any portion of the mortgage balance prior to the scheduled due date. But homeowners do pay off all or part of their mortgage balance prior to the maturity date. Payments made in excess of the scheduled principal repayments are called *prepayments*.

Prepayments occur for one of several reasons. First, homeowners prepay the entire mortgage when they sell their home. The sale of a home may occur because of (1) a change of employment that necessitates moving, (2) the purchase of a more expensive home ("trading up"), or (3) a divorce in which the settlement requires sale of the marital residence. Second, the borrower may be moved to pay off part of the mortgage balance as market rates fall below the mortgage rate. Third, in the case of homeowners who cannot meet their mortgage obligations, the property is repossessed and sold. The proceeds of such a sale are used to pay off the mortgage in the case of a conventional mortgage. For an insured mortgage, the insurer will pay off the mortgage balance. Finally, if property is destroyed by fire or if another insured catastrophe occurs, the insurance proceeds are used to pay off the mortgage.

The effect of prepayments is that the amount and timing of the cash flow from a mortgage is not known with certainty. For example, all that the investor in a $100,000, 8.125 percent, 30-year insured mortgage knows is that as long as the loan is outstanding, interest will be received and the principal will be repaid at the scheduled date each month; then at the end of the 30 years, the investor would have received $100,000 in principal payments. What the investor does not know—the uncertainty—is for how long the loan will be outstanding, and therefore what the timing of the principal payments will be. This is true for all mortgage designs, not just level-payment, fixed-rate mortgages.

The uncertainty about the cash flow of a mortgage due to prepayments is called *prepayment risk.*

MORTGAGE-BACKED SECURITIES

There are three types of mortgage-backed securities: pass-through securities, stripped mortgage-backed securities, and collateralized mortgage obligations. We review each below.

Pass-Through Securities

A mortgage pass-through security, or simply a pass-through, is created when one or more mortgage holders form a pool of mortgages and sell shares or participation certificates in the pool. The three major issuers/guarantors of pass-throughs are Ginnie Mae, Fannie Mae, and Freddie Mac.

The aggregate monthly cash flow for a pool of mortgages consists of three components: (1) interest, (2) scheduled principal repayment, and (3) prepayments (that is, payments in excess of the regularly scheduled principal repayment). Payments are made to security holders each month. The monthly cash flow for a pass-through is less than the monthly cash flow of the underlying mortgages by an amount equal to servicing and other fees. The other fees are those charged by the issuer or guarantor of the pass-through for guaranteeing the issue. The coupon rate on a pass-through, called the *pass-through coupon rate*, is less than the mortgage rate on the underlying pool of mortgage loans by an amount equal to the servicing and guaranteeing fees.

Because of prepayments, an investor in a pass-through is still exposed to prepayment risk. This risk can never be eliminated. The expectation is that while the investor in an individual loan may find it quite difficult to predict the prepayment behavior of the borrower, the same will not be true for a pool consisting of a large number of mortgages. Rather, based on the historical experience of a pool of mortgages, the investor can better project the prepayment behavior.

Stripped Mortgage-Backed Securities

A pass-through divides the cash flow from the underlying pool of mortgages on a pro rata basis to the security holders. A stripped mortgage-backed security is created by altering the distribution of principal and interest from a pro rata distribution to an *unequal* distribution. For example, one class may be entitled to receive all of the principal and the other class all of the interest.

There are two types of stripped MBS: (1) synthetic-coupon pass-throughs, and (2) interest-only/principal-only securities. The first generation of stripped mortgage-backed securities were the synthetic-coupon pass-throughs. This is because the unequal distribution of coupon and principal resulted in a synthetic coupon rate that is different from the underlying collateral. In early 1987, stripped MBS began to be issued in which all of the interest is allocated to one class (the interest-only, or IO, class) and all of the principal to the other class (the principal-only, or PO, class). The IO class receives no principal payments.

Of course, since they are backed by a pool of mortgages, investors in stripped mortgage-backed securities are exposed to prepayment risk. In the case of POs and IOs, their value is highly sensitive to expected prepayments. The owner of a PO benefits from fast prepayments and is hurt by slow prepayments. The opposite is true for an investor in an IO. Moreover, while the owner of a PO is assured of receiving the stated principal, the owner of an IO cannot be assured of recovering the amount invested in the security.

Collateralized Mortgage Obligations

From an asset/liability perspective, fixed-rate pass-throughs are an unattractive investment for many institutional investors because of prepayment risk. More specifically, certain institutional investors are concerned that a pass-through's life will extend while others are concerned that its life will contract.

As an example of the former, consider depository institutions. These institutions raise funds on a short-term basis either through the issuance of certificates of deposit or short-term money market obligations. If they invest the proceeds in a fixed-rate pass-through, they will be mismatched because a pass-through is a long-term security. More specifically, the concern of a depository institution is that the pass-through's average life (defined later) will become even longer than the liabilities. This would occur if rates in the mortgage market rise and prepayments slow down. Under this scenario, the institution would be locked in to a security paying a below-market interest rate and forced to borrow funds at a higher rate. This form of prepayment risk is called *extension risk*. It is so named because the average life of the pass-through would extend.

Now consider a pension fund with a predetermined set of long-term liabilities that must be paid. By buying a pass-through, these institutional investors are exposed to the risk that prepayments will speed up and, as a result, the pass-through's maturity will shorten considerably. Prepayments will speed up if interest rates decline, thereby forcing reinvestment of the principal received at a lower interest rate. In this case, the pension fund is exposed to the risk that the average life of the pass-through will contract. This form of prepayment risk is called *contraction risk*.

Thus some institutional investors are concerned with extension risk and others with contraction risk when they invest in a pass-through. Fortunately, it is possible by redirecting cash flows from a pass-through to different bond classes, to redistribute prepayment risk to investors who want to reduce their exposure to one of these two types of prepayment risk. Since the total prepayment risk of a pass-through is not changed by altering the cash flows, other investors must be willing to accept the unwanted prepayment risk.

The collateralized mortgage obligation (CMO) structure was developed to broaden the appeal of mortgage-backed products to traditional fixed-income investors. A CMO is a security backed by (1) a pool of pass-throughs, or (2) principal-only mortgage-backed securities, or (3) a pool of mortgage loans that have not been securitized.

CMOs are structured so that there are several classes of bondholders with varying maturities. The different bond classes are also called *tranches*. The principal payments from the underlying collateral are used to retire the bonds based on a set of rules specified in the prospectus. There are also rules for the distribution of the net interest (i.e., interest after servicing and other fees). The rules for the distribution of the principal and interest can range from simple (as in the earlier deals) to those that are quite complex, as seen in recent deals.

Exhibit 9-2 shows how a simple CMO structure can be created from a pool of mortgages that has been securitized. Exhibit 9-3 provides generic characteristics of some CMO classes.

PREPAYMENT CONVENTIONS AND CASH FLOW[2]

The analysis of any mortgage-backed security requires a projection of its cash flow. The difficulty is that the cash flow is unknown because of prepayments. The only way to project a cash flow is to make some assumption about the prepayment rate over the life of the underlying mortgage pool. Several conventions have been used as a benchmark for prepayment rates. The convention currently used is the Public Securities Association (PSA) prepayment benchmark. In order to understand the PSA prepayment benchmark, it is necessary to introduce the concept of a conditional prepayment rate.

Conditional Prepayment Rate

The projection of the cash flow of a mortgage-backed security requires an assumption about what fraction of the remaining principal in the pool is prepaid each month for the remaining term of the mortgage. The prepayment rate assumed for a pool, called the *conditional prepayment rate* (CPR), is based on the characteristics of the pool (including its historical prepayment experience) and the current and expected future economic environment. When the same CPR is assumed for each month, it is said that a constant CPR is used.

---

[2] This section and the one to follow are adapted from Chapter 3 of Frank J. Fabozzi, Charles Ramsey, and Frank R. Ramirez, *Collateralized Mortgage Obligations: Structures and Analysis* 2d ed. (Buckingham, PA: Frank J. Fabozzi Associates, 1994).

Exhibit 9-2. Creation of a Simple CMO Structure

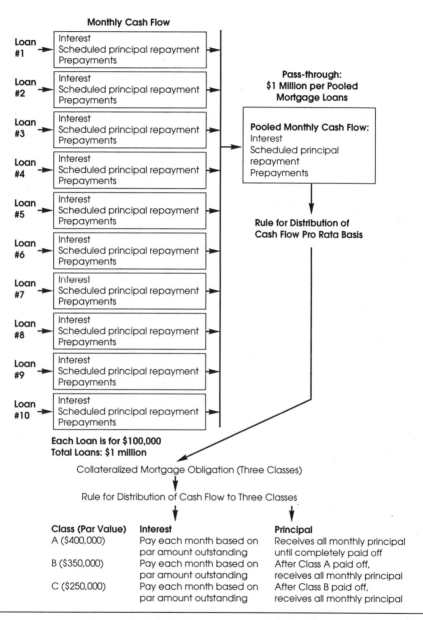

Source: Frank J. Fabozzi, Chuck Ramsey, and Frank Ramirez, *Collateralized Mortgage Obligations: Structures and Analysis* (Buckingham, PA: Frank J. Fabozzi Associates, 1994), p. 6.

Exhibit 9-3. Generic Characteristics of Some CMO Classes

PAC Is: Planned Amortization Class bonds generally exhibit average-life stability and call and extension risk protection inside the PAC bands.

PAC IIs: Second-tier PAC bonds typically have somewhat less average-life stability with correspondingly less call protection and more extension risk.

TACs: Targeted Amortization Class bonds are generally call-protected above the target speed but have substantial extension risk.

Companions: Sometimes referred to as support bonds, these classes exhibit volatile average lives and have cash flows that support the amortization schedule of PAC and TAC bonds.

Z Bonds (Accrual): These are long average-life bonds with no up-front cash flows. Interest accrues to this class over its life.

IOs: Interest-only bonds are sold at high premiums. These classes have a bearish profile and benefit from slowing prepayments.

POs: Principal-only bonds are sold at deep discounts. These classes have a bullish profile and benefit from increasing prepayments.

Sequentials: These are plain vanilla bonds of various average lives, depending on their sequence in the CMO.

Floaters: Floating-coupon rate classes can be created off any of the principal structures.

Inverse Floaters: The inverse floating-rate classes can generally be combined with the floater to re-create the underlying bond.

Source: David T. Yuen, T. Anthony Coffey, Roger A. Bayston, and Shannon R. Owens, "CMO Structure Analysis," in Frank J. Fabozzi, ed., *CMO Portfolio Management* (Summit, NJ: Frank J. Fabozzi Associated, 1994), p. 39.

The Single-Monthly Mortality Rate. The CPR is an annual prepayment rate. To estimate monthly prepayments, the CPR must be converted into a monthly prepayment rate, commonly referred to as the *single-monthly mortality rate* (SMM). A formula can be used to determine the SMM for a given CPR:

$$SMM = 1 - (1 - CPR)^{1/12}$$

Suppose that the CPR used to estimate prepayments is 6 percent. The corresponding SMM is:

$$SMM = 1 - (1 - 0.06)^{1/12}$$
$$= 1 \ (0.94)^{0.08333} = 0.005143$$

The SMM Rate and the Monthly Prepayment. An SMM of w percent means that approximately w percent of the remaining mortgage balance at the beginning of the month, less the scheduled principal payment, will prepay that month. That is,

Prepayment for month t
$$= SMM \times (\text{Beginning mortgage balance for month } t$$
$$- \text{Scheduled principal payment for month } t)$$

For example, suppose that an investor owns a pass-through in which the remaining mortgage balance at the beginning of some month is $290 million. Assuming that the SMM is 0.5143 percent and the scheduled principal payment is $3 million, the estimated prepayment for the month is:

$$0.005143 \times (\$290,000,000 - \$3,000,000) = \$1,476,041$$

PSA Prepayment Benchmark

The Public Securities Association (PSA) prepayment benchmark is expressed as a monthly series of CPRs.[3] The PSA benchmark assumes that prepayment rates are low for newly originated mortgages and then will speed up as the mortgages become seasoned.

The PSA benchmark assumes the following prepayment rates for 30-year mortgages:

1. a CPR of 0.2 percent for the first month, increased by 0.2 percent per year per month for the next 30 months when it reaches 6 percent per year, and

---

[3] This benchmark is commonly referred to as a prepayment model, suggesting that it can be used to estimate prepayments. But characterization of this benchmark as a prepayment model is inappropriate; it is simply a market convention.

Exhibit 9-4. Graphical Depiction of 100 PSA

2. a 6 percent CPR for the remaining years.

This benchmark, referred to as "100 percent PSA" or simply "100 PSA," is graphically depicted in Exhibit 9-4. Mathematically, 100 PSA can be expressed as follows:

if $t \leq 30$, then CPR = 6% $(t/30)$
if $t > 30$, then CPR = 6%

where t is the number of months since the mortgage originated.

Slower or faster speeds are then referred to as some percentage of PSA. For example, 50 PSA means one-half the CPR of the PSA benchmark prepayment rate; 150 PSA means 1.5 times the CPR of the PSA benchmark prepayment rate; 300 PSA means three times the CPR of the PSA benchmark prepayment rate. This is illustrated graphically in Exhibit 9-5 for 50 PSA, 100 PSA, and 150 PSA. A prepayment rate of 0 PSA means that no prepayments are assumed.

The CPR is converted to an SMM. For example, the SMMs for month 5, month 20, and months 31 through 360 assuming 100 PSA are calculated as follows:

for month 5: $CPR = 6\% \ (5/30) = 1\% = 0.01$
                             $SMM = 1 - (1 - 0.01)^{1/12}$
                             $ = 1 - (0.99)^{0.083333} = 0.000837$

for month 20: $CPR = 6\% \ (20/30) = 4\% = 0.04$
                             $SMM = 1 - (1 - 0.04)^{1/12}$
                             $ = 1 - (0.96)^{0.083333} = 0.003396$

for months 31–360: $CPR = 6\%$
                             $SMM = 1 - (1 - 0.06)^{1/12}$
                             $ = 1 - (0.94)^{0.083333} = 0.005143$

The SMMs for month 5, month 20, and months 31 through 360 assuming 165 PSA are computed as follows:[4]

for month 5: $CPR = 6\% \ (5/30) = 1\% = 0.01$
                             $165 \ PSA = 1.65 \ (0.01) = 0.0165$
                             $SMM = 1 - (1 - 0.0165)^{1/12}$
                             $ = 1 - (0.9835)^{0.083333} = 0.001386$

for month 20: $CPR = 6\% \ (20/30) = 4\% = 0.04$
                             $165 \ PSA = 1.65 \ (0.04) = 0.066$
                             $SMM = 1 - (1 - 0.066)^{1/12}$
                             $ = 1 - (0.934)^{0.083333} = 0.005674$

for months 31–360: $CPR = 6\%$
                             $165 \ PSA = 1.65 \ (0.06) = 0.099$
                             $SMM = 1 - (1 - 0.099)^{1/12}$
                             $ = 1 - (0.901)^{0.083333} = 0.007828$

Illustration of Monthly Cash Flow Construction. We now show how to construct a monthly cash flow for a hypothetical pass-through, given a PSA assumption. For the purpose of this illustra-

---

[4] Notice that the SMM assuming 165 PSA is not just 1.65 times the SMM assuming 100 PSA. It is the CPR that is a multiple of the CPR assuming 100 PSA.

Exhibit 9-5. Graphical Depiction of 50 PSA, 100 PSA, and 150 PSA

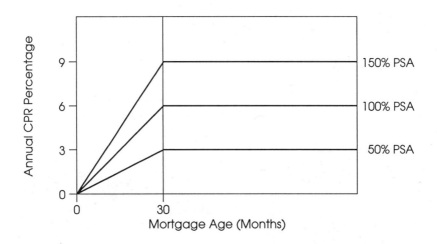

tion, the underlying mortgages for this hypothetical pass-through are assumed to be fixed-rate, level-payment mortgages with a weighted average coupon (WAC) rate of 8.125 percent. It will be assumed that the pass-through rate is 7.5 percent with a weighted average maturity (WAM) of 357 months.

Exhibit 9-6 shows the cash flow for selected months assuming 100 PSA. The cash flow is broken down into three components: (1) interest (based on the pass-through rate), (2) the regularly scheduled principal repayment, (3) prepayments based on 100 PSA.

Let's walk through Exhibit 9-6 column by column.

Column 1: This is the month.

Column 2: This column gives the outstanding mortgage balance at the beginning of the month. It is equal to the outstanding balance at the beginning of the previous month reduced by the total principal payment in the previous month.

Column 3: This column shows the SMM for 100 PSA. Two things should be noted in this column. First, for month 1, the SMM is for a pass-through that has been seasoned three

Exhibit 9-6. Monthly Cash Flow for a $400 Million Pass-Through with a 7.5 Percent Pass-Through Rate, a WAC of 8.125 Percent, and a WAM of 357 Months Assuming 100 PSA

Mo.	Outstanding balance	SMM	Mortgage payment	Net interest	Scheduled principal	Prepay-ment	Total principal	Total cash flow
1	400,000,000	0.00067	2,975,868	2,500,000	267,535	267,470	535,005	3,035,005
2	399,464,995	0.00084	2,973,877	2,496,656	269,166	334,198	603,364	3,100,020
3	398,861,631	0.00101	2,971,387	2,492,885	270,762	400,800	671,562	3,164,447
4	398,190,069	0.00117	2,968,399	2,488,688	272,321	467,243	739,564	3,228,252
5	397,450,505	0.00134	2,964,914	2,484,066	273,843	533,493	807,335	3,291,401
6	396,643,170	0.00151	2,960,931	2,479,020	275,327	599,514	874,841	3,353,860
7	395,768,329	0.00168	2,956,453	2,473,552	276,772	665,273	942,045	3,415,597
8	394,826,284	0.00185	2,951,480	2,467,664	278,177	730,736	1,008,913	3,476,577
9	393,817,371	0.00202	2,946,013	2,461,359	279,542	795,869	1,075,410	3,536,769
10	392,741,961	0.00219	2,940,056	2,454,637	280,865	860,637	1,141,502	3,596,140
11	391,600,459	0.00236	2,933,608	2,447,503	282,147	925,008	1,207,155	3,654,658
12	390,393,304	0.00254	2,926,674	2,439,958	283,386	988,948	1,272,333	3,712,291
13	389,120,971	0.00271	2,919,254	2,432,006	284,581	1,052,423	1,337,004	3,769,010
14	387,783,966	0.00288	2,911,353	2,423,650	285,733	1,115,402	1,401,134	3,824,784
15	386,382,832	0.00305	2,902,973	2,414,893	286,839	1,177,851	1,464,690	3,879,583

194

Mo.	Outstanding balance	SMM	Mortgage payment	Net interest	Scheduled principal	Prepayment	Total principal	Total cash flow
16	384,918,142	0.00322	2,894,117	2,405,738	287,900	1,239,739	1,527,639	3,933,378
17	383,390,502	0.00340	2,884,789	2,396,191	288,915	1,301,033	1,589,949	3,986,139
18	381,800,553	0.00357	2,874,992	2,386,253	289,884	1,361,703	1,651,587	4,037,840
19	380,148,966	0.00374	2,864,730	2,375,931	290,805	1,421,717	1,712,522	4,088,453
20	378,436,444	0.00392	2,854,008	2,365,228	291,678	1,481,046	1,772,724	4,137,952
21	376,663,720	0.00409	2,842,830	2,354,148	292,503	1,539,658	1,832,161	4,186,309
22	374,831,559	0.00427	2,831,201	2,342,697	293,279	1,597,525	1,890,804	4,233,501
23	372,940,755	0.00444	2,819,125	2,330,880	294,005	1,654,618	1,948,623	4,279,503
24	370,992,132	0.00462	2,806,607	2,318,701	294,681	1,710,908	2,005,589	4,324,290
25	368,986,543	0.00479	2,793,654	2,306,166	295,307	1,766,368	2,061,675	4,367,841
26	366,924,868	0.00497	2,780,270	2,293,280	295,883	1,820,970	2,116,852	4,410,133
27	364,808,016	0.00514	2,766,461	2,280,050	296,406	1,874,688	2,171,094	4,451,144
28	362,636,921	0.00514	2,752,233	2,266,481	296,879	1,863,519	2,160,398	4,426,879
29	360,476,523	0.00514	2,738,078	2,252,978	297,351	1,852,406	2,149,758	4,402,736
30	358,326,766	0.00514	2,723,996	2,239,542	297,825	1,841,347	2,139,173	4,378,715

Exhibit 9-6 (Continued).

Mo.	Outstanding balance	SMM	Mortgage payment	Net interest	Scheduled principal	Prepay-ment	Total principal	Total cash flow
100	231,249,776	0.00514	1,898,682	1,445,311	332,928	1,187,608	1,520,537	2,965,848
101	229,729,239	0.00514	1,888,917	1,435,808	333,459	1,179,785	1,513,244	2,949,052
102	228,215,995	0.00514	1,879,202	1,426,350	333,990	1,172,000	1,505,990	2,932,340
103	226,710,004	0.00514	1,869,538	1,416,938	334,522	1,164,252	1,498,774	2,915,712
104	225,211,230	0.00514	1,859,923	1,407,570	335,055	1,156,541	1,491,596	2,899,166
105	223,719,634	0.00514	1,850,357	1,398,248	335,589	1,148,867	1,484,456	2,882,703
200	109,791,339	0.00514	1,133,751	686,196	390,372	562,651	953,023	1,639,219
201	108,838,316	0.00514	1,127,920	680,239	390,994	557,746	948,740	1,628,980
202	107,889,576	0.00514	1,122,119	674,310	391,617	552,863	944,480	1,618,790
203	106,945,096	0.00514	1,116,348	668,407	392,241	548,003	940,243	1,608,650
204	106,004,852	0.00514	1,110,607	662,530	392,866	543,164	936,029	1,598,560
205	105,068,823	0.00514	1,104,895	656,680	393,491	538,347	931,838	1,588,518

Mo.	Outstanding balance	SMM	Mortgage payment	Net interest	Scheduled principal	Prepayment	Total principal	Total cash flow
300	32,383,611	0.00514	676,991	202,398	457,727	164,195	621,923	824,320
301	31,761,689	0.00514	673,510	198,511	458,457	160,993	619,449	817,960
302	31,142,239	0.00514	670,046	194,639	459,187	157,803	616,990	811,629
303	30,525,249	0.00514	666,600	190,783	459,918	154,626	614,545	805,328
304	29,910,704	0.00514	663,171	186,942	460,651	151,462	612,113	799,055
305	29,298,591	0.00514	659,761	183,116	461,385	148,310	609,695	792,811
350	4,060,411	0.00514	523,138	25,378	495,645	18,334	513,979	539,356
351	3,546,432	0.00514	520,447	22,165	496,435	15,686	512,121	534,286
352	3,034,311	0.00514	517,770	18,964	497,226	13,048	510,274	529,238
353	2,524,037	0.00514	515,107	15,775	498,018	10,420	508,437	524,213
354	2,015,600	0.00514	512,458	12,597	498,811	7,801	506,612	519,209
355	1,508,988	0.00514	509,823	9,431	499,606	5,191	504,797	514,228
356	1,004,191	0.00514	507,201	6,276	500,401	2,591	502,992	509,269
357	501,199	0.00514	504,592	3,132	501,199	0	501,199	504,331

months. That is, the CPR is 0.8 percent. This is because the WAM is 357. Second, from month 27 on, the SMM is 0.00514, which corresponds to a CPR of 6 percent.

Column 4: The total monthly mortgage payment is shown in this column. Notice that the total monthly mortgage payment declines over time as prepayments reduce the mortgage balance outstanding. There is a formula to determine what the monthly mortgage balance will be for each month given prepayment.[5]

Column 5: The monthly interest paid to the pass-through investor is found in this column. This value is determined by multiplying the outstanding mortgage balance at the beginning of the month by the pass-through rate of 7.5 percent and dividing by 12.

Column 6: This column gives the regularly scheduled principal repayment. This is the difference between the total monthly mortgage payment [the amount shown in column (4)] and the gross coupon interest for the month. The gross coupon interest is 8.125 percent multiplied by the outstanding mortgage balance at the beginning of the month, then divided by 12.

Column 7: The prepayment for the month is reported in this column. The prepayment is found as follows:

SMM × (Beginning mortgage balance for month t
       − Scheduled principal payment for month t)

So, for example, in month 100, the beginning mortgage balance is $231,249,776, the scheduled principal payment is $332,928, and the SMM at 100 PSA is 0.00514301 (only 0.00514 is shown in the exhibit to save space), so the prepayment is:

0.00514301 × ($231,249,776 − $332,928) = $1,187,608

---

[5] The formula is presented in Chapter 20 of Frank J. Fabozzi, *Fixed Income Mathematics: Analytical and Statistical Techniques* (Chicago: Probus Publishing, 1993).

Column 8: The total principal payment, which is the sum of columns (6) and (7), is shown in this column.

Column 9: The projected monthly cash flow for this pass-through is shown in this last column. The monthly cash flow is the sum of the interest paid to the pass-through investor [column (5)] and the total principal payments for the month [column (8)].

Exhibit 9-7 shows selected monthly cash flows for the same pass-through assuming 165 PSA.

Cash Flow for Stripped MBS and CMO Tranches

The cash flows in Exhibits 9-6 and 9-7 are for a pass-through security. The cash flow for an interest-only security would be that shown in the column "net interest," while for a principal-only security the cash flow would be that shown in the column "total principal." For a CMO, the cash flow for each tranche depends on the rules for the distribution of principal and (net) interest.

To illustrate how the cash flow is determined for a CMO, we will create a simple a sequential-pay CMO structure. The collateral for this hypothetical CMO is a hypothetical pass-through with a total par value of $400 million and the following characteristics: (1) the pass-through coupon rate is 7.5 percent, (2) the weighted average coupon (WAC) is 8.125 percent, and (3) the weighted average maturity (WAM) is 357 months. This is the same pass-through whose cash flow we constructed in Exhibits 9-6 and 9-7 assuming 100 PSA and 165 PSA, respectively.

From this $400 million of collateral, four bond classes or tranches are created. Their characteristics are summarized in Exhibit 9-8. The total par value of the four tranches is equal to the par value of the collateral (i.e., the pass-through security). This structure is a simple sequential-pay structure with the last tranche being an accrual or Z bond. Because the coupon interest for each tranche is less than that of the collateral, there is a residual or equity class that realizes the difference between the total interest from the collateral and the total interest paid to the four tranches. Classes A, B, C, and Z are referred to as regular interest classes.

Exhibit 9-7. Monthly Cash Flow for a $400 Million Pass-Through with a 7.5 Percent Pass-Through Rate, a WAC of 8.125 Percent, and a WAM of 357 Months Assuming 165 PSA

Mo.	Outstanding balance	SMM	Mortgage payment	Net interest	Scheduled principal	Prepay-ment	Total principal	Total cash flow
1	400,000,000	0.00111	2,975,868	2,500,000	267,535	442,389	709,923	3,209,923
2	399,290,077	0.00139	2,972,575	2,495,563	269,048	552,847	821,896	3,317,459
3	398,468,181	0.00167	2,968,456	2,490,426	270,495	663,065	933,560	3,423,986
4	397,534,621	0.00195	2,963,513	2,484,591	271,873	772,949	1,044,822	3,529,413
5	396,489,799	0.00223	2,957,747	2,478,061	273,181	882,405	1,155,586	3,633,647
6	395,334,213	0.00251	2,951,160	2,470,839	274,418	991,341	1,265,759	3,736,598
7	394,068,454	0.00279	2,943,755	2,462,928	275,583	1,099,664	1,375,246	3,838,174
8	392,693,208	0.00308	2,935,534	2,454,333	276,674	1,207,280	1,483,954	3,938,287
9	391,209,254	0.00336	2,926,503	2,445,058	277,690	1,314,099	1,591,789	4,036,847
10	389,617,464	0.00365	2,916,666	2,435,109	278,631	1,420,029	1,698,659	4,133,769
11	387,918,805	0.00393	2,906,028	2,424,493	279,494	1,524,979	1,804,473	4,228,965
12	386,114,332	0.00422	2,894,595	2,413,215	280,280	1,628,859	1,909,139	4,322,353
13	384,205,194	0.00451	2,882,375	2,401,282	280,986	1,731,581	2,012,567	4,413,850
14	382,192,626	0.00480	2,869,375	2,388,704	281,613	1,833,058	2,114,670	4,503,374
15	380,077,956	0.00509	2,855,603	2,375,487	282,159	1,933,203	2,215,361	4,590,848

Mo.	Outstanding balance	SMM	Mortgage payment	Net interest	Scheduled principal	Prepay- ment	Total principal	Total cash flow
16	377,862,595	0.00538	2,841,068	2,361,641	282,623	2,031,931	2,314,554	4,676,195
17	375,548,041	0.00567	2,825,779	2,347,175	283,006	2,129,159	2,412,164	4,759,339
18	373,135,877	0.00597	2,809,746	2,332,099	283,305	2,224,805	2,508,110	4,840,210
19	370,627,766	0.00626	2,792,980	2,316,424	283,521	2,318,790	2,602,312	4,918,735
20	368,025,455	0.00656	2,775,493	2,300,159	283,654	2,411,036	2,694,690	4,994,849
21	365,330,765	0.00685	2,757,296	2,283,317	283,702	2,501,466	2,785,169	5,068,486
22	362,545,596	0.00715	2,738,402	2,265,910	283,666	2,590,008	2,873,674	5,139,584
23	359,671,922	0.00745	2,718,823	2,247,950	283,545	2,676,588	2,960,133	5,208,083
24	356,711,789	0.00775	2,698,575	2,229,449	283,338	2,761,139	3,044,477	5,273,926
25	353,667,312	0.00805	2,677,670	2,210,421	283,047	2,843,593	3,126,640	5,337,061
26	350,540,672	0.00835	2,656,123	2,190,879	282,671	2,923,885	3,206,556	5,397,435
27	347,334,116	0.00865	2,633,950	2,170,838	282,209	3,001,955	3,284,164	5,455,002
28	344,049,952	0.00865	2,611,167	2,150,312	281,662	2,973,553	3,255,215	5,405,527
29	340,794,737	0.00865	2,588,581	2,129,967	281,116	2,945,400	3,226,516	5,356,483
30	337,568,221	0.00865	2,566,190	2,109,801	280,572	2,917,496	3,198,067	5,307,869

Exhibit 9-7 (Continued).

Mo.	Outstanding balance	SMM	Mortgage payment	Net interest	Scheduled principal	Prepay-ment	Total principal	Total cash flow
100	170,142,350	0.00865	1,396,958	1,063,390	244,953	1,469,591	1,714,544	2,777,933
101	168,427,806	0.00865	1,384,875	1,052,674	244,478	1,454,765	1,699,243	2,751,916
102	166,728,563	0.00865	1,372,896	1,042,054	244,004	1,440,071	1,684,075	2,726,128
103	165,044,489	0.00865	1,361,020	1,031,528	243,531	1,425,508	1,669,039	2,700,567
104	163,375,450	0.00865	1,349,248	1,021,097	243,060	1,411,075	1,654,134	2,675,231
105	161,721,315	0.00865	1,337,577	1,010,758	242,589	1,396,771	1,639,359	2,650,118
200	56,746,664	0.00865	585,990	354,667	201,767	489,106	690,874	1,045,540
201	56,055,790	0.00865	580,921	350,349	201,377	483,134	684,510	1,034,859
202	55,371,280	0.00865	575,896	346,070	200,986	477,216	678,202	1,024,273
203	54,693,077	0.00865	570,915	341,832	200,597	471,353	671,950	1,013,782
204	54,021,127	0.00865	565,976	337,632	200,208	465,544	665,752	1,003,384
205	53,355,375	0.00865	561,081	333,471	199,820	459,789	659,609	993,080

Mo.	Outstanding balance	SMM	Mortgage payment	Net interest	Scheduled principal	Prepayment	Total principal	Total cash flow
300	11,758,141	0.00865	245,808	73,488	166,196	100,269	266,465	339,953
301	11,491,677	0.00865	243,682	71,823	165,874	97,967	263,841	335,664
302	11,227,836	0.00865	241,574	70,174	165,552	95,687	261,240	331,414
303	10,966,596	0.00865	239,485	68,541	165,232	93,430	258,662	327,203
304	10,707,934	0.00865	237,413	66,925	164,912	91,196	256,107	323,032
305	10,451,827	0.00865	235,360	65,324	164,592	88,983	253,575	318,899
350	1,235,674	0.00865	159,202	7,723	150,836	9,384	160,220	167,943
351	1,075,454	0.00865	157,825	6,722	150,544	8,000	158,544	165,266
352	916,910	0.00865	156,460	5,731	150,252	6,631	156,883	162,614
353	760,027	0.00865	155,107	4,750	149,961	5,277	155,238	159,988
354	604,789	0.00865	153,765	3,780	149,670	3,937	153,607	157,387
355	451,182	0.00865	152,435	2,820	149,380	2,611	151,991	154,811
356	299,191	0.00865	151,117	1,870	149,091	1,298	150,389	152,259
357	148,802	0.00865	149,809	930	148,802	0	148,802	149,732

Exhibit 9-8. A Hypothetical Four-Tranche Sequential-Pay
Structure with an Accrual Bond Class and a Residual Class

Tranche	Par amount	Coupon rate
A	$194,500,000	6.00%
B	36,000,000	6.50
C	96,500,000	7.00
Z (Accrual)	73,000,000	7.25
R	0	0
Total	$400,000,000	

Payment rules:

1. For payment of periodic coupon interest: Disburse periodic coupon interest to tranches A, B, and C on the basis of the amount of principal outstanding at the beginning of the period. For tranche Z, accrue the interest based on the principal plus accrued interest in the previous period. The interest for tranche Z is to be paid to the earlier tranches as a principal paydown.
2. For disbursement of principal payments: Disburse principal payments to tranche A until it is completely paid off. After tranche A is completely paid off, disburse principal payments to tranche B until it is completely paid off. After tranche B is completely paid off, disburse principal payments to tranche C until it is completely paid off. After tranche C is completely paid off, disburse principal payments to tranche Z until the original principal balance plus accrued interest is completely paid off.
3. Tranche R (the residual class) receives any monthly excess interest payment and reinvestment income.

Now remember that a CMO is created by redistributing the cash flow—interest and principal—to the different tranches based on a set of payment rules. The payment rules at the bottom of Exhibit 9-8 describe how the cash flow from the pass-through (i.e., collateral) is to be distributed to the four tranches. There are separate rules for the payment of the interest and the payment of principal, the principal being the total of the regularly scheduled principal payment and any prepayments.

In our hypothetical CMO structure, the first three tranches receive periodic interest payments based on the amount of the outstanding balance at the beginning of the month. The interest on the accrual bond accrues interest. The disbursement of the principal, however, is made in a special way. A tranche is not entitled to receive principal until the entire principal of the tranche before it has been paid off. More specifically, tranche A receives all the principal payments until the entire principal amount owed to that tranche, $194,500,000, is paid off; then tranche B begins to receive principal and continues to do so until it is paid the entire $36,000,000. Tranche C then receives principal, and when it is paid off, tranche Z starts receiving principal payments and the accrued interest that it is owed. The interest that accrues to the accrual bond is paid to the other tranches in the form of principal repayment.

While the priority rules for the disbursement of the principal payments are known, the precise amount of the principal in each period is not. This will depend on the cash flow, and therefore principal payments of the collateral, which depends on the actual prepayments of the collateral. An assumed PSA speed allows the cash flow to be projected. Exhibit 9-7 shows the cash flow (interest, regularly scheduled principal repayment, and prepayments) assuming 165 PSA. Assuming that the collateral does prepay at 165 PSA, the cash flow available to all four tranches will be precisely the cash flow shown in Exhibit 9-7.

VALUATION TECHNIQUES

There are two approaches used to analyze mortgage-backed securities: static-cash-flow analysis and option-adjusted spread/Monte Carlo simulation analysis. The static-cash-flow yield method is the simplest of the two valuation technologies to apply, although it may offer little insight into the relative value of mortgage-backed securities.

Static-Cash-Flow Yield Method

For mortgage-backed securities, as with all fixed-income securities, the yield is the interest rate that will make the present value of the cash flow equal to the price (plus accrued interest). A yield calculated in this manner for a mortgage-backed security is called a *cash-flow yield*.[6] The problem, of course, in calculating an MBS cash-flow

---

[6] Some market participants also refer to the cash-flow yield as the yield to maturity. This practice will not be followed in this chapter.

yield is that prepayments mean that the cash flow is unknown. Consequently, to determine a cash-flow yield some assumption about the prepayment rate must be made.[7]

Exhibit 9-9 shows the cash-flow yields based on various constant PSA prepayment assumptions for the four regular interest classes assuming different purchase prices. Notice that the greater the discount assumed to be paid for the tranche, the more a tranche will benefit from faster prepayments. The converse is true for a tranche for which a premium is paid. The faster the prepayments, the lower the cash-flow yield.

Vector Analysis. One practice market participants use to overcome the drawback of the PSA benchmark is to assume that the PSA speed can change over time. This technique is called *variable prepay vector array analysis* or, more commonly, *vector analysis*. A vector is simply a single prepay assumption that is held constant for one or more months. In the case of a mortgage-backed security, if the underlying pool is 30-year mortgages, a vector analysis could have as many as 360 prepayment vectors. This type of analysis is crucial in evaluating many CMO structures because differing levels of prepayment activity dramatically affect the cash flows of certain tranche types.

Exhibit 9-10 reports the cash-flow yield using vector analysis. The top panel shows the cash-flow yield for the four regular interest classes and the collateral assuming 165 PSA. Nine vectors are then shown assuming that the PSA is constant from months 1 to 36,

---

[7] The cash flow for an MBS is typically monthly. The convention is to compare the yield on an MBS with that of Treasury coupon securities and corporate bonds by calculating the MBS's bond-equivalent yield. The market practice is to calculate a yield so as to make it comparable to the yield to maturity on a bond-equivalent yield basis. The formula for annualizing the periodic cash-flow yield for an MBS is as follows:

Bond-equivalent yield = $2[(1 + i_M)^6 - 1]$

where i_M is the monthly interest rate that will equate the present value of the projected monthly cash flow to the price (plus accrued interest) of the MBS.

Exhibit 9-9. Price/Cash-Flow Yield Table for the Four Tranches CMO Structure

Tranche A: Orig Par: $194,500,000; Type: SEQ; Coupon: 6.0% (Fixed)

If price paid is	50.00 PSA	100.00 PSA	165.00 PSA	250.00 PSA	400.00 PSA	500.00 PSA	700.00 PSA	1000.00 PSA
90–24	8.37	9.01	9.76	10.61	11.87	12.59	13.88	15.63
91–24	8.09	8.66	9.32	10.07	11.17	11.81	12.94	14.47
92–24	7.82	8.31	8.88	9.53	10.49	11.03	12.01	13.33
93–24	7.56	7.97	8.45	9.00	9.81	10.27	11.10	12.22
94–24	7.29	7.63	8.03	8.48	9.14	9.52	10.20	11.12
95–24	7.03	7.30	7.61	7.97	8.49	8.79	9.32	10.04
96–24	6.78	6.97	7.20	7.46	7.85	8.06	8.45	8.98
97–24	6.53	6.65	6.80	6.97	7.21	7.35	7.60	7.94
98–24	6.28	6.34	6.40	6.48	6.59	6.65	6.76	6.91
99–24	6.04	6.02	6.01	6.00	5.97	5.96	5.94	5.91
100–24	5.79	5.72	5.62	5.52	5.37	5.28	5.13	4.92
101–24	5.56	5.41	5.24	5.05	4.77	4.61	4.33	3.95
102–24	5.33	5.12	4.87	4.59	4.18	3.95	3.54	2.99
103–24	5.10	4.82	4.50	4.14	3.61	3.30	2.77	2.05
104–24	4.87	4.53	4.14	3.69	3.04	2.66	2.01	1.12
105–24	4.65	4.25	3.78	3.25	2.47	2.03	1.26	0.21
106–24	4.42	3.96	3.42	2.81	1.92	1.41	0.52	-0.68
107–24	4.21	3.69	3.07	2.38	1.37	0.80	-0.21	-1.57
108–24	3.99	3.41	2.73	1.96	0.83	0.20	-0.93	-2.44
109–24	3.78	3.14	2.39	1.54	0.30	-0.40	-1.64	-3.29
Average life:	5.09	3.80	2.93	2.33	1.79	1.58	1.31	1.07
Mod. duration:	4.12	3.22	2.57	2.09	1.64	1.46	1.22	1.00

Exhibit 9-9 (Continued).

Tranche B: Orig Par: $36,000,000; Type: SEQ; Coupon: 6.50% (Fixed)

If price paid is	50.00 PSA	100.00 PSA	165.00 PSA	250.00 PSA	400.00 PSA	500.00 PSA	700.00 PSA	1000.00 PSA
90–31	7.85	8.12	8.49	8.95	9.69	10.13	10.89	11.83
91–31	7.69	7.93	8.25	8.66	9.31	9.70	10.36	11.18
92–31	7.54	7.75	8.02	8.37	8.94	9.27	9.84	10.55
93–31	7.39	7.57	7.80	8.09	8.57	8.85	9.33	9.92
94–31	7.24	7.39	7.58	7.82	8.20	8.43	8.82	9.31
95–31	7.10	7.21	7.35	7.54	7.84	8.02	8.32	8.70
96–31	6.95	7.03	7.14	7.27	7.49	7.61	7.83	8.10
97–31	6.81	6.86	6.92	7.00	7.13	7.21	7.34	7.51
98–31	6.67	6.69	6.71	6.74	6.79	6.82	6.86	6.92
99–31	6.53	6.52	6.50	6.48	6.45	6.42	6.39	6.35
100–31	6.39	6.35	6.29	6.22	6.11	6.04	5.92	5.78
101–31	6.26	6.19	6.09	5.97	5.77	5.66	5.46	5.22
102–31	6.13	6.02	5.89	5.72	5.44	5.28	5.00	4.66
103–31	5.99	5.86	5.69	5.47	5.12	4.91	4.55	4.12
104–31	5.86	5.70	5.49	5.22	4.79	4.54	4.11	3.58
105–31	5.74	5.55	5.30	4.98	4.48	4.18	3.67	3.04
106–31	5.61	5.39	5.10	4.74	4.16	3.82	3.23	2.51
107–31	5.48	5.24	4.91	4.50	3.85	3.46	2.80	1.99
108–31	5.36	5.08	4.72	4.27	3.54	3.11	2.38	1.48
109–31	5.24	4.93	4.54	4.04	3.24	2.76	1.96	0.97
Average life:	10.17	7.76	5.93	4.58	3.35	2.89	2.35	1.90
Mod. duration:	7.23	5.92	4.78	3.84	2.92	2.56	2.11	1.74

Tranche C: Orig Par: $96,500,000; Type: SEQ; Coupon: 7.00% (Fixed)

If price paid is	50.00 PSA	100.00 PSA	165.00 PSA	250.00 PSA	400.00 PSA	500.00 PSA	700.00 PSA	1000.00 PSA
90–03	8.34	8.53	8.80	9.15	9.77	10.16	10.89	11.85
91–03	8.20	8.37	8.61	8.92	9.47	9.81	10.46	11.31
92–03	8.06	8.21	8.42	8.70	9.17	9.48	10.05	10.79
93–03	7.92	8.06	8.24	8.47	8.88	9.14	9.63	10.27
94–03	7.79	7.90	8.05	8.25	8.60	8.81	9.22	9.76
95–03	7.66	7.75	7.87	8.03	8.31	8.49	8.82	9.25
96–03	7.53	7.60	7.69	7.82	8.03	8.17	8.42	8.76
97–03	7.40	7.45	7.52	7.61	7.76	7.85	8.03	8.26
98–03	7.28	7.31	7.35	7.40	7.48	7.54	7.64	7.78
99–03	7.15	7.16	7.17	7.19	7.21	7.23	7.26	7.30
100–03	7.03	7.02	7.01	6.98	6.95	6.93	6.88	6.83
101–03	6.91	6.88	6.84	6.78	6.69	6.63	6.51	6.36
102–03	6.79	6.74	6.67	6.58	6.43	6.33	6.14	5.90
103–03	6.67	6.61	6.51	6.39	6.17	6.03	5.78	5.45
104–03	6.56	6.47	6.35	6.19	5.92	5.74	5.42	5.00
105–03	6.44	6.34	6.19	6.00	5.67	5.46	5.07	4.56
106–03	6.33	6.21	6.03	5.81	5.42	5.17	4.72	4.12
107–03	6.22	6.08	5.88	5.62	5.18	4.89	4.37	3.69
108–03	6.11	5.95	5.73	5.43	4.94	4.62	4.03	3.26
109–03	6.00	5.82	5.57	5.25	4.70	4.34	3.69	2.84
Average life:	12.77	10.16	7.98	6.24	4.54	3.87	3.04	2.37
Mod duration:	8.18	7.04	5.92	4.89	3.76	3.28	2.65	2.12

Exhibit 9-9 (Continued).

Tranche Z: Orig Par: $73,000,000; Type: SEQ; Coupon: 7.25% (Fixed)

If price paid is	50.00 PSA	100.00 PSA	165.00 PSA	250.00 PSA	400.00 PSA	500.00 PSA	700.00 PSA	1000.00 PSA
90–01	7.87	7.96	8.09	8.27	8.61	8.84	9.33	10.10
91–01	7.82	7.89	8.00	8.16	8.47	8.68	9.11	9.79
92–01	7.76	7.83	7.93	8.07	8.33	8.51	8.89	9.49
93–01	7.71	7.76	7.85	7.97	8.20	8.35	8.68	9.20
94–01	7.65	7.70	7.77	7.87	8.06	8.19	8.47	8.90
95–01	7.60	7.63	7.69	7.77	7.93	8.04	8.26	8.61
96–01	7.54	7.57	7.62	7.68	7.80	7.88	8.05	8.33
97–01	7.49	7.51	7.54	7.59	7.67	7.73	7.85	8.04
98–01	7.44	7.45	7.47	7.49	7.54	7.58	7.65	7.76
99–01	7.38	7.39	7.39	7.40	7.42	7.43	7.45	7.49
100–01	7.33	7.33	7.32	7.31	7.29	7.28	7.26	7.21
101–01	7.28	7.27	7.25	7.22	7.17	7.14	7.06	6.95
102–01	7.23	7.21	7.18	7.13	7.05	6.99	6.87	6.68
103–01	7.18	7.15	7.11	7.05	6.93	6.85	6.68	6.42
104–01	7.13	7.09	7.04	6.96	6.81	6.71	6.49	6.16
105–01	7.08	7.04	6.97	6.88	6.69	6.57	6.31	5.90
106–01	7.04	6.98	6.90	6.79	6.58	6.43	6.13	5.65
107–01	6.99	6.93	6.84	6.71	6.46	6.29	5.94	5.39
108–01	6.94	6.87	6.77	6.62	6.35	6.16	5.77	5.15
109–01	6.89	6.82	6.70	6.54	6.24	6.03	5.59	4.90
Average life:	22.39	19.57	16.21	12.78	9.01	7.46	5.49	3.88
Mod. duration:	19.42	16.68	13.81	11.08	8.06	6.78	5.11	3.67

Calculated using SFW Software Copyright (c) 1989 by WallStreet Analytics, Inc.

and then changes for months 37 through 138, and again changes for months 139 through 357.

Limitations of Cash-Flow Yield.   All yield measures suffer from problems that limit their use in assessing the potential performance of a bond. The yield to maturity has two major shortcomings as a measure of a bond's potential return, as noted in earlier chapters. To realize the stated yield to maturity, the investor must: (1) reinvest the coupon payments at a rate equal to the yield to maturity, and (2) hold the bond to the maturity date. These shortcomings are equally applicable to the cash-flow yield measure: (1) the projected cash flows are assumed to be reinvested at the cash-flow yield, and (2) the mortgage-backed security is assumed to be held until the final payout based on some prepayment assumption. The importance of reinvestment risk, the risk that the cash flow will have to be reinvested at a rate lower than the cash-flow yield, is particularly important for many mortgage-backed securities, because payments are monthly and include both interest and principal that must be reinvested. Moreover, the cash-flow yield is dependent on realization of the projected cash flow according to some prepayment assumption. If the prepayment experience is different from the prepayment rate assumed, the cash-flow yield may not be realized.

Nominal Yield Spread.   Once the cash-flow yield is calculated according to some prepayment assumption, a nominal yield spread is determined. The nominal yield spread is typically measured relative to a comparable Treasury security, where "comparable" is defined as having a maturity that is close to either the Macaulay duration or the average life of the mortgage-backed security. We described how Macaulay duration is calculated in Chapter 2. The *average life* of a mortgage-backed security is the average time to receipt of principal payments (scheduled principal payments and projected prepayments), weighted by the amount of principal expected. Mathematically, the average life is expressed as follows:

$$\text{Average life} = \sum_{t=1}^{T} \frac{t \times \text{Principal received at time } t}{12(\text{Total principal})}$$

where T is the number of months.

Exhibit 9-10. Vector Analysis of Cash-Flow Yield for Four Tranches and Collateral

Assumptions:

	Coupon	Price	Cash-flow yield at 165 PSA
Tranche A	6.00%	99–24	6.00%
Tranche B	6.50	99–31	6.50
Tranche C	7.00	100–03	7.00
Tranche Z	7.25	100–01	7.25
Collateral	7.50	100–00	7.50

					PSA Vector Scenario				
	(1)	(2)	(3)	(4)	(5)	(6)	(7)	(8)	(9)
Months									
1–36	165	165	165	165	165	165	165	165	165
37–138	50	50	300	400	700	400	400	500	600
139–357	250	400	400	200	400	500	165	200	1000
Tranche/Parameter									
Tranche A:									
Cash-flow yield	6.02	6.02	6.01	6.00	6.00	6.00	6.00	6.00	6.00
Average life	3.51	3.51	2.71	2.63	2.63	2.63	2.63	2.58	2.54
Modified duration	2.97	2.97	2.40	2.34	2.34	2.34	2.34	2.30	2.27
Tranche B:									
Cash-flow yield	6.52	6.52	6.48	6.48	6.48	6.48	6.48	6.47	6.46
Average life	8.51	8.51	4.82	4.39	4.39	4.39	4.39	4.11	3.91
Modified duration	6.35	6.35	4.02	3.71	3.71	3.71	3.71	3.50	3.36

PSA Vector Scenario

Tranche/Parameter	Months	(1)	(2)	(3)	(4)	(5)	(6)	(7)	(8)	(9)
	1–36	165	165	165	165	165	165	165	165	165
	37–138	50	50	300	400	400	400	400	500	600
	139–357	250	400	400	200	700	500	165	200	1000
Tranche C:										
Cash-flow yield		7.03	7.03	6.98	6.97	6.97	6.97	6.97	6.96	6.95
Average life		11.15	11.07	6.24	5.52	5.52	5.52	5.52	5.04	4.68
Modified duration		7.50	7.47	4.89	4.43	4.43	4.43	4.43	4.11	3.87
Tranche Z:										
Cash-flow yield		7.26	7.25	7.21	7.19	7.19	7.20	7.20	7.17	7.14
Average life		17.08	15.29	11.47	10.49	9.55	11.42	10.65	8.92	7.49
Modified duration		15.44	14.19	10.28	9.19	8.76	9.56	9.26	8.01	6.98
Collateral										
Cash-flow yield		7.54	7.53	7.50	7.49	7.49	7.49	7.49	7.48	7.47
Average life		10.90	10.05	6.31	5.68	5.40	5.95	5.72	5.02	4.48
Modified duration		6.47	6.25	4.50	4.14	4.07	4.21	4.16	3.82	3.55

The average life of a mortgage-backed security depends on the PSA prepayment assumption. To see this, the average life is shown below for different prepayment speeds for the pass-through we used to illustrate the cash flow in Exhibits 9-6 and 9-7:

PSA speed	50	100	165	200	300	400	500	600	700
Average life	15.11	11.66	8.76	7.68	5.63	4.44	3.68	3.16	2.78

Given the limitations of the cash-flow yield, the nominal yield spread is not a meaningful measure of the spread over Treasuries. In fact, reliance on this measure can suggest a mortgage-backed security as being an attractive investment, when it is in fact a poor one.

Effective Duration and Convexity.   As explained in the previous chapter, modified duration is a measure of the sensitivity of a bond's price to interest-rate changes, assuming that the expected cash flow does not change with interest rates. Consequently, modified duration is not an appropriate measure for mortgage-backed securities because projected cash flows change as interest rates change and, as a result, expected prepayments change. When interest rates fall, prepayments are expected to increase. As a result, when interest rates fall, duration may decrease rather than increase. This property is referred to as negative convexity.

The impact of negative convexity on the price performance of a mortgage-backed security is the same as for a callable bond. When interest rates fall, a bond with an embedded call option such as a mortgage-backed security will not perform as well as an option-free bond. The effective duration should be calculated. Using the static cash-flow-yield method, the two prices to be used in the effective duration formula are found by discounting the projected cash flow at the new yield levels.

To illustrate the calculation of effective duration for CMO classes and the difference between modified and effective duration, consider once again our hypothetical sequential-pay CMO structure. The second panel of Exhibit 9-11 provides all the data necessary to calculate the modified duration and effective duration of the

Exhibit 9-11. Calculation of Effective Duration and Convexity for Four Tranches and Collateral

Class	Par amount	Coupon rate
A	$194,500,000	6.00%
B	36,000,000	6.50
C	96,500,000	7.00
Z (Accrual)	73,000,000	7.25
R	0	0
Collateral	$400,000,000	7.50

Class	Cash-flow yield	Initial price	New price: 165% PSA CFY change (b.p.) +25 b.p.	New price: 165% PSA CFY change (b.p.) −25 b.p.	New price: CFY change (b.p.)/new PSA +25/150	New price: CFY change (b.p.)/new PSA −25/200
A	6.00%	99.7813	99.0625	100.5313	99.0313	100.4375
B	6.50	100.0313	98.6250	101.5000	98.5625	101.2813
C	7.00	100.2813	98.4063	102.1875	98.3438	101.9063
Z	7.25	100.6250	98.0625	103.2500	98.0313	103.0313
Coll.	7.50	100.1250	98.7500	101.5000	98.7188	101.3438

Modified Duration/Convexity and Effective Duration/Convexity

Class	Modified duration	Effective duration	Standard convexity	Effective convexity
A	2.94	2.82	25.055	− 75.164
B	5.75	5.44	49.984	−174.945
C	7.54	7.11	24.930	−249.299
Z	10.31	9.94	49.689	−149.068
Coll.	5.49	5.24	0	−149.813

four regular interest classes and the collateral. This panel shows the assumed cash-flow yield and the corresponding initial price for the four regular interest classes assuming a prepayment speed of 165 PSA. The two columns following the initial prices give the new prices if the cash-flow yield is changed by 25 basis points and assuming no change in the prepayment speed. The last two columns show new prices if the cash-flow yield changes by 25 basis points and the prepayment speed is assumed to change; it decreases to 150 PSA if the cash-flow yield increases by 25 basis points, and it increases to 200 PSA if the cash-flow yield decreases by 25 basis points.

Exhibit 9-11 reports the modified duration and effective duration. To illustrate the calculation, consider tranche C. The data for calculating modified duration using the approximation formula are

$P_0 = 100.2813$

$P_- = 102.1875$

$P_+ = 98.4063$

$\Delta y = 0.0025$

Substituting into the formula:

$$\text{Modified duration} = \frac{102.1875 - 98.4063}{2(100.2813)(0.0025)} = 7.54$$

The effective duration for the same bond class is calculated as follows:

$P_0 = 100.2813$

$P_- = 101.9063 \text{ (at 200 PSA)}$

$P_+ = 98.3438 \text{ (at 150 PSA)}$

$\Delta y = 0.0025$

Substituting into the formula for duration:

$$\text{Effective duration} = \frac{101.9063 - 98.3438}{2(100.2813)(0.0025)} = 7.11$$

Notice that for all four tranches and the collateral, the effective duration is less than the modified duration. The divergence between modified duration and effective duration is much more dramatic for tranches trading at a substantial discount from par or at a substantial premium over par. To demonstrate this, we can create another hypothetical CMO structure that differs from the hypothetical structure that we have been using by including a PO class and an IO class created from tranche C. Let's look at the duration for that PO class. Assuming that the cash-flow yield for the PO class is 7 percent, based on 165 PSA, the following prices are obtained:

	New price		New price	
Initial	*165 PSA*	*165 PSA*	*150 PSA*	*200 PSA*
price	*7.25% CFY*	*6.75% CFY*	*7.25% CFY*	*6.75% CFY*
60.3125	59.2500	61.3750	57.6563	64.5938

The modified duration for this PO is 7.05. The effective duration of 23.01 is dramatically different.

The effective convexity for each tranche can also be calculated. Exhibit 9-11 also shows the standard convexity and the effective convexity for the four regular interest classes for our hypothetical CMO structure and the collateral. Note the significant difference in the two convexity measures in Exhibit 9-11. The standard convexity indicates that the four regular interest classes have positive convexity, while the effective convexity indicates they have negative convexity. The difference is even more dramatic for bonds not trading near par. For a PO created from tranche C, the standard convexity is close to zero, while the effective convexity is 2,155!

Option-Adjusted Spread (Monte Carlo Simulation) Method[8]

The second method for valuing mortgage-backed securities is the Monte Carlo simulation, or simply Monte Carlo, method. A byprod-

---

[8] Portions of the material in this section and the one to follow are adapted from Frank J. Fabozzi and Scott F. Richard, "Valuation of CMOs," Chapter 6 in Frank J. Fabozzi ed., *CMO Portfolio Management* (Summit, NJ: Frank J. Fabozzi Associates, 1994).

uct of the Monte Carlo method is a security's option-adjusted spread. The Monte Carlo method involves simulating a sufficiently large number of potential interest-rate paths in order to assess the value of a mortgage-backed security along these different paths.

This method is commonly used for valuing interest-rate-sensitive instruments where the history of interest rates is important. That is, for some fixed-income securities and derivative instruments, the periodic cash flows are *path-dependent*. This means that the cash flow received in one period is determined not only by the current and future interest-rate levels, but also by the path that interest rates took to get to the current level.

In the case of mortgage pass-through securities (or simply, pass-throughs), prepayments are path-dependent because this month's prepayment rate depends on whether there have been prior opportunities to refinance since the underlying mortgages were originated. Unlike pass-throughs, the decision as to whether a corporate issuer will elect to refund an issue when the current rate is below the issue's coupon rate is not dependent on how rates evolved over time to the current level.

For CMOs there are typically two sources of path dependency in a tranche's cash flows. First, the collateral prepayments are path-dependent as discussed above. Second, the cash flow to be received in the current month by a tranche depends on the outstanding balances of the other tranches in the deal. Thus, we need the history of prepayments to calculate these balances.

Conceptually, the valuation of pass-throughs using the Monte Carlo method is simple. In practice, however, it is very complex. The simulation involves generating a set of cash flows based on simulated future mortgage refinancing rates, which in turn imply simulated prepayment rates.

Valuation modeling for CMOs is similar to valuation modeling for pass-throughs, although, the difficulties are amplified because the issuer has sliced and diced both the prepayment risk and the interest-rate risk into smaller pieces (i.e., tranches). The sensitivity of the pass-throughs comprising the collateral to these two risks is not transmitted equally to every tranche. Some of the tranches wind up more sensitive to prepayment risk and interest-rate risk than the collateral, while some of them are much less sensitive.

The objective of the money manager is to figure out how the OAS of the collateral, or, equivalently, the value of the collateral, gets transmitted to the tranches. More specifically, the objective is to find out where the value goes and where the risk goes so that the money manager can identify the tranches with low risk and high value: the ones we want to buy.

Using Simulation to Generate Interest-Rate Paths and Cash Flows. The typical model that Wall Street firms and commercial vendors use to generate these random interest-rate paths takes as input today's term structure of interest rates and a volatility assumption. The simulations are calibrated to the market so that the average simulated price of the on-the-run Treasury issues equals today's actual price.

Each model has its own model of the evolution of future interest rates and its own volatility assumptions. Typically, there are no significant differences in the interest-rate models of dealer firms and vendors, although their volatility assumptions can be significantly different.

The random paths of interest rates should be generated from an arbitrage-free model of the future term structure of interest rates. By arbitrage-free it is meant that the model replicates today's term structure of interest rates, an input of the model, and that for all future dates there is no possible arbitrage within the model.

The simulation works by generating many scenarios of future interest-rate paths. In each month of the scenario, a monthly interest rate and a mortgage refinancing rate are generated. The monthly interest rates are used to discount the projected cash flows in the scenario. The mortgage refinancing rate is needed to determine the cash flow because it represents the opportunity cost the mortgagor is facing at that time.

If the refinancing rates are high relative to the mortgagor's original coupon rate, the mortgagor will have less incentive to refinance, or even a positive disincentive (i.e., the homeowner will avoid moving in order to avoid refinancing). If the refinancing rate is low relative to the mortgagor's original coupon rate, the mortgagor has an incentive to refinance.

Prepayments are projected by feeding the refinancing rate and loan characteristics, such as age, into a prepayment model. Given the projected prepayments, the cash flow along an interest-rate path can be determined. These cash flows are then analyzed as described below for a pass-through. In the case of a CMO tranche, the cash flow is obtained by distributing the collateral's cash flow to the tranche based on the rules for distribution of interest and principal.

Determining the Theoretical Value. Given the cash flow on an interest-rate path, the present value of a mortgage-backed security can be calculated. The discount rate for determining the present value is the simulated spot rate for each month on the interest-rate path plus an appropriate spread. The spot rate on a path can be determined from the simulated future monthly rates.

The present value of a given interest-rate path can be thought of as the theoretical value of a mortgage-backed security if that path is actually realized. The theoretical value of a mortgage-backed security can be determined by calculating the average of the present values of all the interest-rate paths.

While the theoretical value is the simple average of the present value of each interest-rate path, there is important information in the simulation results. An investor should examine the distribution of the present values. For example, a well-protected PAC structure would have present values that do not vary significantly around the theoretical value. A support bond could have substantial variability around the theoretical value.[9]

Calculation of the OAS. As explained in the previous chapter, the OAS is a measure of the yield spread that can be used to convert dollar differences between value produced by a model and the market price. In the Monte Carlo model, the OAS is the spread that when added to all the spot rates on all interest-rate paths will make the average present value of the paths equal to the observed market price (plus accrued interest).

---

[9] For examples, see Robert W. Kopprasch, "A Further Look at OAS Analysis," Chapter 30 in Frank J. Fabozzi, ed., *The Handbook of Mortgage-Backed Securities* (Chicago: Probus Publishing, 1995).

Effective Duration and Convexity.   Effective duration and effective convexity can be calculated using the Monte Carlo method as follows. First the mortgage-backed security's OAS is found using the current term structure of interest rates. Next the mortgage-backed security is repriced holding OAS constant, but shifting the term structure. Two shifts are used in order to get the prices needed to apply the effective duration and effective convexity formulas; in one, yields are increased, and in the second, they are decreased.

Simulated Average Life.   The average life reported in a Monte Carlo analysis is the average of the average lives for the interest-rate paths. That is, for each interest-rate path, there is an average life. The average of these average lives is the average life reported in an OAS model. Once again, additional information is conveyed by the distribution of the average life. The greater the range and standard deviation of the average life, the more uncertainty there is about the tranche's average life.

TOTAL RETURN

Neither the static cash-flow-yield method nor the option-adjusted spread method will tell a money manager whether investment objectives can be satisfied. The potential performance of an individual mortgage-backed security or a portfolio requires specification of an investment horizon. As we have pointed out throughout this book, the measure that should be used to assess the performance of a security or a portfolio over some investment horizon is the total return.

The total dollars received from investing in a mortgage-backed security consists of

1. the projected cash flow of the mortgage-backed security from

   a. the projected interest payments

   b. the projected principal repayment (scheduled plus prepayments)

2. the interest earned on reinvestment of the projected interest payments and the projected principal repayments

3. the projected price of the mortgage-backed security at the end of the investment horizon

To obtain the cash flow, a prepayment rate over the investment horizon must be assumed. The second step requires assumption of a reinvestment rate. Finally, either of the methodologies described in this chapter—static cash-flow yield or option-adjusted spread—can be used to calculate the security's price at the end of the investment horizon under a particular set of assumptions. Either approach requires assumption of the prepayment rate and the Treasury rates (i.e., the yield curve) at the end of the investment horizon. The static cash-flow-yield approach uses an assumed nominal yield spread to a comparable Treasury to determine the required cash-flow yield, which is then used to compute the projected price. The OAS method requires an assumption of what the OAS will be at the investment horizon. From this assumption, the OAS method can produce the theoretical value. In practice, a constant OAS is sometimes assumed (i.e., it is assumed that the OAS will not change over the investment horizon).

For a monthly-pay CMO, the monthly total return is then found using the formula:

$$\left(\frac{\text{Total future dollars}}{\text{Total proceeds paid}} \right)^{1/\text{Number of months in horizon}}$$

where total proceeds paid is the purchase price plus accrued interest.

The monthly total return can be annualized on a bond-equivalent yield basis as follows:

Bond-equivalent annual return
$$= 2\,[(1 + \text{Monthly total return})^6 - 1]$$

or, by computing the effective annual return as follows:

Effective annual return $= (1 + \text{Monthly total return})^{12} - 1$

To illustrate how to calculate total return for a CMO, we will use tranche C of our hypothetical CMO structure. The assumptions are:

1. The investment horizon is one year.

2. The amount purchased of this tranche is $9.65 million of the original par value at the issue date for a price of 100-09 and a cash-flow yield of 7 percent assuming 165 PSA.

3. Interim cash flows are reinvested at 4 percent per year.

4. At the investment horizon, interest rates for similar sequential-pay bonds decrease by 200 basis points to 5 percent.

5. A drop in interest rates of 200 basis points increases the prepayment speed at the end of the investment horizon to 250 PSA from 165 PSA.

According to these assumptions, the cash flow generated from principal repayments, coupon interest, and reinvestment income would be $682,100. The price of the tranche at the end of the investment horizon would be 111-17. The sale price plus accrued interest for $9,650,000 of original par value is $10,819,100. The total future dollars would then be $11,501,200.

Since the bonds are assumed to be purchased at 100-09, the price paid for this tranche is $9,677,141 (100.2812 for $9,650,000 of original par value) plus accrued interest. The accrued interest is $56,292, so the total proceeds paid for this tranche would be $9,733,433. The monthly total return is then:

$$\left(\frac{\$11,501,200}{\$9,733,433}\right)^{1/12} - 1 = (1.181618)^{1/12} - 1 = 0.014004$$

The bond-equivalent yield is found as follows:
$2[(1.014004)^6 - 1] = 0.1740 = 17.4\%$

The effective annual yield would be:
$(1.014004)^{12} - 1 = 0.1816 = 18.17\%$

Difficulty of Estimating Terminal Price

The most difficult part of estimating total return is projecting the price of the mortgage-backed security at the horizon date. The price depends on the characteristics of the MBS and the relevant spread to Treasuries at the termination date. The key determinants are its average life (or duration), its convexity, and, in the case of a CMO tranche, its quality.

The quality for a CMO tranche refers to the type of bond. Consider, for example, that an investor can purchase a CMO tranche that is a planned amortization class (PAC) bond but as a result of projected prepayments, could become a sequential-pay tranche because all support bonds prepay. As another example, suppose a PAC bond is the longest-average-life tranche in a reverse PAC structure. Projected prepayments in this case might occur in an amount to change the class from a long-term average-life PAC tranche to effectively a support tranche. The converse is that the quality of a tranche may improve as well as deteriorate.

Exhibit 9-12 demonstrates how the average life and Macaulay duration can change materially, depending on the scenario, although perhaps not in the desired direction. For example, consider once again tranche C. From Exhibit 9-12 we can see that if interest rates increase by 400 basis points, the Macaulay duration increases from 7.3 years to 8.11 years, and the average life increases from 10.26 years to 14.92 years. Thus, one year later this tranche will become a longer-term security, and in all likelihood it will be priced relative to a longer-benchmark Treasury security. Rather than rolling down the yield curve, this security would roll up the yield curve. For support bonds and other exotic bond classes, the drift of Macaulay duration and average life can be quite substantial.

While we have not focused on convexity in our discussion, the same is true for this parameter. It can drift to an undesirable value, thereby adversely affecting price.

OAS-Total Return

The total return and OAS frameworks can be combined to determine the projected price at the horizon date. This requires an OAS model and a prepayment model. At the end of the investment horizon, it is necessary to specify how the OAS is expected to change. The horizon price can be "backed out" of the OAS model. We explained earlier how to obtain the two prices needed to calculate effective duration and effective convexity. This technique can be extended to

Exhibit 9-12. Scenario Analysis for Four Regular Interest
Classes and Collateral

Assumptions:

One-year investment horizon
Horizon yield based on interest-rate shift
Priced at: 165.00 PSA
Interest rates shift in 1 step of 1 month each
Cash flows reinvested to horizon point at 4%

Collateral prepayment assumptions:

Interest-rate shift	PSA
+400 b.p.	100
+300 b.p.	130
+200 b.p.	140
+100 b.p.	150
+0 b.p.	165
−100 b.p.	200
−200 b.p.	250
−300 b.p.	300
−400 b.p.	400

Exhibit 9-12 (Continued). Scenario Analysis for Tranche A

Original Par: $194,500,000; Type: SEQ; Coupon: 6.00% (fixed); Price: 99–25

Interest-rate shift (b.p.)	Ending prepayment (PSA)	Horizon A/L (yrs)	Performance Dur (yrs)	Yield (%)	Reinvest. cash ($1000s)	Sale price ($1000s)	Sale price (32nds)	Total cash ($1000s)	Total return (% BEY)
+400	100	4.17	3.37	10.01	22,836	161,333	87–08	184,168	–5.66
+300	130	3.35	2.87	9.01	25,019	167,286	91–20	192,305	–1.41
+200	140	3.15	2.75	8.01	25,673	171,788	94–16	197,461	1.23
+100	150	2.96	2.64	7.01	26,323	175,908	97–06	202,231	3.65
0	165	2.72	2.48	6.01	27,344	179,328	99–23	206,671	5.87
–100	200	2.29	2.14	5.01	29,857	180,361	101–26	210,218	7.63
–200	250	1.86	1.78	4.01	33,477	178,851	103–06	212,329	8.67
–300	300	1.56	1.52	3.01	37,076	176,652	104–07	213,728	9.36
–400	400	1.18	1.18	2.01	44,384	168,879	104–11	213,263	9.13

Scenario Analysis for Tranche B

Original Par: $36,000,000; Type: SEQ; Coupon: 6.50% (fixed); Price: 100–01

Interest-rate shift (b.p.)	Ending prepayment (PSA)	Horizon A/L (yrs)	Performance Dur (yrs)	Yield (%)	Reinvest. cash ($1000s)	Sale price ($1000s)	Sale price (32nds)	Total cash ($1000s)	Total return (% BEY)
+400	100	9.96	6.89	10.51	2,428	27,566	76–01	29,994	–17.97
+300	130	8.06	6.08	9.50	2,417	30,289	83–19	32,706	–9.91
+200	140	7.56	5.87	8.50	2,406	32,291	89–05	34,697	–4.21
+100	150	7.12	5.66	7.51	2,395	34,260	94–20	36,655	1.24
0	165	6.53	5.33	6.51	2,384	36,184	99–31	38,568	6.42
–100	200	5.46	4.63	5.51	2,374	37,815	104–16	40,189	10.71
–200	250	4.39	3.85	4.51	2,363	38,940	107–20	41,303	13.61
–300	300	3.65	3.28	3.51	2,352	39,750	109–28	42,102	15.67
–400	400	2.71	2.50	2.51	2,341	39,795	110–00	42,136	15.76

Exhibit 9-12 (Continued). Scenario Analysis for Tranche C

Original Par: $96,500,000; Type: SEQ; Coupon: 7.00% (fixed); Price: 100–09

Interest-rate shift (b.p.)	Ending prepayment (PSA)	Horizon A/L (yrs)	Performance Dur (yrs)	Yield (%)	Reinvest. cash ($1000s)	Sale price ($1000s)	Sale price (32nds)	Total cash ($1000s)	Total return (% BEY)
+400	100	14.92	8.11	11.00	7,008	69,922	71–28	76,930	−22.19
+300	130	12.44	7.68	10.00	6,977	77,371	79–19	84,347	−13.82
+200	140	11.75	7.63	9.00	6,945	83,764	86–07	90,709	−6.93
+100	150	11.11	7.54	8.00	6,914	90,429	93–04	97,343	0.01
0	165	10.26	7.30	7.00	6,883	97,274	100–07	104,157	6.89
−100	200	8.65	6.56	6.00	6,852	103,516	106–22	110,368	12.97
−200	250	7.00	5.63	5.00	6,821	108,191	111–17	115,011	17.40
−300	300	5.84	4.89	4.00	6,790	111,749	115–07	118,539	20.71
−400	400	4.32	3.79	3.00	6,759	112,232	115–23	118,990	21.13

Scenario Analysis for Tranche Z

Original Par: $73,000,000; Type: SEQ; Coupon: 7.25% (fixed); Price: 100–20

Interest-rate shift (b.p.)	Ending prepayment (PSA)	Horizon A/L (yrs)	Performance Dur (yrs)	Yield (%)	Reinvest. cash ($1000s)	Sale price ($1000s)	Sale price (32nds)	Total cash ($1000s)	Total return (% BEY)
+400	100	23.69	9.01	11.25	5,491	50,127	68–02	55,617	−26.49
+300	130	21.71	9.34	10.25	5,466	55,237	75–02	60,703	−18.73
+200	140	21.04	9.75	9.25	5,442	60,666	82–16	66,108	−10.83
+100	150	20.36	10.12	8.25	5,417	66,871	91–00	72,288	−2.19
0	165	19.37	10.36	7.25	5,393	73,874	100–19	79,267	7.14
−100	200	17.19	10.12	6.25	5,368	81,243	110–22	86,611	16.52
−200	250	14.53	9.44	5.25	5,344	88,041	120–00	93,385	24.83
−300	300	12.41	8.71	4.25	5,320	94,041	128–07	99,360	31.91
−400	400	9.36	7.21	3.25	5,295	96,390	131–14	101,686	34.61

Exhibit 9-12 (Continued). Scenario Analysis for the Collateral

Original Par: $400,000,000; Type: SEQ; Coupon: 7.50% (fixed); Price: 100–00

Interest-rate shift (b.p.)	Ending prepayment (PSA)	Horizon A/L (yrs)	Performance Dur (yrs)	Yield (%)	Reinvest. cash ($1000s)	Sale price ($1000s)	Sale price (32nds)	Total cash ($1000s)	Total return (% BEY)
+400	100	11.01	5.49	11.50	41,790	311,971	79–16	353,760	-12.50
+300	130	9.49	5.23	10.50	43,876	332,289	85–07	376,165	-6.65
+200	140	9.06	5.30	9.50	44,441	349,990	89–31	394,431	-2.01
+100	150	8.66	5.36	8.50	45,002	368,462	94–30	413,465	2.71
0	165	8.10	5.34	7.50	45,933	387,079	100–02	433,012	7.44
-100	200	7.01	5.02	6.50	48,347	402,901	104–29	451,249	11.77
-200	250	5.83	4.54	5.50	51,863	413,782	108–27	465,645	15.12
-300	300	4.95	4.12	4.50	55,357	421,667	112–02	477,025	17.73
-400	400	3.76	3.36	3.50	62,540	416,867	113–03	479,407	18.27

Note: This analysis was performed using the Multiscenario Analysis Feature of WallStreet Analytics, Inc.

the total return framework by making assumptions about the required variables at the horizon date.

Assumptions about the OAS value at the investment horizon reflect the expectations of the money manager. It is common to assume that the OAS at the horizon date will be the same as the OAS at the time of purchase. A total return calculated using this assumption is sometimes referred to as a *constant-OAS total return*. Alternatively, active total return managers will make bets on how the OAS will change—either widening or tightening. The total return framework can be used to assess how sensitive the performance of a mortgage-backed security is to changes in the OAS.

Chapter 10

Using Futures, Options, and Swaps to Modify Total Return

Futures, options, and swaps are derivative contracts that allow portfolio managers to control interest-rate risk more effectively and, under special circumstances, enhance total return. In this chapter, we explain how derivative contracts can be used in total return portfolio management. In a total return context, risk control really means the shaping of the return profile of the portfolio to fit the needs and goals at hand. For balanced fund managers who allocate funds between fixed-income securities and equities, futures and options provide a means for more effectively implementing an asset allocation strategy.

FUTURES CONTRACTS

A futures contract is an exchange-traded agreement between the buyer or seller and the exchange in which the buyer agrees to take delivery of *something* and the seller agrees to make delivery of that *something* at a specified future date. When the *something* to be delivered is either a fixed-income security or a basket of fixed-income securities, the futures contract is referred to as an *interest-rate futures contract*.

When an investor takes a position in the market by buying a futures contract, the investor is said to be in a *long position* or *long the futures*. If, instead, the investor's opening position is the sale of a

233

futures contract, the investor is said to be in a *short position* or *short the futures*. To liquidate or close a position prior to the delivery date, the investor must take an offsetting position in the same contract. For a long position this means selling an identical number of contracts; for a short position this means buying an identical number of contracts. The alternative is to wait until the delivery date. At that time the investor liquidates a long position by accepting delivery of the underlying instrument at the agreed-upon price and liquidates a short position by delivering the instrument at the agreed-upon price.

There are several interest-rate futures contracts that represent the fixed-income markets. They are based on Treasury obligations in the maturity sectors of 2, 5, and 10 years and on the long bond. There are also short-term futures, such as the Treasury bill contract and the Eurodollar contract. The Chicago Board of Trade's long bond contract is the most liquid, and we will use it in our examples. This contract is more complex than other futures contracts in that there are a number of different bonds deliverable against the contract. The delivery price is determined by the futures prices times a normalization factor, known as the *conversion factor*, for each deliverable bond. Usually, the price of the future's contract follows that of the bond that is considered most likely to be delivered, known as the *cheapest-to-deliver bond* (CTDB).

Modifying Interest-Rate Risk with Treasury Bond Futures

In order to use interest-rate futures to modify a portfolio's exposure to interest rates, we can use the portfolio's dollar duration as a measure of interest-rate risk. As defined in Chapter 2, dollar duration is the dollar change in portfolio value for a 100-basis-point change in interest rates. Dollar duration is the product of duration (percentage expressed as a decimal) and the market value of the portfolio. When stated without any specific reference to a portfolio or a holding, the dollar duration is most often expressed using a notional par amount of $100.

The dollar duration of a Treasury bond (or note) futures contract is obtained by dividing the dollar duration (per $100 par value) of the CTDB by the conversion factor associated with that bond and multiplying the result by 1,000. The multiplication reflects the $100,000 par value of the futures contract. For example, suppose the CTDB for a Treasury bond futures contract has a dollar duration for a notional par amount of $100 of 9.146 at a price of 85 18/32 and a conversion factor of 0.9176. The dollar duration of the futures contract is $9,967.31 (1,000 × 9.146/0.9176).

The purchase of a Treasury bond futures contract increases the dollar duration of a portfolio. The sale of a Treasury bond futures contract reduces a portfolio's dollar duration. Hedging a portfolio is a special case of controlling interest-rate risk. With hedging, the portfolio manager seeks to reduce the dollar duration of a portfolio to zero.

Because the dollar duration of the futures contract depends on the CTDB and because this can change, there is some uncertainty in determining the interest-rate risk of a futures position precisely. Some amount of error due to maturity mismatches can be mitigated by using combinations of the different acceptable Treasury issues that are deliverable into the futures contracts.

Yield Enhancement with Treasury Bond Futures

If the Treasury bond futures contracts are cheap relative to the cash market, there are opportunities to enhance return by following a synthetic strategy using long positions in Treasury bond futures rather than Treasuries. Since the primary use of futures is to sell Treasury bond futures to hedge assets, it is argued that futures should be cheap to buy.

An argument could be made that if futures are indeed cheap, then arbitrage activity will bring them up to their fair price. However, because of the complex terms of the futures contract—for example, the choice of the deliverable bond—it is not always easy either to structure an arbitrage or to determine what the fair price should be. Thus, market inefficiency definitely exists. A corollary to this is that short positions in the bond futures could reduce the returns obtained.

In the context of yield enhancement, the advantage of futures comes with an associated cost, negative convexity, described below.

The complexity of the futures contract that makes arbitrage imperfect also generates this cost.

Trading in Anticipation—Time Shifting

Another application of interest-rate futures is to use them for time shifting, letting them stand as place holders until the completion of the transaction in the cash security. Such time shifting can be advantageous in many situations. A portfolio manager might wish to wait to receive funding for a purchase or to postpone the recognition of gain (or loss) due to sale. Or we might consider the market condition unsuitable for obtaining the right price for the security under consideration.

For example, suppose a portfolio manager wishes to purchase a long Treasury bond. Assume, however, that the funding for the purchase will be available only after one month. In this case, the manager can hedge her decision to purchase the long bond by buying the CBT long Treasury bond contracts. If the market rallies, the price she will have to pay to purchase the bond will be greater, but a corresponding gain on the futures position will bring down the net cost of purchase. Similarly, if the market price declines, she can buy the bond at a lower price, but there will be a loss on the futures position, bringing the net cost of purchase up. In either case, the effective purchase price of the bond will be close to the price locked in today. This price will be approximately equal to the forward purchase price for the bond.

If a portfolio manager is contemplating the future sale of a bond already in the portfolio, then he can hedge this action by selling bond futures. The sale price of the bond is effectively locked in by the hedge.

Convexity Risk in a Futures Contract

The dollar duration or eqivalently the price value of a basis point (PVBP) of a bond or a portfolio is not a constant. It changes with time as well as with market levels. If the PVBP of a portfolio increases as the market rallies, then the portfolio is said to be convex. Convexity is a desirable property because a convex portfolio gains value at an increasing rate for every successive basis-point rally in the interest rates. For some portfolios, the PVBP actually decreases in rallying markets. They are said to have negative convexity. In general, the more convexity, the better.

However, convexity, being a desirable property, can be obtained only by giving up something else desirable. Even though the popular literature contains voluminous discussions of the trade-off between convexity and yield give-up, as explained in Chapter 4 it turns out that this trade-off is not easily determined or quantified. The advantage of convexity depends on many factors, including the volatility of interest rates, and the yield is not necessarily a good measure of return. The actual rate of return obtained over a given horizon is a much better measure.

The futures contract has associated with it certain options characteristics known as delivery options. The major ones are the rights retained by the short seller as to the timing of the delivery as well as the bond that is delivered. In effect, the buyer of the futures contract has sold these options and therefore is subject to some risk.

The market price of the bond futures contract closely follows that of the CTDB. As the market rallies, shorter-duration bonds typically become CTDs. As the market declines, longer-duration bonds become CTDs. This tendency of the shorter and longer bonds to become CTDs at low and high levels is dominated by the relative yield spreads among the deliverable bonds.

Because the duration of the futures contract follows that of the CTDB, its duration tends to fall as rates fall and to rise as rates rise. As we stated earlier, this property is an undesirable property known as negative convexity. A consequence of negative convexity is that a long position in futures tends to underperform a cash portfolio of equal duration but higher convexity. Thus, the possible yield enhancement of using futures comes at a price.

It should be noted that the duration of the futures contract can change even without the CTDB changing. This change in duration is not as abrupt as a change in the CTDB. To this extent, our formula for the computation of the duration of the futures is approximate.

The effect of the delivery option is relatively large in the case of the long bond futures. In their case, a large number of bonds are deliverable, the range of their maturities extends from 15 to 30 years, and the coupons vary from 7.25 percent to 14 percent. The dollar duration of these deliverable bonds can vary substantially. In the case of the shorter futures on 10-, 5-, and 2-year Treasury notes, the effect is smaller and the ranges of dollar durations for these contracts are less.

Negative convexity is undesirable because it makes the portfolio underperform another with a greater convexity. In our case, the synthetic security could underperform the cash bond. Thus, even if the futures contract appears to be cheap at the outset, it might turn out otherwise when the effect of the seller's options is included.

Fortunately, it is possible to address negative convexity. The obvious solution is to add convexity to the portfolio by purchasing appropriate quantities of highly convex instruments, such as long zero-coupon bonds and options.

Advantages of Using Futures

The use of interest-rate futures provides a portfolio manager with numerous advantages in addition to potential yield enhancement and time shifting. Two primary advantages are lower transaction costs and liquidity. Transaction costs can be viewed as having two components: the stated commission, or fees, and market impact. Treasury bond futures contracts involve negligible market impact. Treasury bond futures contracts are very deep and liquid. Large volumes can be transacted relatively quickly and efficiently. Bond futures are the most liquid market in the world, routinely trading over $25 billion daily.

For a balanced-fund manager who pursues a tactical asset allocation (TAA) strategy, there are other advantages of using Treasury bond futures contracts. A TAA strategy is an active management technique that attempts to take advantage of the opportunities occurring in the fixed-income and equities markets. Properly executed TAA should capture value in the market by changing the asset mix in response to changing market patterns.

Both Treasury bond futures and stock index futures contracts can be used in TAA. A portfolio managed under TAA will show a turnover of perhaps 100 percent per annum. Therefore, transaction costs can be a critical factor in the implementation of strategy selection. It has been estimated that the transaction costs can be 200 basis points for stocks and 100 basis points for bonds. Use of futures can cut these costs to 10–20 basis points. Thus, the added cost of active management is acceptably low.

Another advantage of the use of futures in TAA is that it is possible to execute simultaneous trades in different markets. For example, a portfolio manager pursuing a TAA strategy can shift large amounts of bond exposure to cash and increase stock exposure literally in minutes. In a simultaneous transaction in the underlying securities, the different lengths of delay before settlement (e.g., five business days for stocks and one business day for Treasury bonds) is a nuisance. The use of futures avoids this complexity.

Disadvantages of Using Futures

Notwithstanding the numerous advantages in using futures, there are also certain disadvantages. Regulatory restrictions prevent many potential investor groups from effectively using futures. Other disadvantages are (1) daily mark to market; (2) need for liquidity to meet variation margin calls; (3) tracking error; and (4) mispricing cost.

Daily Mark to Market.   In order to ensure the integrity of the futures markets, the exchanges require that futures positions be marked to market daily. This results in a significant data processing burden, as well as the need to transfer funds to and from the broker. In addition, the mark-to-market process leads to immediate recognition of gains and losses. In certain circumstances, it might be more advantageous to postpone the recognition of gains and losses, an option not available with futures.

Need for Liquidity.   In order to meet the daily variation margin calls resulting from the settlement process, the investor will be required to maintain a reserve fund. As a consequence, some portion of the portfolio is forced to be in liquid assets, such as money-market securities, rather than in actively managed assets. Also, large market moves might require additional assets to be liquidated in order to meet margin calls.

Tracking Error. Futures are not necessarily ideal representations of the broad markets a portfolio manager might wish to track. This is especially true in the case of interest-rate futures. For example, the CBT long bond futures tend to track a single bond, the cheapest deliverable bond, rather than an index of long bonds. In addition, the cheapest deliverable bond itself can change as a function of market conditions. Thus, there can be significant uncertainty in the behavior of the futures contract.

On the other hand, the fixed-income sectors are highly correlated (relative to stock market sectors) and the tracking error is small. To the extent that any uncertainty in the behavior of the futures contract is already incorporated in the futures price, there is no cost to the investor in using futures due to this uncertainty.

Finally, when using futures in a TAA strategy, it is best to view the allocation process at a gross level rather than as having a fine, arbitrage-like precision. That is, the allocator should have a good tolerance for tracking error relative to a market index.

Mispricing Cost. The true cost of using futures is in the possibility of mispricing the futures contracts at the time they are bought and sold. Notwithstanding the very high liquidity and size of the futures markets, there is potential for favorable as well as unfavorable mispricing. The available analytical pricing models are not adequate to handle the complexities of the futures contracts, such as the largely ignored daily mark-to-market process and the numerous delivery options.

However, there is no reason to believe that the cost due to mispricing is significantly higher in futures than in the underlying securities. In fact, it is possible to take the view that the futures prices are closer to fair price than the cash-market instruments because of the size and liquidity of the futures markets.

The Effect of Variation Margin. For most analytical purposes, futures contracts are approximated by forward contracts. Unlike forward contracts, futures contracts are marked to market daily. The futures contract effectively is settled every day. This results in daily cash flow to the holder of futures positions. The cash flow is positive if the position is long and the futures price goes up or if the position is short and the futures price goes down. The cash flow is negative otherwise. This daily cash flow, known as the variation margin, has two important effects on the futures contract.

The first effect is on pricing. Consider the following: Suppose that the price of the underlying security in a futures contract is positively correlated with interest rates. Then, if we are long in the futures contracts, any margin that we receive due to an increase in the price of the security is likely reinvested at higher interest rates, resulting in higher returns. Similarly, any margin flows that results from a fall in price of the underlying security can be financed at lower interest rates, resulting in lower cost. Thus, the futures contract is attractive to buy. Therefore, its price should also be correspondingly higher.

Similarly, if the underlying security and the interest rates are negatively correlated, then the variation margin has a negative effect on the price of the futures because the margin outflows are financed at higher rates and inflows are invested at lower rates. In this case, the futures price is expected to be lower. This is perhaps the case in the fixed-income markets, where the correlation between interest rates at different maturities is high. This causes a negative correlation between the short-term rate and the price of the deliverable bonds, thus forcing down the futures price. This effect partly explains why the interest-rate futures prices appear cheaper compared to forward prices.

The second effect is on the hedge ratio, or the number of futures contracts needed for hedging. To illustrate this effect, suppose we wish to sell one month from now a $25 million portfolio with a duration of 5. The dollar duration of the portfolio is 5 percent of the market value, or $1.25 million ($25 million times 0.05). Assume that delivery is in one month. If the cheapest deliverable bond has a dollar duration (per $100) of 9.146 and a conversion factor of 0.9176, the dollar duration of a futures contract, using the earlier derivation, is $9,967.31 ($1000 × 9.146/0.9176). Therefore, to represent a dollar duration of $1.25 million, we need 125 futures contracts.

Suppose now that market rates immediately drop by 100 basis points and stay there for a month. The value of the portfolio will increase by $1.25 million, and we will receive approximately $26.25 million ($25 million initial value + $1.25 million increase) for our portfolio. On the futures side, because we have matched the dollar durations, the corresponding loss will also be $1.25 million. However, this cash amount has to be delivered immediately as variation margin. The cash requirement can be funded by borrowing or by liquidating interest-earning securities. In either case, the total cost to us from the futures position will be not just the $1.25 million, but the interest cost on the amount for the one month to the horizon.

Similarly, if the market rates rise by 100 basis points, we will have a loss of approximately $1.25 million, but the equal gain on the futures position is earned immediately. We can earn interest on this gain for the one month to horizon and thus more than make up the loss on the portfolio.

The implication here is that we are *overhedged* by a small amount. A little reflection will reveal that the overhedge amount depends on the interest rate at which the variation margin flows can be financed or invested and on the time to delivery. More precisely, to be properly hedged we have to multiply the hedge by a factor equal to the present value of one dollar payable at delivery, discounted at the short-term rate. For example, if the interest rate is 9 percent and the time to delivery is one month, then the factor would be 0.9926 $(1/(1 + 0.09/12))$. Therefore, the correct number of futures contracts to use would be 124 (125 × 0.9926).

In other words, the futures contract has the price sensitivity (dollar duration) of a forward contract that delivers a little more than the par amount of the futures. This effective amount is obtained by multiplying the par amount by the futures value of a dollar on the delivery date, or, equivalently, by dividing the present value of a dollar payable on the delivery date.

Clearly, given that the short-term rate (say the one-day rate) is not a constant, the futures position needs rebalancing in response to rate changes. As we approach the delivery date, the adjustment becomes smaller. For long horizons, the correction due to variation margin financing can be significant. For example, for a one-year time period, assuming a 10 percent interest rate, we would use just over 90 percent of the usual number of contracts.

OPTIONS

In Chapter 7 we reviewed option contracts and their investment characteristics. Recall that an option is a contract in which the writer of the option grants the buyer of the option the right to purchase from (in the case of a call option) or sell to the writer (in the case of a put option) a designated instrument at a specified price within a specified period of time.

Options can be written on cash instruments or on interest-rate futures. Exchange-traded options on cash-market instruments are not as liquid as options on interest-rate futures contracts.

Institutional investors who want to purchase an option on a specific Treasury security or mortgage pass-through can do so on an over-the-counter basis. There are government and mortgage-backed securities dealers who make a market in options on specific securities. Over-the-counter (or dealer) options are typically purchased by institutional investors who want to hedge the risk associated with a specific security. Typically, the maturity of the option coincides with the time period over which the buyer of the option wants to hedge. Thus, the buyer of an over-the-counter option is typically not concerned with the liquidity of the option.

Futures Options

An option on a futures contract, commonly referred to as a *futures option*, gives the buyer the right to buy from or sell to the writer a designated futures contract at a designated price at any time during the life of the option. If the futures option is a call option, the buyer has the right to purchase one designated futures contract at the exercise price. That is, the buyer has the right to acquire a long futures position in the designated futures contract. If the buyer exercises the call option, the writer (seller) acquires a corresponding short position in the futures contract.

A put option on a futures contract grants the buyer the right to sell one designated futures contract to the writer at the exercise price. That is, the option buyer has the right to acquire a short position in the designated futures contract. If the put option is exercised, the writer acquires a corresponding long position in the designated futures contract.

Upon exercise, the futures price for the futures contract will be set equal to the exercise price. The position of the two parties is then immediately marked to market based on the then-current futures price. Thus, the futures position of the two parties will be at the prevailing futures price. At the same time, the option buyer will receive from the option seller the economic benefit from exercising. In the case of a call futures option, the option writer must pay the difference between the current futures price and the exercise price to the buyer of the option. In the case of a put futures option, the option writer must pay the option buyer the difference between the exercise price and the current futures price.

For example, suppose an investor buys a call option on some futures contract in which the exercise price is 85. Assume also that the futures price is 95 and that the buyer exercises the call option. Upon exercise, the call buyer is given a long position in the futures contract at 85 and the call writer is assigned the corresponding short position in the futures contract at 85. The futures position of the buyer and the writer is immediately marked to market by the exchange. Since the prevailing futures price is 95 and the exercise price is 85, the long futures position (the position of the call buyer) realizes a gain of 10 while the short futures position (the position of the call writer) realizes a loss of 10. The call writer pays the exchange 10 and the call buyer receives from the exchange 10. The call buyer who now has a long futures position at 95 can either liquidate the futures position at 95 or maintain a long futures position. If the former course of action is taken, the call buyer sells a futures contract at the prevailing futures price of 95. There is no gain or loss from liquidating the position. Overall, the call buyer realizes a gain of 10. If the call buyer elects to hold the long futures position, then he will face the same risk and reward of holding such a position. But he still has realized a gain of 10 from the exercise of the call option.

Suppose instead that the futures option is a put rather than a call, and the current futures price is 60 rather than 95. Then if the buyer of this put option exercises it, the buyer would have a short position in the futures contract at 85; the option writer would have a long position in the futures contract at 85. The exchange then marks the position to market at the then-current futures price of 60, resulting in a gain to the put buyer of 25 and a loss to the put writer of the same amount. The put buyer who now has a short futures position at 60 can either liquidate the short futures position by buying a futures contract at the prevailing futures price of 60 or maintain the short futures position. In either case the put buyer realizes a gain of 25 from exercising the put option.

Directional Use of Options

Just as futures represent a leveraged position in underlying securities, so do options. However, the leverage, or the participation in the market in the case of options, varies with the level of the market. For example, a call option on the Treasury bond futures contract participates in market rallies and effectively withdraws from the market in a decline. Buying a put option increases the exposure of a fixed-income portfolio to market declines and effectively withdraws from the market in a rally. Depending on whether an option is purchased or sold, there would be an up-front cost or income to the portfolio.

Factors to Consider

Options basically price market volatility. To the extent that the actual volatility differs from the volatility implied by the price of the option, the expected returns will vary. Therefore, if there is a strong opinion on the volatility, then it is relatively more straightforward to determine the appropriate options strategy. If we believe that the implied volatility is low, we would tend to use those strategies in which we buy options. Similarly, if we believe that the implied volatility is high, we would seek strategies selling options.

Options are wasting assets; their value decreases as expiration approaches. Because of this time decay, options might not be appropriate for some long-term strategies that require repeated purchases of options. The rate of time decay is not a constant. It is possible to construct strategies that make use of this fact; for example, we can purchase an option with a low time decay. This might mean buying an option with a longer time to expiration than necessary, which would minimize time decay.

Unlike futures, there is an up-front payment necessary in the case of options.

Any factor that affects the value of options will also change the effective market exposure of a portfolio using the options strategy. These include volatility, time to expiration, market level, and the short-term interest rate. Of these, change in the market level is by far the most important.

Using Options for Hedging

Hedge strategies involve a position in an option and a position in the underlying bond in such a way that one position will offset any unfavorable price (interest-rate) movement in the other position. The two popular hedge strategies are protective put-buying strategy and covered call-writing strategy.

Protective Put-Buying Strategy.   A portfolio manager may want to protect the value of bonds held in his portfolio. A way of doing this with options is to buy a put option. By doing so, the investor is guaranteed the strike price of the put option less the cost of the option. Should market rates fall, thereby increasing the price of the bonds, the investor is able to participate in the price increase; however, the profit will be reduced by the cost of the option. This strategy is called a *protective put-buying strategy* and consists of a long position in a bond held in the portfolio and a long put position (buying a put option) in which the bond held in the portfolio is the underlying bond for the put option.

When futures options are used to implement a protective put-buying strategy, the amount of futures options to purchase must be determined. This requires using the duration or the price sensitivity to equate the futures options position to the alternative futures or cash position. For example, an at-the-money call option on the Treasury bond futures contract has a *delta* of about 0.5; that is, its value changes about half as much as that of the futures contract. Therefore, it would be necessary to use twice as many futures options as futures.

Covered Call-Writing Strategy.   A *covered call-writing strategy* involves writing a call option on bonds held in the portfolio. That is, the investor is in a short position in a call option and a long position in the underlying bond. If the price of the bond declines because interest rates rise, there will be a loss on the long bond position. However, the income generated from the sale of the call option will either (1) fully offset the loss in the long bond position, (2) partially offset the loss in the long bond position, or (3) more than offset the loss in the long bond position so as to generate a profit.

In the covered call-writing strategy, the portfolio manager does not match the price sensitivity of the futures option to that of an alternative futures position. Rather, the portfolio manager simply purchases an equal par value of the option.

Anticipatory Strategies

A portfolio manager can also use options in anticipation of buy or sell transactions. For example, if a manager is planning to purchase bonds, he could instead purchase call options. Then, if the market rallies, the call options would put the manager in bonds at a lower cost. If the bond market declines, then the manager would either not purchase the bonds or purchase them in the open market at the new lower price.

An alternative strategy is for a manager to sell put options. However, the net cost of the purchase can be higher than the market, and if the market rallies, the manager would have to purchase them at a higher price in the open market.

In both of the above applications using puts and calls, the manager can increase the certainty of the purchase by using options that are deep in-the-money. The deeper the option is in-the-money, the closer the transaction would resemble a cash (or futures) transaction.

INTEREST-RATE SWAPS

The two derivative instruments that we have discussed thus far—interest-rate futures and options—have become standard tools for portfolio managers. More recently, some of the more sophisticated portfolio managers have realized the importance of the interest-rate swap market and begun to study and deal in this market. Pension funds, for example, are expected to be more active players in the swap market due to a recent favorable ruling by the Internal Revenue Service.

An interest-rate swap is an agreement whereby two parties (called *counterparties*) agree to swap interest payments based on a notional amount. The only amount exchanged between the parties is interest payments, not the notional amount. In the most common type of swap, one party agrees to pay the other fixed interest payments at designated dates for the life of the contract. This party is referred to as the fixed-rate payer. The other party agrees to make floating interest-rate payments and is referred to as the floating-rate payer.

We believe that the study of the swap market, its products and strategies, is an essential requirement for *every* prudent fixed-income portfolio manager for several reasons. First, interest-rate swaps are among the most significant innovations in finance. They were introduced in the early 1980s and within the short period since then, the swap market has attained an enormous size sufficient to pervade almost all other markets as well as to exert significant influence on them. For example, in the U.S. dollar market, the swap yield curve is almost on a par with the Treasury curve in its use as a basis relative to which other securities are measured. In many other currencies, it is the swap curve that defines the dominant standard.

Second, swaps are extremely flexible. Since they are private contracts between two counterparties, they can be structured with almost unlimited precision to match any need at hand. Such structuring flexibility is not available in any of the traditional securities or derivatives, such as interest-rate futures contracts.

Third, the interest-rate swap market offers the fruits of a large number of innovations that have characterized it since its inception. These include elimination of (or acceptable solutions to) the problems of liquidity, credit risk, cross-border regulations and withholding taxes, and legal and accounting issues. For every situation, there appears to be a swap solution that is more efficient.

Finally, participants in the swap market have also contributed in no small way toward developing a consistent and unified way to value various securities.

A Simple Interest-Rate Swap

To understand how a swap works, let us look at a situation that can use a simple, so called "plain vanilla" swap.

Suppose RB is a regional bank. RB has just issued $100 million of a fixed-rate Eurobond of 5-year maturity at a spread of 40 basis points over the 5-year Treasury. The Treasury yield is at 8.20 percent and therefore the coupon on the bond is 8.60 percent. RB is using the proceeds from the bond issue to fund a $100 million floating-rate loan. The loan is of 5-year maturity and has a rate of 3-month LIBOR plus 50 basis points. The situation is depicted in Exhibit 10-1.

In this case, RB has a floating-rate asset, the loan, but a fixed-rate liability, the bond. This situation is known as an asset/liability *gap*. The gap is much more than an intellectual curiosity. It can have significant financial implications on RB in the following way: If rates fall, the cash flow from the loan will decrease but the cash flow due

Exhibit 10-1. The Floating Asset/Fixed Liability Gap

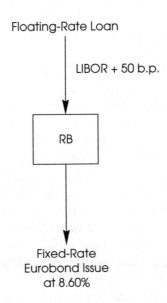

Floating-Rate Loan

LIBOR + 50 b.p.

RB

Fixed-Rate
Eurobond Issue
at 8.60%

on the liability remains constant, resulting in a loss of the spread earned. Similarly, if the rates rise, the spread increases due to the higher level of cash flow from the asset. The spread that RB earns is thus subject to interest-rate risk.

To continue with our simple interest-rate swap illustration, suppose that SMM is a swap market maker. SMM serves its clients by offering to enter into swap transactions of various kinds. SMM can help RB bridge the asset/liability gap and lock in the spread by providing an interest-rate swap. Assuming that the swap spreads are at 65 basis points, RB can contract with SMM to pay, for a period of 5 years, 3-month LIBOR on a notional principal amount of $100 million in return for fixed annual cash receipts from SMM of 8.85 percent (8.20 percent Treasury rate plus the 65-basis-point swap spread) on the same notional amount. RB pays LIBOR to SMM out of the cash flow received from the loan, retaining the 50-basis-point spread. The 8.60 percent interest payments due on the bond issue are covered by the 8.85 percent swap payments from SMM. Even here, RB retains the 25-basis-point spread. Thus, RB earns a total of 75 basis points (50-basis-point spread over LIBOR from the loan, 25-basis-point spread over the bond coupon from the swap) from the combined transaction. This is illustrated in Exhibit 10-2.

More importantly, this spread is locked in, assuming the borrower who was granted the loan by RB does not default. The earned spread is immune to interest-rate changes. As the interest receipts from the loan change, the payments due on the swap change in lock-step, effectively insulating RB from rate volatility.

The swap transaction between RB and SMM is usually illustrated diagrammatically as in Exhibit 10-2, with each party in a box and cash flows represented by arrows. If more details are necessary or if the cash-flows are more complex, a swap can be represented by means of a cash flow profile, as in Exhibit 10-3. Here, payment flows are represented by arrows pointing upward and cash receipts are represented by arrows pointing downward. A cash flow can be fully described by means of a cash-flow table, as in Exhibit 10-4. In practice, a combination of a diagram for summary representation and a cash-flow table for full details is used.

Several important characteristics of a swap can be illustrated using the simple transaction above.

Exhibit 10-2. A Simple Swap Transaction to Bridge
the Asset/Liability Gap

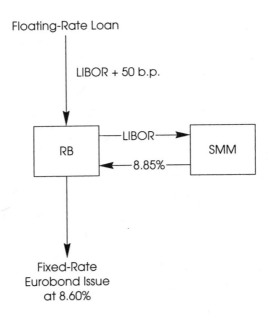

Floating-Rate Loan

LIBOR + 50 b.p.

RB ──LIBOR──▶ SMM
◀──8.85%──

Fixed-Rate
Eurobond Issue
at 8.60%

1. In an interest-rate swap transaction, only payments
   resembling or corresponding to the interest payments
   on a notional (loan) amount are exchanged, the principal amount itself is not. This fact has important
   implications on the amount of credit risk in a swap
   transaction.

2. One party pays a floating rate; the other party pays a
   fixed rate. This is typical of most interest-rate swap
   transactions even though both parties could pay floating or fixed.[1] Typical U.S. dollar floating-rate indexes

---

[1] If both parties pay fixed or floating, the payments would differ in one
or more attributes, such as frequency or timing of payment, floating-rate
index used, and compounding method.

used are LIBOR, commercial paper, Fed funds rate, prime rate, and Treasury bill rate. Most (about 75 percent) of the swaps in dollars are based on LIBOR.

3. The swap has a specific notional amount and maturity. The floating side has a specified index, e.g., 3-month LIBOR.

Exhibit 10-3. Cash Flow Profile of a Swap

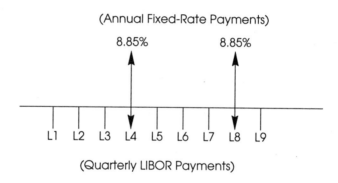

Exhibit 10-4. Cash Flow Table for a Swap

Year	RB pays	RB receives
0.00		
0.25	L_1	
0.50	L_2	
0.75	L_3	
1.00	L_4	8.85%
1.25	L_5	
1.50	L_6	
1.75	L_7	
2.00	L_8	8.85%
2.25	...	

4. The swap rate, i.e., the fixed rate, is quoted as a spread over the appropriate-maturity current coupon Treasury. The payments on the floating side are usually made flat, i.e., at the selected index rate without any spread.

Exhibit 10-5 explains the terminology used in the swap market.

Exhibit 10-5. Terminology Used in the Swap Market

Interest-Rate Swap. Refers to the contractual agreement to exchange specified cash flows between the two parties.

Counterparties. The two principal parties involved in a swap transaction.

Floating-Rate Payer. This is the party that pays floating rate in a swap. This party also receives fixed-rate cash flows and is said to be long the swap.

Fixed-Rate Payer. This is the party that pays fixed rate in a swap transaction. This party also receives floating-rate cash flows and is said to be short the swap.

Notional Amount. This is the amount that is used to determine the actual cash flows paid or received by applying the corresponding interest rates for the appropriate calendar periods.

Coupon. The swap coupon refers to the fixed rate of interest in a swap. This is also known as swap price, swap rate, and swap strike.

Term. This refers to the period commencing from the first day of coupon accrual and ending on the maturity date.

Trade Date. This is the date on which the counterparties enter in a swap transaction. The swap rate is also agreed upon on this date.

Settlement Date or Effective Date. This is the date on which the coupon starts accruing. This is the first day of the swap term, and is usually two business days after the trade date.

Reset Date. The date on which the floating rate is set. The rate set on this date is generally applicable for the subsequent period until next reset date.

Reset Frequency. Number of times reset dates occur in a year. Generally, reset frequency reflects the floating-rate index. This frequency is not necessarily the same as the number of payment dates in a year.

Exhibit 10-5 (Continued).

Maturity Date. Interest stops accruing on this date. This date is also referred to as the termination date.

Intermediary. A third party that stands between two principal parties in a swap transaction.

At-Market or At-the-Money Swap. An interest-rate swap in which no up-front payment by either party is necessary, that is, the value of the swap is zero. The corresponding swap rate is the at-market or at-the-money swap rate.

Off-Market Swap. There are two types of off-market swaps—an above-market swap and a below-market swap. The swap is above-market if the rate is greater than the at-the-money swap rate. The value of the swap is positive. In this case, the fixed payer will receive an adjustment, e.g., up-front premium. In a below-market swap, the fixed rate is less than the at-the-money swap rate. The swap value is negative. In this swap, the fixed receiver will receive an adjustment or premium.

Use of Interest-Rate Swaps in Fixed-Income Portfolios

There are countless ways of using interest-rate swaps to manage cash flows. Generally, swaps are used by institutional investors for the following major purposes:[2]

1. To hedge, or to modify for risk-management purposes, a genuine existing (or future expected) asset. This is the most straightforward case and is the most common use of swaps.[3]

---

[2] There are also a wide range of use of swaps by borrowers/issuers. Our focus here is only on institutional investors.

[3] For an illustration of how the risk point method described in Chapter 6 can be used to hedge with interest-rate swaps, see Ravi E. Dattatreya, Raj E. S. Venkatesh, and Vijaya E. Venkatesh, *Interest Rate and Currency Swaps* (Chicago: Probus Publishing, 1994).

2. To sculpt an existing cash flow to a desired structure. This is similar to hedging.

3. To capture value in the market, e.g., to enhance returns. Value capture is usually achieved either by arbitraging different market segments or by taking advantage of market anomalies. The swap market also offers interesting risk-reward trade-offs not easily available in the traditional debt markets.

Chapter 11

Practical Considerations

In this chapter we focus on the practical considerations in implementing the framework that we presented in this book.

ONE-FACTOR MODELS

There are several methods that can be used to implement a consistent framework that we discussed in Chapter 5. Each method involves numerous choices in the details of implementation. Because of such variety, the development of a consistent framework is still something of an art. A reasonable but relatively simple approach assumes that the yield curve at any point in time can be fully determined by knowing one independent variable. In many such models, known as *one-factor models*, the variable can be interpreted as the short-term rate.[1] We use the one-factor model to clarify certain points.

---

[1] There are also models that assume that bond prices are affected by more than one interest rate. For example, the Brennan-Schwartz model assumes that a short-term and long-term interest rate determine the price of a bond. (See Michael Brennan and Eduardo Schwartz, "Alternative Methods for Valuing Debt Options," Working Paper 888, University of British Columbia, BC, 1982.) The Cox-Ingersoll-Ross model assumes that in addition to the short-term interest rate, changes in the market portfolio will influence bond prices. (See John Cox, John Ingersoll, and Stephen Ross, "A Reexamination of Traditional Hypotheses About the Term Structure of Interest Rates," *Journal of Finance* (September 1981), pp. 769–799.) Richard proposes a two-factor model in which the second factor is the inflation rate. (See Scott Richard, "An Arbitrage Model of the Term Structure of Interest Rates," *Journal of Financial Economics* (March 1978), pp. 33–58.)

It is usual to assume a tractable, stochastic or random process that is in line with market experience for the short rate. The short rate then determines the yields of bonds at all maturities at any point in time; that is, it determines the full yield curve. The internal consistency condition discussed in Chapter 5 places some restraints on the relative movements of the rates at different maturities. For example, parallel changes in the yield curve are prohibited because they are considered to be inconsistent. The external consistency condition discussed in Chapter 5 can be satisfied by tuning the parameters of the stochastic process for the short rate.

INTEREST-RATE PATHS AND SCENARIOS

Paths.   In a one-factor model, the short-term rate (or the factor) can take on values from a large set of possible values according to the assumed random process. A sequence of such values, which can be attained by the short rate, is known as an *interest-rate path*. In mathematical terminology, this is known as a *realization* of the random process.

Note that the interest-rate path not only represents the short-term rate, but also the evolution of the entire yield curve as a function of time. This is because in a one-factor model, the factor completely determines the rates and yields at all maturities. In addition to the paths, the model also provides the probability that any *given* path will be realized under the assumed parameters of the model. Therefore, if we can compute a value of interest for any given realization of an interest-rate path, we can compute the corresponding average values, aggregated over *all* paths. It is in this aggregate or average value that we are interested.[2]

For example, the fair value of a security can be computed by determining the cash flows from the security for any given path and then discounting the cash flows using the realized interest rates

---

[2] As we saw in our discussion on average yields in Chapter 4, care must be taken when using average values. There are pitfalls that must be avoided when applying statistical intuition to the valuation of securities. It can be shown that aggregating values over interest-rate paths is appropriate, but the theoretical basis for this is beyond the scope of this book.

along the path. The procedure is repeated for each path, and an aggregate present value, which is averaged over all paths, is determined. This is the fair value of the security.

In total return analysis, we compute the *present value* of all expected cash flows that occur *after* the horizon by discounting the cash flows along each path using realized interest rates. We also compute the *future value* of all cash flows that occur *before the horizon* by reinvesting the cash flows at the realized rates along the path. The path total return is then computed by adding the present and future values along each path. The path-specific returns are then aggregated as desired.

Representing Scenarios. The collection of interest-rate paths with common properties represents a scenario. For example, if we wish to represent scenarios based on the short-term rates at horizon, then the scenario return for a terminal rate of say 8 percent is determined by aggregating returns over all paths that have a terminal rate of 8 percent. Similarly, if we wish to represent a scenario that corresponds to rates rising steeply and then declining, we simply aggregate returns over all paths satisfying this property. The interest-rate path concept thus provides enormous flexibility in choosing and representing scenarios.

Computing Aggregates. Depending on the situation, either analytical methods or Monte Carlo simulation can be used to estimate path averages. The analytical methods are computationally less expensive, while the simulation methods can address certain complex situations and are at times easier to implement.

INVESTMENT HORIZON VERSUS TRADING HORIZON

We can define two types of horizons for an investor who trades actively:

Investment Horizon. This represents the period over which the investor is seeking to maximize returns. In this case, the horizon is usually tied to a specific event such as the timing of a future liability. In most cases, the investment horizon tends to be on the longer side. The length of an investment horizon usually enters into a framework when strategic decisions regarding the management of the portfolio must be made. These decisions include the selection of a portfolio management technique, such as dedication and immunization, and some broad portfolio-wide parameters, such as total duration. For active trading purposes, long horizons generally are not suitable as they tend to mask the relative market performance of securities.

Trading Horizon. It is difficult to make reliable judgments and assumptions relative to a distant investment horizon. Therefore, active traders usually have a shorter horizon in mind, which is referred to as the trading horizon. This is used to evaluate and compare most transactions. Thus, the investment period is composed of a sequence of trading horizons. By achieving incremental returns in every transaction over the short trading horizon, the investor seeks to achieve significant improvement in return over the entire investment period. The shorter horizon provides more opportunities to take advantage of any values that can be found in the market, and to tune the portfolio, bringing it in line with long-term strategic goals.

Since the trading horizon is short, the effect of the relative performance of the securities is emphasized. Therefore, static analytical tools such as yield computations are of little use in revealing the risks and rewards of a transaction. Thus, a consistent framework for valuation becomes all the more important.

RETURN PROFILES

Total return analysis provides us with a *return profile* for any given security or portfolio. A return profile numerically or graphically represents the returns projected under each scenario subject to the assumptions of the framework. Returns can be expressed as annualized rates of return or as the total dollar values at horizon. We prefer to use the latter; since dollars are additive, it is much easier to work with profiles expressed this way. Since any security or a collection of securities can be mapped to a return profile, we have a common denominator for comparative analysis.

We borrow terminology from chemical engineering to describe two major ways to use the framework: *analysis*[3] and *synthesis.*

---

[3] The word *analysis* is used in this context not to mean investigation or inquiry, but dissection or decomposition into simpler parts.

Analysis.   In the analysis of securities, we break down a complex entity into its component parts, each part presumably being easier to value. The value of the security or its behavior is then the algebraic sum of the values or behavior of the parts.[4]

Synthesis.   Here we try to mimic the return profile of a given security (or a portfolio) by combining other securities in appropriate proportions. Parametric descriptions of the securities under consideration can provide good clues as to the proportions that work. If we can create a combination whose return dominates that of the original security, then we have successfully and efficiently synthesized the latter. We could consider selling the security and purchasing the combination instead.

Two points can be made in this context. First, domination need not mean that the return from one portfolio is greater than that from another in each and every scenario. It need be greater only in those scenarios that we consider likely. Thus, total return analysis allows us to use the results selectively. Second, the closure property discussed in Chapter 5 can be used to simplify relative value trading when used with synthesis. The property implies that if a combination of two bonds is cheap, then at least one of them is cheap. If we can determine or assume that one of the bonds in the combination is either rich or fairly priced, then we can conclude that the second bond is cheap and simply purchase this second bond. We would buy the full combination only if we are specifically trying to synthesize the original security, not just to determine relative value.

AN IMPLEMENTATION EXAMPLE

With total return management as our goal, we can develop a simple implementation of a portfolio that takes advantage of the framework developed here. A fixed-income portfolio is usually set up to satisfy:

- Short-term cash needs
- Long-term return expectations

---

[4] This is what we did when we analyzed callable bonds and mortgage-backed securities.

- The ability to move quickly in order to capture values in the market that are revealed by appropriate analytical or empirical procedures

In order to meet these three needs, we propose a three-pronged portfolio approach. We would conceptually divide the fixed-income holdings into three parts to satisfy the three requirements:

1. *The Liquidity Portfolio.* This portfolio meets all immediate cash-flow needs and represents 10 percent to 20 percent of the total holding. As such, it would consist mainly of short-term money-market-type instruments. We can also include the so-called dedicated or cash-flow-matched securities as they too satisfy specific cash-flow needs. Since the cash flow from this portfolio is paid out, the portfolio rolls over periodically and is replenished from fresh exogenous cash inflow or from other parts of the holding. It is unlikely that complex securities are present here, and thus the need for extensive analysis is minimal.

2. *The Strategic Portfolio.* This represents the bulk of the holding—about 50 percent to 80 percent—and therefore is also called the *core portfolio.* The summary characteristics of the strategic portfolio reflect the long-term goals of the fund. In those cases in which the long-term liabilities are *known* or can be estimated with some degree of confidence, the risk posture of this portfolio reflects the properties of the liabilities. Essential market judgments can be represented here. For example, a bullish stance means that the portfolio is more sensitive to market conditions than the liability; a less sensitive portfolio indicates a bearish stance. If the goal is to be neutral, then the portfolio matches the liability stream as closely as possible. We could use duration along with other parameters to compare the relative riskiness of assets and liabilities. It is important to note here that riskiness, i.e., bullish or bearish stance, is measured relative to the liabilities, not in an absolute manner; we

would consider a short-duration portfolio more risky if the liabilities are long in duration. The neutral portfolio, as defined above, is least risky.

The strategic portfolio would require periodic course correction or "rebalancing" to align its attributes with the goals or changes in market judgments or liabilities. The portfolio can be actively managed by swapping securities within the constraints in accordance with a chosen framework. For example, the constraints could include limits on the proportional representation of different sectors.

3. *The Tactical Portfolio.* This portfolio represents about 10 percent to 25 percent of the holdings and is mainly designed to provide the manager with enough agility to react quickly to changing market conditions. It can be used to realign the strategic portfolio on a temporary basis. For example, if the decision has been made to lengthen duration, the manager could take action quickly in the tactical portfolio to achieve the desired duration and then slowly transfer the duration attribute to the strategic portfolio as opportunities arise.

Another important function of the tactical portfolio is to capture exceptional values in the market. For this reason it is best to have few restrictions as to the class of securities that can be purchased. Thus, the tactical portfolio is not necessarily similar to the strategic portfolio in investment goals or content.

Finally, the tactical portfolio, given its relative freedom of investment, can be used as a scouting portfolio to investigate pilot project ideas. Uses of instruments such as options and futures can be explored here. When enough experience has been gained in a new sector or strategy, it can be considered for inclusion in the core portfolio.

This approach is obviously only one of the several ways one can implement a portfolio under total return management. But the basic ideas are common to most such approaches.

EMPIRICAL ANALYSIS

The total return framework focuses on market risk and reinvestment risk, and on the corresponding returns from capital gains and reinvestment of cash flows. Other risk attributes of fixed-income securities, such as credit risk and liquidity differences, are specifically not quantified. In the absence of a model to value these risks, it is possible to use empirical or historical data analysis techniques to modify and enhance the results of total return analysis.

In order to avoid error, it is always best to use empirical data analysis in conjunction with a theoretical model. For example, when comparing yield spreads of corporate bonds to corresponding Treasury bonds, any widening or tightening of the spreads might be due to call features in the corporate bonds. The call feature makes a corporate bond "look" cheaper in rallying markets even though it is not, by allowing a high yield to maturity. Similarly, in the empirical analysis of Treasury bonds, consideration should be given to the use of coupon-adjusted yields. In addition, caution should be exercised, as conclusions from historical analysis may not hold true in the future; history may not repeat—or reverse—itself.

Chapter 12

Conclusions and Summary

Investment returns in the fixed-income markets are related to the risks taken. In general, higher-risk investments are associated with higher return possibilities. Our assertion is that a *framework* that relates an investment's risk and return characteristics is needed in order to manage a portfolio. A framework helps us evaluate the trade-off between risk and return.

The simplest approach is the *duration framework*, which treats price sensitivity to yield changes as risk and yield to maturity as reward. In Chapter 2 we studied transactions, such as yield curve swaps and barbell-bullet swaps, that looked attractive within this framework. In the barbell-bullet swap we found a barbell with a lower average yield than that of a bullet, while both had the same duration. Therefore, under the duration framework, the bullet appeared more attractive than the barbell. In a positively sloping yield curve, barbells usually have a lower average yield than equal-duration bullets.

We extended this method to obtain the *parametric framework*, which recognizes that duration is not a constant, and defined an additional parameter, *convexity*. Convexity is the property that the dollar-weighted duration of many fixed-income securities increases in rallying markets and decreases in declining markets. Convexity is a desirable property. Different securities, even with the same duration, can have different convexities. In Chapter 3, we concluded that the barbell-bullet swap we examined under the duration framework may not necessarily be attractive considering that the convexity of the bullet is lower than that of the barbell. We attributed the yield pickup in a bullet to the convexity give-up, relative to the barbell. We concluded that there are no free lunches; we have to *pay for convexity.*

In the barbell-bullet swap we compared the average yield of the barbell to the yield of the bullet. Upon reexamining this procedure in Chapter 4, we concluded that it is incorrect to use average yield in this context; cash-flow yield is a much better measure. Upon computing the cash-flow yield of the barbell, which is approximately equal to its dollar-duration-weighted average yield, we may find suddenly that the barbell looks more attractive, having a higher yield than the bullet. This would very often be the case in an upwardly sloping yield curve.

A more surprising fact is that a barbell may have both a higher yield *and* higher convexity. This contradicts our premise that convexity must be paid for by means of a yield spread. Instead of jumping to the wrong conclusion that barbells in general are more attractive, we decided that yield is not a good measure of return. Thus, the parametric framework is not an acceptable approach.

We then proposed the *total return framework* in Chapters 4 and 5 as a solution to the problems encountered thus far. The total return concept replaces a summary number, such as yield, with a series of values, one for each *scenario.* For each scenario the returns depend on the future course of interest rates both in terms of the reinvestment of all cash flows received until the horizon, and in the determination of the horizon value of the investment. In a way, scenario returns are an opinion about the future. Therefore, the use of total return alone does not guarantee consistent results; incorrect assumptions about interest-rate movements will still produce incorrect results.

Fortunately, as we explained in Chapter 5, it is possible to state conditions that assumptions regarding the interest rates should satisfy so that we can obtain useful results from total return analysis. First, the assumptions should be *internally consistent.* This means that there should be no implied riskless profitable arbitrage among fairly priced securities. An intuitive restatement of this condition, also known as the no-arbitrage condition, is the *closure property,* which states that all combinations of fairly priced securities should themselves be fairly priced. The no-arbitrage condition is a theoretical requirement; it basically establishes the fundamental structure of the framework and addresses *values* of securities.

A second condition is that the framework should be *externally consistent*. That is, the values implied by the assumptions within the framework should match market prices. This condition is a practical requirement; it calibrates the structure set up by the no-arbitrage condition and deals with market *prices*. It is important to distinguish between making assumptions about rate movements and forecasting. Intuitively, interest-rate assumptions that are internally and externally consistent are devoid of any implicit or explicit predictive element. Thus, they help create an impartial, objective platform to value securities.

Interestingly, even when limiting ourselves to straight Treasury securities and thereby avoiding credit risk, call risk, etc., the duration and parametric frameworks proved inadequate. The superiority of total return analysis is clearer when analyzing more complicated securities, such as callable bonds and mortgage-backed securities, discussed in Chapters 8 and 9, respectively.

The duration of a fixed-income security is a measure of its price sensitivity relative to its own yield. It is well recognized that duration fails to capture the exposure of a portfolio to changes in the shape of the yield curve. This form of interest-rate risk, referred to as yield curve risk, can be significant in portfolios containing options, some mortgage derivatives, and most exotic securities. In Chapter 6 we discussed a risk measure that is more complete compared to a simple measure such as duration that can be used in measuring yield curve risk. We refer to this measure as the risk point measure.

Admittedly, total return analysis is more tedious and can be computationally expensive. However, we should overcome the natural tendency to dismiss the analysis presented here as just theory. On the contrary, theoretical consistency is a fundamental requirement rather than a utopian luxury. Indeed, the analysis is laborious, but in the pursuit of excellence there are no shortcuts.

The model we looked at is clearly a simplification of the actual market. We made no attempt, for example, to model credit risk or liquidity. However, it is possible to enhance the knowledge obtained from total return analysis with results from empirical data analysis.

In using historical analysis, some skepticism is always healthy, as history may not repeat itself. Also, it is best to use empirical analysis in conjunction with some theoretical model, as there might be valid reasons for the seemingly random deviations observed in the market.

On average, the market seems to know that duration and other parameters do not describe securities completely. That is why we find differences in prices and yields among securities and portfolios that are parametrically similar. When completeness is attributed to the parameters, these differences produce the *illusion* of profitable transactions.

Notwithstanding their drawbacks in the determination of relative value, we acknowledged that parameters of fixed-income securities, such as duration and convexity, do provide useful summary information about these securities and portfolios. Such summary attributes are powerful tools in hedging and asset/liability applications. The error occurs only when we attribute more meaning to these parameters than they merit in the valuation of securities.

There are several methods that can be employed to implement a consistent framework; each method involves numerous choices in the details of implementation. Because such variety exists, the development of a consistent framework is still something of an art. A reasonable but relatively simple approach assumes that the yield curve at any point in time can be fully determined by knowing the value of one independent variable. In many such models, known as *one-factor models*, the variable can be interpreted as the short-term rate. Because of its simplicity, a one-factor model can not only provide valuable insight into the modeling process but also be of actual practical value.

Appendix

The price-yield function of a standard noncallable bond is given by

$$P = \sum_{t=1}^{M} \frac{C(t)}{(1+r)^{\tau}}$$

P = Price (including accrued interest)

$C(t)$ = Cash flow at time t

r = Periodic yield in decimal form

t = Time subscript in periods

τ = Discounting factor[1]

M = Maturity in terms of the number of cash flows remaining

Macaulay duration is defined as the present-value-weighted average of the lengths of time prior to the cash flows. The mathematical formula corresponding to this definition is:

$$\text{Macaulay duration (in periods)} = \frac{\displaystyle\sum_{t=1}^{M} \frac{\tau C(t)}{(1+r)^{\tau}}}{\displaystyle\sum_{t=1}^{M} \frac{C(t)}{(1+r)^{\tau}}}$$

---

[1] $\tau = t + [(\omega T) - 1]$, where ω is the time remaining until the next cash flow and T is the total time between cash flows.

Note that because the time subscript is in periods, the duration calculated from this formula is in periods. It can be converted to years by dividing it by the number of periods or cash flows per year.

To determine the relationship between Macaulay duration and the behavior of price when yields change (price volatility), we take the derivative (rate of change) of price with respect to yield and compare it to the formula for Macaulay duration.

$$\frac{dP}{dr} = \left(\frac{-1}{1+r}\right)\sum_{t=1}^{M}\frac{\tau C(t)}{(1+r)^\tau}$$

We observe that the summation in this expression is the numerator of the equation for Macaulay duration. Because the denominator of the duration expression is simply the price (i.e., the present value of all cash flows, plus accrued interest), we can write:

$$\frac{dP}{dr} = \left(\frac{-1}{1+r}\right)\sum_{t=1}^{M}\frac{\tau C(t)}{(1+r)^\tau} = \frac{-\left[\text{Macaulay duration (in periods)}\right]}{1+r}\times\text{Price}$$

For semiannual bonds, we can substitute $Yield/200$ for r, where $Yield$ is the annual yield stated as a percentage. Also, it is preferable to know the price volatility with respect to the annual percentage yield (dP/dY) instead of with respect to the periodic yield in decimal form (dP/dr). To make this conversion, we first convert Macaulay duration to years and then divide both sides of the equation by 100. The result is the relationship between duration and price volatility that was given in the text.

$$\frac{dP}{dY} = \frac{-\left(\text{Macaulay duration}\right)}{1.0 + \dfrac{Yield}{200}}\times\frac{\text{Price}}{100}$$

A CLOSED-FORM SOLUTION FOR DURATION

The duration of a standard noncallable bond can be expressed in terms of a closed-form equation.

$$\text{Macaulay duration} = \frac{C\left([1+r]^M - 1\right)\left(\dfrac{1}{r} + \dfrac{\omega}{T}\right) + 100r\left(M - 1 + \dfrac{\omega}{T}\right) - CM}{C\left([1+r]^M - 1\right) + 100r}$$

C = Size of each coupon cash flow

r = Periodic yield in decimal form

ω = Time remaining until next cash flow

T = Total time between cash flows

M = Maturity in terms of the number of cash flows remaining

This formula gives a result in periods. To convert to years, it is divided by the number of periods of cash flows per year.

Index